Getting the Triangle Straight:
Managing China-Japan-US Relations

Getting the Triangle Straight

Managing China-Japan-US Relations

Copyediting by Kimberly Gould Ashizawa and Lilian Haney.
Cover by Patrick Ishiyama.
Cover map adapted from *The American Practical Navigator*, 2002 ed.
(Bethesda MD: National Imagery and Mapping Agency, 2002).

Printed in Japan.
ISBN 978-4-88907-080-4

Japan Center for International Exchange
4-9-17 Minami Azabu, Minato-ku, Tokyo 106-0047 Japan
URL: www.jcie.or.jp

Japan Center for International Exchange, Inc. (JCIE/USA)
274 Madison Avenue, Suite 1102, New York NY 10016 USA
URL: www.jcie.org

Table of Contents

Economic Integration and Trilateral Relations

Mutual Perceptions in China-Japan-US Relations

Foreword

THE TRAJECTORY OF the China-Japan-US triangular relationship is likely to have greater bearing on the future of global affairs than that of almost any other international relationship. For that reason, it is extremely important that we think more deeply about how to skillfully manage its dynamics. I am delighted that the authors of this volume have been willing to grapple with this critical issue by taking part in a three-year Japan Center for International Exchange (JCIE) study that was launched in 2007 and has culminated in this book. The three senior figures who have served as leaders of this study—Gerald Curtis, Ryosei Kokubun, and Wang Jisi—are among the most prominent and thoughtful foreign policy experts in their respective countries. In order to encourage the development of a new generation of experts in each country who are equipped to go beyond bilateral approaches and to think in trilateral terms, they have been willing to give guidance to and share their insights with the other contributors to this volume, a team of some of the most promising younger scholars from the three countries.

Of course, the question of how to best manage trilateral relations is not necessarily a new one. In fact, in 1996, JCIE launched a similar set of interrelated studies on China-Japan-US relations that eventually resulted in five publications on the topic. These were part of the first wave of studies to identify relations among China, Japan, and the United States as one of the most potentially volatile and consequential factors in the region. Remarkably, there was some debate at that time over whether the terms "trilateral" or "triangular" were even appropriate to describe the relationship given that relations were so asymmetrical, primarily because China's power was still more potential than actual. For example, the United States and Japan boasted the largest and second-largest economies in the world at the time, while China ranked seventh. The mismatch among the three countries in terms of military force and political influence was similarly stark.

However, tensions in the region were clearly growing. In December 1995, in response to Chinese missile tests over the Taiwan Strait, the United States dispatched an aircraft carrier battle group to the waters off of Taiwan as a show of force. Shortly thereafter, in April 1996, Japan and the United States began a review of their alliance framework, and the new US-Japan defense guidelines that were released in 1997 signaled for the first time that alliance obligations might extend to military action against China in order to maintain the status quo in the Taiwan Strait.

By 2007, a decade later, the big news was China's rise as a global power. China had climbed in economic rankings to the number three position, behind only the United States and Japan, and its growing influence in regional and even global affairs was increasingly palpable. In the span of just a decade, it had become accepted wisdom that the relationship between the three countries would be key to the future of Asia. In fact, everywhere we looked there was growing evidence of how interconnected the political and economic dynamics of the three bilateral legs of these relations—i.e., the China-Japan, US-China, and US-Japan relationships—had become. It was clear to observers that discussions between Tokyo and Washington were affecting how the US and Japanese governments were dealing with China, that tensions in China-Japan relations were complicating US policy in the region, and that Japanese policy was affected by the course of US-China relations.

In sum, by 2007, the dynamics of the trilateral relationship had proven to be even more complex and consequential than we had anticipated a decade earlier. For this reason, we launched a new study on "Managing China-Japan-US Relations and Strengthening Trilateral Cooperation." Conceived out of the conviction that a better understanding of the trilateral dynamics is essential for leaders in the three countries to minimize the potential for conflict in the region, this study set out to assess how China, Japan, and the United States have become more interconnected, what impact the trilateral dynamics have on the bilateral legs of the relationship, and how the three countries can build mutual confidence and cooperate in ways that spill over to other aspects of their relations.

I hope and expect that the final result, this volume, will encourage policymakers in all three countries to think trilaterally even while acting bilaterally and will encourage them to explore how to better manage their crucial relations and deal with the increasing number of shared challenges before them. These include issues particular to trilateral relations as well as traditional and nontraditional challenges at the regional and global levels. And, of course, the ultimate aim in stabilizing trilateral relations is to encourage leaders in the three countries to find a way to avoid the clashes that have arisen so many times throughout history when there have been shifts in the regional and global balances of power—shifts that are comparable to what we are seeing today in Asia.

One aspect of this project that has been particularly gratifying is that this was an intensely trilateral endeavor. The three senior experts who agreed to lead this project convened a stellar group of emerging intellectual leaders from the three countries who have worked together closely as a team over the three years of the study, engaging in deep and thoughtful debate, expanding upon one another's analysis, and generously offering suggestions, feedback, and encouragement to one another. The entire research team came together for workshops in Tokyo, Beijing, and Honolulu—and it was heartening to see how they developed a common sense of purpose. Their participation in the project represented a major commitment of time and energy, and I wish to profusely thank Wang Jisi, Ryosei Kokubun, and Gerald Curtis for their guidance and the entire team for their efforts.

Going beyond the project team, there is a long list of people who should be acknowledged for making this endeavor a success. First and foremost, I wish to express my gratitude to the Henry Luce Foundation and especially to Terry Lautz and Helena Kolenda for generously funding the project and, moreover, for providing the encouragement and inspiration to undertake this important endeavor in the first place. I also wish to relay our deep appreciation to the Shibusawa Eiichi Memorial Foundation and MRA House for providing the additional funding that has made this study possible. In addition, we are grateful to Peking University for supporting our Beijing workshop and to the East-West Center, and especially its president Charles Morrison, for serving as host for our Honolulu workshop.

Also, I wish to recognize and thank the JCIE staff who have contributed so much to this study. This includes Jim Gannon and Ryo Sahashi, who have overseen the editing of this volume and who coordinated the project with assistance from Atsuko Geiger, Hiyuko Fujita, Yuka Inabata, and others. In addition, Kimberly Gould Ashizawa, Susan Hubbard, and Lilian Haney played key roles in editing this book, and Patrick Ishiyama adeptly prepared the layout and graphics, along with David Monico.

If the last 10 years are any indication, the coming years will bring many unanticipated challenges that threaten to shake relations among China, Japan, and the United States. However, I believe that all of the project participants join in my hope that leaders in the three countries will be able to manage the dynamics of the relationship with wisdom and dexterity and that the seeds of trilateral cooperation that are currently being planted through the intense efforts of many individuals in the three countries may blossom and grow.

Tadashi Yamamoto
President
Japan Center for International Exchange

The Trilateral Dynamics of China-Japan-US Relations

1 | Getting the Triangle Straight: China, Japan, and the United States in an Era of Change

GERALD CURTIS

COMPARED WITH SOUTH ASIA, the Middle East, and other parts of the world plagued by political instability, violence, pervasive poverty, death, and destruction, East Asia offers a stark contrast as a region that is the dynamic center of the world economy and that is at peace, or at least not at war. This reality is rendered all the more remarkable by the fact that this is an area where the interests of three great powers—China, Japan, and the United States—intersect. There are dangers of course. North Korea and Taiwan in particular are potential triggers for armed conflict, which, were it to occur, would in one way or another involve all three of these countries. Perhaps even more worrisome is the fragility of the global financial system, posing as it does the ever-present danger of renewed economic turmoil, increased protectionism, and the weakening of a relatively free trade regime that makes it possible for China, Japan, Korea, and the countries of Southeast Asia to pursue successful export-led growth policies.

China, Japan, the United States, and other countries in East Asia face the same essential strategic question of how to keep the region at peace and sustain the economic vitality that not only is raising the living standards of people in East Asia but, in the globalized system in which we live, is contributing to improving the lives of people around the world. Successfully responding to this strategic challenge is no easy task, to be sure, but it is far preferable to the alternative faced in other parts of the world where there is still a need to figure out how to bring about political stability, economic growth, and the termination of war.

It is not surprising that the attention of policymakers and of media opinion makers should be drawn more to crisis situations than to the less headline-grabbing issues of how to manage relations among the great and the lesser powers of East Asia—not surprising, but worrisome nonetheless. East Asia is too important to be treated with a kind of benign neglect, approached with the easy assumption that since the region is at peace and is economically vibrant, what has worked in the past to keep it that way can be relied upon to do the same well into the future.

This is especially true for relations among the United States, China, and Japan. The consequences for the region and for the world of China's remarkably rapid transformation are at this point impossible to gauge. China's rise to great power status by definition upsets the status quo. That does not make conflict inevitable, but whether there is conflict or cooperation will depend on how policymakers respond to the history-changing reality of China's emergence, or rather reemergence, as one of the world's most powerful countries.

In terms of domestic politics, economics, and social structure, both Japan and the United States are undergoing transformations more far-reaching than anything either of them has experienced for decades. Though still the world's singular military superpower, the United States' unilateral moment has passed. The distribution of national power—a combination of economic strength, military capability, political will, and diplomatic skill—among the United States, China, and Japan is shifting. And it is doing so in a regional and global environment that itself is changing in dramatic ways. A new and complex multilateral international system is in the process of formation, but its structure is as yet inchoate; the old world order is gone and a new one has not yet been created.

Bilateral relationships within the China-Japan-US triangle, and the trilateral relationship itself, are free of major discord at the current time, but it would be facile to assume that they necessarily will continue to be so. Managing relations among the three great powers of the Asia Pacific so as to deepen and expand cooperation and reduce the dangers of discord will test the abilities of the leaders of all these countries—none more so than that of the United States.

PAYING ATTENTION TO ASIA

Upon assuming the presidency in January 2009, President Barack Obama moved quickly to ratchet up the level of US attention to East

Asia—consulting more closely with the nations in the region, reassuring the Japanese and South Koreans of the administration's commitment to maintaining strong alliances with both of them, and signaling its intention to engage much more closely with the countries in Southeast Asia. In February 2009, within weeks of the administration coming into power, Secretary of State Hillary Clinton made her first overseas trip, choosing East Asia as the destination for a whirlwind tour that took her to Tokyo, Jakarta, Seoul, and Beijing. She made Japan her first stop in order to reassure the Japanese that the new administration attached as much importance to the US-Japan relationship as had its predecessors. In Seoul, she reaffirmed America's commitment to its alliance with South Korea, warning North Korea that any hostile action against the South would be met by a firm and united response. In Beijing, she stressed the importance of Sino-American cooperation, especially in dealing with global issues, commenting publicly that human rights concerns would not be allowed to get in the way of working with the Chinese on pressing political and economic matters.

Secretary Clinton took a detour between Tokyo and Seoul to visit Jakarta, President Obama's childhood home, the most populous Muslim country in the world, a fledgling democracy, and a key regional player in ASEAN. The ASEAN countries had been critical of President George W. Bush and Secretary of State Condoleezza Rice for their apparent lack of interest in cultivating relations with the region; Secretary Clinton promised that things would be different under the Obama administration. She quickly followed through on that promise when, at a meeting with the 10 ASEAN foreign ministers in July 2009, she signed the ASEAN-sponsored Treaty of Amity and Cooperation. Though involving no binding commitments on the part of the United States, accession to this nonaggression pact sent a clear signal that the Obama administration intended to take Southeast Asia seriously and give it more high-level attention than had the previous government in Washington.

Secretary Clinton's trip to Asia came at the very beginning of the administration, when expectations were high about the foreign policy changes the Obama administration would bring about and when the new president's popularity both at home and abroad were at record high levels. By the time President Obama made his own visit to the region, in November 2009, the situation was far more complicated. The purpose of the trip was to attend a summit meeting of the Asia Pacific Economic Cooperation (APEC) organization in Singapore, with additional stops in Tokyo, Shanghai, Beijing, and Seoul.

As with Secretary Clinton's visit, the hierarchically conscious Japanese were pleased that they were first on the president's schedule. But the Tokyo visit came as the United States and the new Hatoyama government were at loggerheads over what to do about an agreement that the Liberal Democratic Party (LDP) government had signed with the United States in 2006—after more than a decade of negotiation—to relocate an American military base away from a congested area in Okinawa. President Obama tried to keep this dispute from dominating media coverage of his short stay in Tokyo but, unlike when Secretary Clinton visited a few months earlier, there was now a new government in Tokyo that had come into office advocating change—including a change in the way the United States and Japan manage their bilateral relationship.

Back at home, what the media seemed to find most significant about the president's trip to Tokyo was his bowing deeply to the emperor, something many commentators and Republican members of Congress claimed was demeaning. In fact, it was nothing other than a gesture of politeness and respect that evoked no negative comment anywhere in the region and was hardly remarked upon at all until people became aware of criticism of it in the United States.

President Obama's visit to China did not go over well with the US media either. He was criticized for allowing the Chinese government to stage-manage a public forum in Shanghai so as to avoid any questions being raised that might prove embarrassing to the government. He was also attacked for not publicly raising the issue of human rights and China's treatment of dissidents.

In reality, President Obama was no different from his predecessors in this regard. Once in power, President William Clinton quickly walked away from his campaign commitment to make most-favored-nation treatment of China dependent on its human rights behavior. And George W. Bush, for all his talk about spreading democracy everywhere, did not say a word publicly about the Chinese government rounding up dissidents or putting them under house arrest during his visit there in 2005. Nor did he hesitate to warn the Taiwanese that US support of democratic movements and self-determination did not extend to tolerating a Taiwanese move toward independence. But historical memory is in short supply among pundits and politicians out to score points against the sitting president.

By the end of his first year in office, President Obama had little to show in the way of concrete policy accomplishments in East Asia. There had been no progress in getting North Korea to stop its nuclear weapons program. Security relations with Japan were strained because of a dispute over repositioning American forces in Okinawa. Strategy toward China seemed to be based on the hope that, if the United States treated China as a geopolitical as well as an economic partner, China would behave as a "responsible stakeholder" that would provide "strategic reassurance" to the United States, to use expressions coined in the first case by the Bush administration and in the latter by the Obama administration.

But to expect a lot of progress on specific and difficult issues in a new administration's first year is to expect too much. What is most important about President Obama's first year in office is that he changed the climate of opinion about the United States throughout East Asia. Although it did not draw headlines back home, his meeting with the leaders of the 10 ASEAN countries during his visit to Singapore—a first for a US president—his decision to open a dialogue with the military regime in Myanmar, and his emphasis on close consultation with both South Korea and Japan in evolving his North Korea policy have been welcomed as signaling a higher level of engagement with the region and a move away from unilateralism. Making the United States popular once again in the region and raising expectations that the United States is serious about engaging deeply with the countries in East Asia are no mean accomplishments for a government that has been in power for less than a year. It is an impressive beginning. But it begs the question of whether the Obama administration is going to be successful in managing the difficult issues that it faces in relations with China, Japan, and the rest of the region.

THE CONTEXT AND THE CHALLENGE

The United States, China, and Japan are each in a transformative period in their history with respect to their domestic affairs, foreign policy orientations, and relations with each other. Each is trying to define anew its role in the world, and they are doing so at a time when the world order itself is being transformed.

Recovery from the global financial crisis will not return us to the world in which the United States reigned supreme, either economically or politically. There is no going back to a system in which prosperity was sustained by easy money, excess consumption, and huge budget and trade deficits. American personal saving rates ranged close to 10 percent in the postwar years up to the mid-1970s, but they subsequently moved toward zero and finally, in 2008, into negative territory. The saving was done by China, Japan, and oil-rich Middle Eastern countries, which recycled that money back to the United States for Americans to borrow so that they could buy more products made by China and Japan and more oil from the Middle East.

This global system has now crashed. Americans have already begun to save more. That trend doubtless will continue and will bring personal spending more into line with personal income, with profound effects on both the American and the world economy.

Countries such as China, Japan, and others that have depended on exports to the United States as the driving force in their export-led growth strategies will have to make major adjustments in light of decreasing American demand for their products. This inevitably will mean greater emphasis on intra-Asian trade and investment for all Asian countries. Japanese, Korean, and ASEAN trade with China already exceeds that with the United States, and the gap is bound to grow wider.

Many of the exports from other Asian countries to China, it needs to be pointed out, consist of components for products that are assembled in China for export to the United States and to other countries. The US market will remain critically important for all Asian economies, but its relative importance will continue to decline, especially as the Asian middle class grows larger and consumes a larger share of the products produced by Asia's cross-border production networks.

The United States, for its part, will have to adopt policies that reassure foreign holders of American treasury bonds—particularly China and Japan, which are the largest holders of those bonds—that the value of their holdings is secure.

Leverage, of course, is not all on one side. China's huge holdings of US Treasury bills creates something of an economic equivalent to the theory of mutually assured destruction that is applied to the balance of nuclear terror: China could impose devastating damage on the US economy by disposing of these assets, but not without creating substantial distress to its own economy. Japan is in a similar situation, though its heavy dependence on the United States for its security makes it more unlikely than in China's case that it would take actions that the United States would perceive as hostile. Nonetheless, the reality that the United States depends on foreign financing of its government deficit changes the dynamic between the United States and the countries whose willingness to buy that debt is crucial to America's economic wellbeing.

Change in East Asia obviously encompasses much more than just trade and finance. Environmental degradation, pandemics, competition for energy resources, North Korea's development of nuclear weapons capability, the threat of nuclear proliferation, China's growing military capabilities, and Japan's groping for a new foreign policy vision all go into the dynamic mix that is transforming East Asia. That has led some analysts to argue that the region needs a new security "architecture."

The architecture imagery, however, seems far too grandiose for what is needed and what is feasible in East Asia. For the United States, the key feature of the postwar East Asian architecture has been a hub-and-spokes arrangement of bilateral security alliances. There is no reason to believe that this will not or should not continue to be the case for many years to come. There has been a proliferation of regional organizations and there is much talk about the emergence of an East Asia community, but it is questionable whether all this innovation on the multilateral front amounts to something that can usefully be considered as the basis for a new architecture.

It is important to be realistic about what regional institutions can achieve. The Six-Party Talks in Northeast Asia that were created to try to get the North Koreans to give up their nuclear weapons, for example, have been notable mainly for their failure to achieve their objective. It is hard to fathom what a five-party format—the United States, China, Japan, South Korea, and Russia—would seek to achieve or indeed what this talk shop would actually talk about.

The so-called East Asia community is a "community" characterized by deep distrust among its key members—China and Japan in particular—by political systems that range from democratic to autocratic, by large disparities in levels of economic development, and by religious and cultural diversity. The United States should welcome the development of regional institutions that can help bridge these differences, as President Obama has done.

It also should take a relatively relaxed attitude toward the emergence of an East Asia community. Unlike the EU, community in East Asia is developing as a multilayered set of regional institutions. There are the Six-Party Talks, the ASEAN Regional Forum, the East Asia Summit, APEC, and several functionally specific organizations. For the United States, the need is not for more architecture. The challenge is to pay attention to the region, deal with it in a flexible and imaginative manner, and participate actively in multilateral institutions where it is appropriate to do so. But more than anything else, the United States needs to manage its bilateral relations with China and Japan skillfully and get the triangular relationship with China and Japan straight.

9

CHINA'S RISE, AMERICA'S RESPONSE

Ever since Richard Nixon initiated the process of normalizing relations with the People's Republic of China in 1972, there has been basic continuity in America's China policy. Whether Republican or Democrat, every American president from Nixon to Obama has taken the position—some only after initially promising to reverse the supposedly soft China policy of the previous administration—that it is in the vital national interest of the United States to deepen economic and political ties with China and to encourage it to become fully enmeshed in the international system. Each administration has also emphasized the importance of maintaining strong alliances, especially with Japan, to enable the United States to retain military and political preeminence in East Asia. A major purpose of that preeminence is to prevent China from securing a hegemonic position in the region.

But while the basic strategy, often described as entailing a combination of engagement and hedging, has not changed for nearly four decades, China itself has been transformed. It has made a truly great leap forward, becoming virtually overnight a major force in the economy of the East Asian region and that of the world and one of the leading players on the international political stage. China's GDP was US$390 billion in 1990; it had risen to about US$5 trillion by 2010. Because its phenomenal growth has been driven by exports, China has rather suddenly become a leading trading partner for the United States, Japan, South Korea, ASEAN, and the European Union. The United States is China's largest export market, and Japan is second.

But China is still a developing economy. It is the third biggest economy in the world in terms of nominal GDP and shortly will surpass Japan to become second only to the United States. In terms of per capita income and the living standards of the great majority of its huge population, however, China is a poor country. Even under the best of circumstances, it will take decades for its people to reach the living standards enjoyed by Japanese or Americans. The temptation to extrapolate current growth trends well into the future seems virtually irresistible, even though we know that what cannot go on forever will not go on forever. It is worth remembering that only a little more than 20 years ago, the conventional wisdom was that the 21st century would be Japan's century.

But uncertainties notwithstanding, China is joining the ranks of the world's great powers. The policies it pursues will have a profound impact on the global economy, on regional security, and on the international system.

History is replete with examples of interstate conflicts spawned by the competition between rising new powers seeking to expand their influence and established powers endeavoring to hold on to their power position. However, it is not inevitable that China's rise should have such a destabilizing impact. China does not seek to impose its ideology on other countries, as did the Soviet Union. It does not deny the legitimacy of existing international institutions but rather wants to be an active participant in them. And Chinese leaders appear far more skeptical than many foreign observers that China will become a superpower in the sense that the United States is anytime in the near future.

Ever since Deng Xiaoping set China on the path of rapid modernization, China's rulers have been unwavering in giving priority to domestic development, keenly aware that China has many years to travel and many obstacles to overcome before it becomes a truly prosperous country. China needs a stable international environment in order to accomplish its development goals, and it has been seeking in recent years to create that environment by pursuing a pragmatic and sophisticated foreign policy. The hallmarks of that policy are efforts to develop cooperative relations with the United States, defuse tensions with Japan, avoid controversies with Southeast Asian countries over territorial disputes in the South China Sea, engage with existing international institutions, and convince the world that it has no intention to use its increasing power to upset the existing international system.

Still, whatever China's intentions may be, the reality is that its emergence as a great power changes the status quo. That is true whether it harbors hegemonic ambitions or not, whether it looks forward to acquiring the power that would position it to challenge the United States for influence in the world or instead sees its interests as lying in the evolution of an international system characterized by cooperation between China and the United States.

China makes no secret of its determination to become a great power in all dimensions. Its goals contrast sharply with those of Japan, whose peaceful postwar rise did not challenge US power. Japan's rise to great power status was unidimensional. Japan became a great economic power while foreswearing the option to become a political and military power as well. China has no such inhibitions. Its strategic thinkers are not like the Japanese, who tend to think reactively, trying to gauge what Japan should do to maximize its advantages in the world as they find it. The Chinese are more like Americans, inclined to think strategically about how to shape the world order to achieve their objectives.

American policymakers should have no illusion about this reality. China's acquisition of great power status will to some degree come at the expense of American power. Even more importantly, the United States does not have the power to decide whether or not China is going to acquire great power status.

This is a reality that American policymakers seem to be reluctant to accept. The two phrases coined by successive deputy secretaries of state under President Bush and President Obama to characterize the US views of China's rise imply that it is somehow within America's power to decide whether the world will "accept" China's rise. For Deputy Secretary Robert Zoellick, it was China as a "responsible stakeholder" in the international system. For his successor, James Steinberg, it is "strategic reassurance."

The idea that China's rise can best be accommodated within the existing international system if China develops important stakes in the institutions of that system makes a great deal of sense. But what does it mean to be a "responsible" stakeholder? And who is to decide whether it is acting in a responsible manner or not, or what to do about it if it does not? China is certain to claim that its behavior is "responsible"—it is hardly likely to admit that it is irresponsible. But, being "responsible," as Zoellick used the word, can have only one meaning: that the United States will decide what is responsible and what is not. The Chinese are not likely to agree that the United States should be the judge of what constitutes responsible Chinese behavior. Nor is it apparent what the United States can do if China does not behave "responsibly." This catch phrase seems to be rooted in the unrealistic assumption that the United States is in a position to decide whether the world order is going to accommodate China's rise.

Even more problematic is the concept of "strategic reassurance." According to Deputy Secretary Steinberg, "Strategic reassurance rests on a core, if tacit, bargain. Just as we and our allies must make clear that we are prepared to welcome China's 'arrival' . . . China must reassure the rest of the world that its development and growing global role will not come at the expense of [the] security and well-being of others. Bolstering that bargain must be a priority in the US-China relationship. And strategic reassurance must find ways to highlight and reinforce the areas of common interest, while addressing the sources of mistrust directly, whether they be political, military or economic."[1]

There are a lot of weighty words in this statement, but they do not add up to much more than an American assertion of its right to decide whether China's "arrival" will be welcomed or not. The bargain that Steinberg seems to offer is that the United States will acquiesce to a growing global role for

China as long as China provides strategic reassurance to the United States. But China is going to "arrive" whether the United States welcomes it or not. Moreover, if strategic reassurance involves "addressing the sources of mistrust directly," does that mean that the United States is prepared to offer strategic reassurance to China about Tibet, Taiwan, ballistic missile defense, Internet censorship, or any other of a number of issues that make the Chinese apprehensive about US policy? And if China somehow provides the strategic reassurance the United States is looking for, does that then mean that the United States will look the other way when China engages in behavior that it finds repugnant, in the way it deals with minorities within its own borders for example or in its persecution of dissidents?

As a great power, China will have great power ambitions. There is no hedging strategy that can prevent that from happening. The United States needs to guard against a false sense of confidence that it has the power to decide whether or not China will become a great power. It also should avoid exaggerating China's strengths. In terms of living standards, technological development, and many other indicators, China is not among the top-ranking countries. The idea that a Sino-American "G2" can be a key element in resolving regional and global problems grossly exaggerates China's power. And the view that the United States should temper its criticism of Chinese policies that it finds inimical to American interests and values out of a desire not to incur China's wrath is similarly misguided. In dealing with an increasingly powerful China, the United States needs to pursue a policy mix that seeks avenues for cooperation with China across a whole gamut of issue areas and that at the same time strives to maintain a balance against Chinese power—not to punish it for misbehavior, but because a stable international order requires balance among the powerful.

THE UNITED STATES AND JAPAN: THE "CORNERSTONE" SHIFTS

Japan has been in a deep funk ever since the early 1990s, when the Cold War ended, its real estate and stock market bubble burst, and the long-ruling LDP realized that, after achieving Japan's more than century-long goal to catch up with the West, it had no idea what to do for an encore. Japan stumbled through a "lost decade" averaging a 1 percent annual growth rate. The government's response to the economic crisis was a fiscal policy that was not expansionary enough to jumpstart the economy but was large enough to balloon the government deficit. Corruption scandals multiplied, ensnaring not only leading politicians but senior bureaucrats as well. Japan's lifetime employment system came under severe stress as companies shifted to recruiting more contract and part-time workers. The banking system tottered on the verge of collapse under the weight of huge amounts of nonperforming loans. Public confidence in government and key social institutions plummeted, as did hopes for the country's future.

In 2001, a maverick LDP politician, Junichiro Koizumi, tapped into a reservoir of voter frustration to engineer a kind of intra-party coup, becoming president of the party and prime minister by rallying the support of the LDP's rank and file against the party's bosses. Koizumi's message that there could be no economic growth without structural reform, his attack on the leaders of his own party as the "forces of opposition," his charisma, even his lion-mane hairstyle, all struck a positive chord with a public that finally had become fed up with the LDP's traditional political game. Koizumi became the most popular prime minister in Japanese history.

Once he left office in 2006, however, the LDP lost little time in trying to turn back the clock to play politics the old-fashioned way. Despite their best efforts, however, they could not revive a system that had been gravely weakened by Koizumi's reforms and that the public opposed. Over the next three years, Japan had three LDP prime ministers—Shinzo Abe, Yasuo Fukuda, and Taro Aso. The LDP enjoyed a large majority in the Lower House but it was in the minority in the Upper House as a result of its losses in an election held in the summer of 2007. Fearing that the party would lose its Lower House majority the next time the voters had the opportunity to express their preferences, the LDP delayed calling an election for as long as possible. Finally, just weeks before the full four-year term of those elected to the Diet in 2005 would have ended, Prime Minister Aso dissolved the Lower House.

When voters cast their ballots on August 30, 2009, they confirmed the LDP's worst fears. As they headed to the polls, there was little indication that they felt enthusiastic about the opposition Democratic Party of Japan (DPJ), but the enthusiasm for political change was palpable. Some DPJ candidates had campaigned on Barack Obama's slogan of "change you can believe in." Japanese voters seemed to be moved by a somewhat different sentiment: "change, believe in it or not."

The election gave the DPJ 308 seats and only 119 to the LDP, a precipitous drop from the 303 seats the latter had held prior to the vote. From the end of World War II until 2009, the LDP had been the only party to win a majority of seats in the Lower House. The DPJ's victory therefore was unprecedented. On September 16, 2009, power transferred to a new government led by

Yukio Hatoyama as prime minister. Tellingly, only two DPJ cabinet members, Hirohisa Fujii, the minister of finance, and Naoto Kan, the head of the National Strategy Bureau (who replaced an ailing Fujii as finance minister in January 2010), had previous cabinet experience. A team of untested, largely younger politicians now took the reins of power.

The DPJ had been elected on a platform of change and it began almost immediately upon taking power to begin the process of implementing promises the party had made in its campaign manifesto: to change the government's decision-making processes to make them more transparent and reduce the discretionary authority of the bureaucracy; to center decision-making responsibility on the elected politicians in the cabinet; to reorder domestic policy priorities to emphasize direct payments to consumers rather than indirect support through investments in roads and other infrastructure projects; and to modify the country's foreign policy.

Upon taking office, the Hatoyama administration did not have a clearly defined foreign policy strategy or vision of the role it sees Japan playing in international affairs. Moreover, as a result of decades of one-party dominance, there was no system in place in Japan to help facilitate a smooth transition from one ruling party to another. There was no transition team, no intelligence briefings for the incoming administration, little access to the hard data in the possession of the bureaucracy on economic and foreign policy issues, and very little time between winning the election on August 30 and forming a cabinet on September 16.

Inexperience showed. The prime minister and other key cabinet ministers made contradictory and uncertain statements about the government's policies with respect to both the US alliance and relations with China and other East Asian countries. The United States, in turn, overreacted.

President Obama had been elected on a platform promising change, and he moved quickly once in office to make change happen—taking initial steps to close Guantanamo and to withdraw troops from Iraq, canceling plans to place a missile defense system in Eastern Europe, and seeking dialogue with Iran and Syria and with North Korea. But political change in Japan was another matter entirely. The Obama administration did not hide its irritation with the Hatoyama government's decision to take a fresh look at an agreement that had been reached between the LDP government and the United States to relocate a US Marine air station in Okinawa, or with Prime Minister Hatoyama's call for the creation of an "East Asian Community," which some in the administration believed reflected a desire to downgrade the US-Japan alliance in favor of closer ties with China and other Asian states.

The US-Japan discord over the relocation of the Marine air base is still unresolved at the time of this writing. No matter how it is finally settled, however, there is no question that it has sowed a considerable amount of ill will toward Prime Minister Hatoyama among the officials who deal with Japan in the Obama administration and that it has taken a toll on the Hatoyama government's attitude toward the Obama administration as well.

Neither Prime Minister Hatoyama nor his foreign minister, Katsuya Okada, was adept in the way they handled this issue. There was too much thinking out loud about possible alternatives to the relocation agreement that had been concluded by the Bush administration and the LDP government in 2006, too many half-baked or totally unbaked ideas floated that only made the situation more confusing.

But the lack of sophistication of the DPJ's leadership in dealing with foreign policy is not the primary reason for discord between the United States and Japan over this basing issue. Whether the Hatoyama government lasts or not, whether the DPJ stays in office for several years or not, Japanese foreign policy and the dynamics of Japan's relations with the United States are changing. Americans are fond of referring to the alliance with Japan as the "cornerstone" of US policy in East Asia. It is an apt metaphor because a cornerstone just sits there; it is inanimate and reliable, something you can confidently build upon. But the Japanese cornerstone is shifting.

Japan can be deceptive for those who do not look below the surface at the currents that are churning Japanese society and influencing how people think about their country and about the world in which they must live and survive. Japan is going through a major political transformation, one important aspect of which is a generational shift in political leadership.

DPJ politicians are mostly young, and the LDP, now that so many of its incumbents have been defeated, is beginning to turn to younger candidates as well to try to revive its fortunes. This younger generation brings with it a more cosmopolitan perspective than has been the norm for Japan's political class. Many of them have studied in the United States or for other reasons have had experience living abroad. For the most part, they do not have the stomach for old-style machine politics; they are more comfortable talking about national and global policy issues than about how to get the pork barrel to roll more largesse into their constituencies.

Young or old, whether in the DPJ or LDP, the great majority of Japanese politicians accept that alliance with the United States is in Japan's vital interest. But younger politicians have not inherited that complex of attitudes of gratitude and injured pride that so many older politicians who experienced the American Occupation and its aftermath exhibit. Nor do they believe that relations with Asian neighbors necessarily need to be seen through the prism of Japan's relations with the United States.

Ever since the Meiji period, when Yukichi Fukuzawa argued that Japan had to "get out of Asia," the Japanese people have debated whether to give priority to relations with Asia or with the West. But for younger politicians, and for a considerable number of older ones as well, the idea that Japan has to choose one or the other does not ring true. Close relations with the United States are vital for Japan, but so too are close relations with China. The leaders now in power in Tokyo, and even more so those who are going to succeed them, take the view that it is Japan's leaders and not America's who are to decide the terms of Japan's Asian engagement. In an important sense, it is far easier for American officials to talk with Japan's younger politicians, especially those who have lived in the United States and are English speakers. But American officials are used to dealing with an older generation of Japanese political leaders for whom the preservation of Japan's "special relationship" with the United States was seen as the nation's primary foreign policy goal. They need to recognize that that is no longer the case and that the dynamics of the relationship are changing.

For the eight years of the Bush administration, both American and Japanese officials crowed that US-Japan relations had never been better. And that is certainly true for the relationship between officials in the Bush administration and those in the Japanese government who constantly reassured them that this was indeed the case. But it was not true for the Japanese public. The belief that Japanese policy is subservient to the United States, that Japanese foreign policy is made in Washington even as Washington pays less and less attention to Japan, grew stronger over the past decade. When Yasuhiro Nakasone was prime minister in the 1980s, the "Ron-Yasu" relationship between him and President Ronald Reagan was widely seen by Japanese as a source of leverage for Japan. But to many Japanese, all Prime Minister Koizumi's close personal relationship with President Bush seemed to have accomplished was to get Japan to send Self-Defense Forces to support the United States in an unpopular war in Iraq. There is a serious reconsideration of Japan's foreign policy currently underway in Tokyo. The Obama administration is doing far too little to tune in to this debate and too little to reach out beyond Japanese whom American officials know well to engage people who now are in power and those who have influence with those in power in a strategic dialogue about the alliance's future and about the region.

Prime Minister Hatoyama and President Obama share a similar world-view in the importance they attach to so-called nontraditional security threats—global warming, environmental degradation, pandemics, and other issue areas that provide opportunities for meaningful cooperation between the United States and Japan. There is also an essential common-ality in their views of China. The DPJ government is enthusiastic about deepening relations with China, but this is less of a departure from the policies pursued by recent LDP governments than some people are wont to assume. Political leaders in both the LDP and the DPJ are well aware that Japan's prosperity is increasingly dependent on its economic relations with its Asian neighbors and with China in particular. Like the United States, Japan is deepening economic ties with China and at the same time striving to maintain a balance of power in the region. Given Japan's constraints—constitutional restrictions on the roles and missions of its military, severe budgetary conditions that have frozen defense spending, and continued public opposition to a larger Japanese regional security role—Japan's hedging strategy toward China depends on maintaining a strong security alliance with the United States.

The Obama administration has ratcheted up the economic dialogue that the Bush administration had initiated with the Chinese into a more encompassing "Strategic and Economic Dialogue." It needs to initiate an equally high-level and broad-based dialogue with Japan. Japan should not be taken for granted. The United States cannot afford to put relations with Japan on a kind of autopilot and expect to avoid a lot of turbulence. The US-Japan relationship will change, but whether that change results in a stronger alliance or not depends on the leadership exercised by both Washington and Tokyo.

Getting the Triangle Straight

The urgent tends to drive important but less urgent issues to the bottom of the president's inbox, where they sit until some event compels his attention and forces a policy response. Those at the center of East Asia policymaking in the Obama administration need to push back against this tendency. The Obama administration needs to engage closely with China and Japan, both of which are in the midst of a period of dynamic change. It needs a well-thought-through strategy for dealing with China and Japan, bilaterally and trilaterally, if the president is to avoid finding himself constantly caught up in a game of catch-up, reacting tactically to events after they occur rather than thinking strategically about how to further American interests in a region that is the center of the global economy and that is undergoing far-reaching political, social, and economic change.

The challenge posed by East Asia is fundamentally different from what President Obama confronts in the Middle East, South Asia, and other areas where a sharp break from the failed policies of the Bush administration is imperative. The legacy of previous administrations' policies toward China and Japan is a positive one upon which President Obama can build his own East Asia strategy. But build he must.

China is far more powerful today than it was just a few years ago. American policy must respond to that reality, accepting China as a major player not only in regional but also in global economic and political affairs, while also balancing China's growing power. Balance requires robust alliances in the region and a willingness to take a strong stance toward China on issues where it is called for. The United States should not underestimate the historic importance of China's emergence as a major power; nor should it exaggerate its strengths. Engagement and balance both need to be made part of the policy mix in US policy.

In some ways, Japan poses more of a problem for the Obama administration than China does. Senior Obama administration officials understand how significant China's rise is and recognize the importance of engaging in a strategic dialogue with China across a whole range of bilateral, regional, and global issues. The same cannot be said for the administration's handling of relations with Japan. An administration whose president was elected with a commitment to change has reacted negatively and in a shortsighted manner to political change in Japan. This may be because the issues at stake have not seemed important enough to engage the attention of the president himself, and thus their handling has been left in the hands of officials who are too invested in policies inherited from previous governments. The Hatoyama government got off to a shaky start with its key leaders lacking both governmental decision-making experience and deep knowledge of important issues. But insisting that the Japanese government, which came to power in opposition to the LDP, should ignore its campaign pledges to satisfy the United States—or believing that the application of enough public pressure by American officials will cause the Japanese government to accept US demands—will only make it more difficult to manage what is a crucially important relationship for both the United States and Japan.

Neither the Obama administration nor preceding governments have given enough attention to developing trilateral relations with China and Japan. The pattern has been to focus on bilateral ties and to give short shrift

19

to a trilateral dialogue and little attention to the development of trilateral programs. There is a need for a new approach.

For one thing, bilateral relations have a way of refusing to stay bilateral. In the interconnected world in which we live, those relationships are more akin to a game of billiards than they are to the more familiar chessboard of international politics. Billiards is a two-person game in which when one hits a ball it hits another, setting that ball in motion and moving other balls on the table. It is an apt metaphor for international politics, where what may be intended as a solely two-party interaction, whether between the United States and China, the United States and Japan, or some other combination, takes on the characteristics of a multiparty game. As the United States deepens its relations with China, it has to reassure Japan that this does not amount to a downgrading of the US-Japan relationship, that America's relations with China and with Japan are a positive-sum and not a zero-sum game.

Conversely, as the DPJ government of Prime Minister Hatoyama emphasizes its desire to strengthen relations with China and to build an East Asia community, there is a need for Japan to reassure a suspicious Obama administration that this does not amount to a downgrading of the US alliance or an effort to build a regional structure that excludes the United States. The only way to do that is to enhance a strategic dialogue between Japan and the United States, not just on bilateral issues but also on regional and global issues and on policy toward third countries such as China.

There are limits to what a trilateral dialogue can achieve. Many of the most important issues in US relations with China and Japan are bilateral in nature. And many of those that are not bilateral involve the interests of other countries as well. Institutionalizing a China-Japan-US "G3" is no more desirable than a US-China "G2." The South Koreans would be concerned about being left out and anxious about how trilateral consultations might impinge on their own interests. Nor is it necessarily the case that China and Japan would welcome trilateral consultations that might result in the United States taking a position that tilts toward one of the other two parties. In addition, the United States would need to be careful not to let such consultations draw it into taking sides on controversial issues that it would rather avoid being drawn into, such as the Sino-Japanese territorial dispute over the Senkaku (Diaoyu) Islands.

There is an important role, nonetheless, for a trilateral dialogue among China, Japan, and the United States. These are, after all, the three most powerful countries in East Asia, with many common interests that could be furthered by coordinating their policies. Japan's pollution control technology, for example, is among the world's best. A joint China-Japan-US program to combat water and air pollution in China, for example, could make an important contribution to dealing with an issue that not only affects the health of the Chinese population but also has an adverse impact on nearby countries as well.

There is also considerable merit in convening a regularized trilateral dialogue on hard security issues. Strengthening the US-Japan alliance, which should be a goal of the Obama administration, should be pursued in a manner that does not provoke Chinese suspicions that the US objective is to enlist Japan in a containment strategy against China.

Trilateralism should be only one of several approaches used to foster dialogue among the United States and countries in East Asia. But it should be one of them. It is especially important that the United States and Japan, whose alliance is the core element in the East Asian international order, engage in a much deeper and broader dialogue on a range of bilateral, trilateral, and multilateral issues. The importance of skillfully managing relations with a rising China is well understood by Washington. Regrettably, the equally important need to pay greater attention to skillfully managing relations with a changing Japan is not as well understood.

President Obama, in a major policy address in Tokyo in November 2009, referred to himself as America's first "Pacific president." Given his personal history it is quite natural that he should look out at the world across the Pacific as much as he does across the Atlantic. Throughout Asia, people get the sense that Obama is interested in Asia and is comfortable dealing with people there. His emphasis on consultation and dialogue, his recognition of the limits of American power, and his respect for the opinions of others provide the foundation for a new positive era in US relations with China and Japan and with the East Asian region as a whole.

But getting the China-Japan-US triangle straight will require a commitment of time, energy, and resources greater than what the administration invested in its first year. The opportunities to strengthen this trilateral relationship are there. Leadership from the top is required to realize them.

NOTES

1. James Steinberg, deputy secretary of state, US Department of State, "Administration's Vision of the US-China Relationship" (keynote address at the Center for a New American Security, September 24, 2009), www.state.gov/s/d/2009/129686.htm.

2 | The China-Japan-US Triangle: A Power Balance Analysis

WANG JISI

THE POWER BALANCE among China, Japan, and the United States, and perceptions of that balance, are major determinants in shaping the trilateral relationship among the three great powers. In two of my earlier essays on this subject, written in 1997 and 2001, I presented the assessment that the United States remained the strongest power among the three, followed by Japan, and that China was the weakest in terms of economic development, technological prowess, and other measurable indicators of modernization.[1] However, at the beginning of the 21st century, the power balance seems to have changed drastically in China's favor.

As one of the fastest-growing economies in the world, China's gross domestic product (GDP) has now surpassed that of Germany and may catch up with Japan's in the near future. China's military forces are becoming increasingly formidable and have expressed their intention to build aircraft carrier battle groups. In Asia, Europe, Africa, Latin America, and literally every corner of the world, China's influence is expanding along with the spread of consumer goods marked "made in China." While China has also considerably narrowed its power gap with the United States, few analysts expect China's power status to be on par with the United States anytime soon. However, more and more observers in all three countries now view China as a more powerful nation than Japan.

This snapshot of the shifting power balance has tremendous policy implications. Drawing on traditional balance-of-power theories of international politics, the conventional view is that China, as a rising power that is challenging the existing world order, will pose a growing problem—if not a threat—to the United States and Japan. China's newly enhanced power status can be expected to give impetus to a more assertive foreign policy. In addition, there have been increasing expressions of nationalist sentiments in China, reinforcing the view that China will inevitably try to compete with the United States in assuming leadership in world affairs.[2] Therefore, the argument goes, the status quo power, in this case the United States, should hedge against Chinese geopolitical ambitions. The best approach to doing this, as some Americans propose, is to consolidate US alliance relationships in the Asia Pacific region, especially with Japan. Meanwhile, as a "declining power," Japan's natural choice vis-à-vis China is to balance Chinese influence by leaning closely toward the United States and building up political and security ties with other neighboring countries and areas, including covert military cooperation with Taiwan.

These perceptions of the new reality, however, miss a number of important factors that are also shaping the dynamics of interaction among the three nations. In particular, these nations must also take into account considerations of "soft power" or "smart power," a range of nontraditional security challenges, and the ramifications of the global financial crisis, and all of these elements must be weighed in order to accurately assess the trilateral power balance. This chapter, therefore, reviews the real and perceived shift in the power balance among China, Japan, and the United States, with emphasis placed on soft power and sustainable development measurements. Based on this new emphasis, a set of conclusions and policy recommendations is provided that point toward a new direction for China and trilateral relations.

PERCEPTIONS OF THE TRILATERAL POWER BALANCE

Chinese Perceptions

The ascendance of China's power has had strong repercussions not only in the outside world but also in China itself. The official media promote the notion that China's economic boom has benefited the whole world and that the increase in China's cultural and political influence is, and should be, embraced by the international community. This is expected to boost Chinese patriotism and national confidence, which are needed to sustain social stability and fend off international pressures on China for Western-style democracy and liberalization.

Meanwhile, the Chinese official media portray the Western world, including Japan, as attempting to set up obstacles to China's rise to great power status. It is widely reported that Western countries are resisting mergers between their companies and Chinese enterprises, making excuses (like the defects in Chinese consumer goods) to protect their domestic markets, criticizing China's lack of political transparency and its human rights record, worrying about China's expansion of its military power, and sympathizing with the Dalai Lama and his followers as well as with Chinese political dissidents. The basic message to the Chinese population is that the United States, Japan, and other Western nations are jealous of, and ideologically biased against, China's reemergence.

These media reports and comments echo the sentiments among China's political and intellectual elites, particularly against the larger background of the global financial turbulence and economic recession. In a recent collection of Chinese observations on the 2008–2009 financial crisis and its implications for a global power shift, China's leading policy analysts reached the consensus that the new momentum in emerging powers, especially China, along with the deepening economic crisis in the developed world, is accelerating the multipolarization of world politics.[3] Shi Yinhong, a professor at Renmin University, observed that the scale of the debilitation of US power caused by the financial crisis is comparable to the collapse of the Soviet Union. Shi shares a view that became popular in China during the global crisis—that the superiority of the capitalist market economy and liberal democracy is now dubious and that China's social system, values, and policies are increasingly appreciated and praised in the Western world.[4]

However, other Chinese commentators are more cautious about forecasting the decline of the United States in world affairs, pointing to the resilience of the US economy and the existence of a self-corrective mechanism in US politics. A widely shared projection is that the United States will remain the only superpower in the foreseeable future despite its weakened position. The United States is still very relevant in Asian regional affairs. In comparison with some criticisms in other parts of Asia that Washington has neglected Asia while fighting fires in the Middle East, the official Chinese understanding is that "the United States has increased its strategic attention to and input in the Asia Pacific region, further consolidating its military alliances, adjusting its military deployment, and enhancing its military capabilities."[5]

Meanwhile, Japan's relevance in China's overall strategic vision has diminished remarkably. In the 1980s, when the Chinese were envious of Japan's economic expansion, there was little doubt among Chinese policymakers and analysts that Japan's strategic and economic importance to China was second only to that of the United States. In recent years, however, the European Union as a whole has become China's biggest trading partner, and its political influence has risen accordingly. With its newly regained power, Russia has loomed larger in China's strategic calculations, and an increasing number of Chinese analysts now regard Russia as a more important country than Japan. A recent public opinion poll showed that Russia is perceived by the Chinese people to be a much more popular and a more powerful nation than Japan.[6] Other emerging powers, including India, Brazil, and South Africa, are also gaining more importance in Chinese perceptions of the global power equation.

Japanese Perceptions

With its economic stagnation in recent years, and in particular with the heavy blow of the current financial crisis, Japan's self-confidence in world affairs has plummeted. Having relied on overseas demand to drive growth, Japan in the spring of 2009 found itself in its deepest recession since World War II. In addition, Japan's aging and shrinking population poses a long-term threat to its ability to sustain economic growth. In contrast to Japan, China has demonstrated annual growth of over 8 percent for the last 30 years, and its political and cultural influence, as seen through Japanese eyes, also appears to have been enhanced. Few Japanese commentators fail to acknowledge the emergence of China, and even fewer portray Japan as a rising power.

Japan's political elites harbor ambivalent feelings about China's renewed power and confidence. It is difficult to trace the attitudes of Japanese leaders by reading their publicized comments on China, as there is little consistency there. While Junichiro Koizumi was prime minister, he reiterated the view that China's development was not a threat to Japan but an opportunity.[7] Taro Aso, as foreign minister in the Koizumi cabinet, contradicted that statement in December 2005 by proclaiming, "China has 1 billion people and owns nuclear weapons. China's military budget has increased in the last 17 years successively, and its content is extremely opaque. China is becoming a threat to a considerable degree."[8] Nevertheless, Aso repeatedly said he was the first foreign minister of Japan to welcome the rise of China. Then, as prime minister, Aso remarked during his visit to Beijing in April 2009, "There is indeed a voice expressing concern that, with its economy developed, China might embark upon the road of a great military power. We understand that in recent years China has stuck to the strategy of peace and development and made efforts to build a world of lasting peace and common prosperity. We expect China to take actions according to this strategy and dispel such worries and concerns."[9]

Judging from the tone of such statements and from numerous public opinion polls, it is very clear that Japanese concerns about China's growing power are widespread and that China's image in Japan is largely negative.[10] Ideological differences between China and Japan are an important factor in exacerbating Japanese concerns, but the perceptions of the shifting power balance seem to be more fundamental. Regardless of the state of the bilateral relationship, as long as the power balance changes in China's favor, Japanese suspicions of Chinese ambitions and intentions are likely to persist and increase.

Japan continues to pay respect to the United States' strength and leadership role and works to maintain the US-Japan alliance relationship. Nonetheless, Tokyo is concerned that when the Americans are tied up in Iraq, Afghanistan, Pakistan, and other flashpoints in the greater Middle East, and when the Chinese are seen as a more crucial partner, Washington may give short shrift to East Asia in general and to Japan in particular. To many Japanese observers, a lessening of relevance of the United States to the Asia Pacific region is deplorable but anticipated in the long run, given China's rise in capacity and influence.

The anticipation of this shift has been reinforced by some recent developments, which can be interpreted as revealing America's weaknesses and unreliability as a strategic ally. For one, the Americans have not indicated support for Japan's territorial claims in its disputes with South Korea and China. Washington expressed, almost openly, displeasure about Japan's insistence on solving the abduction issue with North Korea as a precondition for a more forthcoming attitude in the Six-Party Talks on Korean denuclearization. Also, despite its vocal support for Tokyo's endeavor to join the UN Security Council as a permanent member, Washington has not made vigorous efforts to fulfill that commitment.

To prepare for a seemingly inevitable reduction in American influence in Asia, some Japanese elites are calling for a more independent strategy and a more proactive diplomacy vis-à-vis China. Hence we find the recurrence of such ideas as "values diplomacy" and the construction of an "arc of freedom and prosperity," as well as more recent attempts to reach out to India, Australia, and ASEAN. Quietly, a number of Japanese politicians feel sympathetic to the pro-secession movement in Taiwan as a counterweight to the Chinese mainland, and there have been occasional reports of clandestine military cooperation between Japan and Taiwan in the form of sharing intelligence. All of these developments have implications for the dynamics of the trilateral China-Japan-US relationship.

US Perceptions

Global Trends 2025, a report prepared by the National Intelligence Council (NIC) of the United States in November 2008, presents the following description of China:

> Few countries are poised to have more impact on the world over the next 15–20 years than China. If current trends persist, by 2025 China will have the world's second largest economy and will be a leading military power. It could also be the largest importer of natural resources and an even greater polluter than it is now. US security and economic interests could face new challenges if China becomes a peer competitor that is militarily strong as well as economically dynamic and energy hungry.[11]

In terms of Japan's future, this report predicts, "Japan will face a major reorientation of its domestic and foreign policies by 2025 yet maintain its status as an upper middle rank power . . . On the foreign front, Japan's policies will be influenced most by the policies of China and the United States."[12] By linking this characterization of Japan with that of China, the writers of the NIC report seem to regard China as carrying heavier weight than Japan in the US strategic vision.

Many influential American writers, including those who prepared the *Global Trends 2025*, believe that international politics will become increasingly multipolar in nature. Richard Haass, president of the Council on Foreign Relations, concludes, "The only certainties in today's world are that geopolitics are becoming more multipolar and that America will not stay on top forever."[13] Fareed Zakaria, editor of *Newsweek*, also envisions a "post-American" multipolar world where the United States will no longer be in a dominant position.[14] Zakaria predicts,

> For some countries, the current economic crisis could actually accelerate the process (of multipolarization). For the past two decades, for example, China has grown at approximately 9 percent a year and the United States at 3 percent. For the next few years, American growth will likely be 1 percent and China's, by the most conservative estimates, 5 percent. So, China was growing three times as fast as the United States, but will now grow five times as fast, which only brings closer the date when the Chinese economy will equal in size that of the United States. Then contrast China's enormous

surplus reserves to America's massive debt burden: the picture does not suggest a return to American unipolarity.[15]

While noting China's ascending power, a great many American commentators are still confident that the United States will remain superior to China in overall strength in the foreseeable future and are not as alarmed as their Japanese counterparts. There appear to be three schools of American thinking regarding how the United States should respond to China as a resurgent power versus Japan as a status quo power.

The first school, represented by a number of distinguished thinkers like Henry Kissinger and Zbigniew Brzezinski, holds traditional realist or geostrategic views about the changing balance of power. These strategists see the rise of Chinese power as inevitable and advocate a strong US-China relationship. They by no means neglect Japan's importance in economics or the necessity of maintaining the US-Japan alliance. However, in geopolitical terms, China appears to play a more active role and to have more influence than Japan. According to Brzezinski, an "informal G2" is needed to cope with the global financial crisis and other current problems.

> The relationship between the US and China has to be truly a comprehensive global partnership, parallel [to] our relations with Europe and Japan. Our top leaders should therefore meet informally on a regular schedule for truly personal in-depth discussions regarding not just about bilateral relations but about the world in general. We have a common interest in global stability, in social progress worldwide, in successful domestic renewal and development, and in a renovated international system.[16]

The G2 is a popular notion among some economists and economic decision makers. Robert Zoellick, president of the World Bank, and Justin Yifu Lin, his deputy and a renowned economist from China, noted in a joint article that "for the world's economy to recover, these two economic powerhouses must cooperate and become the engine for the Group of 20. Without a strong G2, the G20 will disappoint."[17]

The second school of thinkers regards China as more of a rising strategic competitor—or even a strategic rival—rather than a global partner. They would like to see the maintenance and strengthening of Japan's power position, although practically speaking they may not deny the reality of China being a growing global player. Japan, therefore, is viewed as an ideological and political ally that is expected to play the role of balancing an "autocratic" China. As Robert Kagan, an American strategic thinker, argues,

> The global competition between democratic governments and autocratic governments will become a dominant feature of the twenty-first-century world. The great powers are increasingly choosing sides and identifying

themselves with one camp or the other. India, which during the Cold War was proudly neutral or even pro-Soviet, has begun to identify itself as part of the democratic West. Japan in recent years has also gone out of its way to position itself as a democratic great power, sharing common values with other Asian democracies but also with non-Asian democracies. For both Japan and India the desire to be part of the democratic world is genuine, but it is also part of a geopolitical calculation—a way of cementing solidarity with other great powers that can be helpful in their strategic competition with autocratic China.[18]

Obviously, to this school of thinkers, the solidification of the US-Japan alliance should be the priority in trilateral interactions, and they emphasize "common values" as well as common security goals between the United States and Japan plus Europe. Some of the thinkers in this school of thought may be labeled as "neoconservatives," who are already sufficiently distrustful of China's long-term strategic intentions regardless of its power position vis-à-vis other nations.

Thinkers in the third school could be characterized as "liberal institutionalists" in some cases or "constructivists" in others. This school of thought believes that, at a time when China is gaining more strategic and economic importance, Japan should remain the cornerstone for America in Asia. Meanwhile, the United States should also encourage China to join global and regional arrangements while preventing it from getting a free hand and dominant position. Noting more uncertainties in the power balance and in the trilateral relationship, some Americans propose a "hedging strategy" toward China while working with Japan and other nations to coordinate their China policies. This school of thought casts doubt on the notion of a G2 but is also skeptical of the proposal to contain China by simply cementing solidarity with Japan. In the May/June 2009 issue of *Foreign Affairs*, Elizabeth Economy and Adam Segal, both senior fellows at the Council on Foreign Relations, countered the G2 concept, asserting that Washington should embrace a more flexible and multilateral approach to dealing with China. "A heightened bilateral relationship may not be possible for China and the United States, as the two countries have mismatched interests and values," they wrote. "As a first step, the Obama administration should sit down with Japan, the EU, and other key allies to begin coordinating their policies toward China."[19]

Given the remarkable consistencies in US policy toward East Asia from the Bush administration to the Obama administration, as well as the pragmatic nature of Obama's foreign policy, the mainstream policy thinking in Washington toward Tokyo and Beijing may lie somewhere between the first and the third schools. Policymakers in Washington will never openly embrace a G2 formula, but they do work closely with Beijing on all important global issues. In the meantime, Japan remains a valuable ally in helping the United States meet the challenges it faces, including those resulting from China's rising power and influence.

DIFFERENT MEASUREMENTS OF POWER

The perceptions of the three bodies politic, as described above, are based predominantly on traditional measurements of power: economic size and growth rates, financial assets, trade volume, military capabilities, geopolitical presence, diplomatic influence, and so on. These measurements do make a great deal of sense, as they have a tremendous impact on how national leaders conceptualize their foreign policy and on how the general public views world politics.

Economic Growth

If one assesses the power balance among China, Japan, and the United States on the basis of traditional measurements, the trends are definitely in China's favor. Based on recent economic forecasts, China's GDP may catch up with that of Japan in two to three years, if not sooner, and with that of America in about 20 years. However, even when China's economy becomes equal in size to Japan's, the population of China is likely to be 10.5 times that of Japan and 4.3 times that of the United States, meaning its per capita GDP may be only one-tenth and one-twelfth that of Japan and America respectively.[20]

Since the global financial crisis deepened toward the end of 2008, analysts have debated as to which of the three economies will take the lead in recovering from the crisis, making the future balance more obscure and unpredictable. In all likelihood, however, in both the short run and the long run, China's economy will grow much faster than those of the United States and Japan, and the US economy may continue to grow faster than Japan's.

Military Capabilities

The momentum in the military balance is tilted toward China as well. China's defense budget doubled between 2000 and 2005 and then increased by 14.7 percent in 2006, 17.8 percent in 2007, and 17.6 percent in 2008.

According to a Chinese official report, its military spending in 2009 was set to increase by another 14.9 percent.[21] Reportedly, China is planning to build aircraft carriers to add to the blue water navy of the People's Liberation Army (PLA), and the Chinese armed forces already have a formidable nuclear missile force.

In comparison, the US military budget was to increase by 5.7 percent in 2009. The Japanese government–approved fiscal 2009 defense budget proposal represented a decline of 0.8 percent from the preceding year.[22] Nonetheless, in recent years, the US military budget has been almost as large as the rest of the world's defense spending combined and is over eight times larger than the officially announced military budget of China (compared at the nominal US dollar–renminbi rate, not the PPP rate). Despite the growth in China's military power, there is no doubt that the United States remains by far the strongest military power both in the Asia Pacific region and globally. Another common understanding is that Japan's armed forces are better equipped, bettered trained, and more modernized than the PLA.

In addition to its military weaknesses, China has no military allies and is faced with multifaceted security threats from both within and without. A major part of China's large military machine has been directed at the need to deter the pro-secession movement in Taiwan. There are quite a few potential flashpoints along China's borders with its Asian neighbors, including domestic tensions in North Korea, Pakistan, and Afghanistan that might explode. China's territorial disputes with India, Vietnam, and other Southeast Asian countries remain unresolved. Furthermore, as illustrated by the incidents in Tibet in March 2008 and Xinjiang in July 2009, China has to be prepared to resort to military force, at least occasionally, to cope with riots and tensions in sensitive areas.

Therefore, the missions and responsibilities of China's military power are vastly different from those of the United States and Japan, and the increase in its defense budget could be easily "absorbed" by needs unrelated to the United States and Japan. As an independent force, the Chinese military's power is inferior to the US-Japan military alliance (plus the US–South Korea alliance). US arms sales to Taiwan and covert US-Japan-Taiwan military cooperation also serve the purpose of preventing China from obtaining more military advantages. Given all these factors, the overall military balance among China, Japan, and the United States will not change dramatically in the foreseeable future.

Sustainable Development

While the above measurements are important, they offer only a partial picture. To obtain a clearer and more nuanced understanding of trilateral interaction requires alternative and additional measurements, of which "sustainable development" and "soft power/smart power" are perhaps the two most relevant elements for analyzing the power equation.

In recent years, observers both inside and outside of China have become increasingly concerned about China's development model, which has been dependent on international trade and investment from overseas (including Taiwan, Hong Kong SAR, Macau SAR, and ethnic Chinese in other countries). The high growth rate of the export-oriented economy has been attained at the expense of the environment and low-income laborers. The environmental degradation and the social disparities caused by this pattern of growth, in turn, are creating increasing tensions, dislocations, and pitfalls for China on the road ahead.

The Chinese government has realized the necessity of changing the current development model in order to sustain economic growth and social progress. It has officially adopted the concept of the "Scientific Outlook on Development," with a set of policies to redress many serious problems, such as the alarming income gaps, spiritual decay, and environmental pollution.[23]

Despite this realization, stark realities remain that contradict the "Scientific Outlook." For example, China has replaced the United States as the number one emitter of greenhouse gases. China's energy efficiency is only one-third to one-seventh that of the industrialized countries. Sixteen out of the 20 most polluted cities in the world are in China.[24] Over 54 percent of rivers in China contain contaminants that are harmful to human beings. More than 1.15 billion Chinese residents have to drink unsafe water. Desertification is progressing at an alarming rate, with deserts now claiming 27.4 percent of China's land.[25] Currently, only 18 percent of the country's landmass is covered by forest (compared with 67 percent in Japan and 33 percent in America).[26] Natural calamities in China are increasingly frequent and disastrous (e.g., the winter storms in southern China and the Sichuan earthquake, both in 2008, and the drought that struck the north in 2009). Official reports show that the economic costs resulting from environmental pollution were US$700 billion in 2004, more than 3 percent of China's GDP, which means a striking portion of its impressive economic growth was "swallowed" by pollution.[27]

The Chinese government and people have made impressive and strenuous efforts to contain water and air pollution. However, China's official targets to reduce pollution and greenhouse gas emissions are seen by many as unachievable. In the Chinese media, many government officials and political commentators are even expressing their suspicion that climate change is yet another policy tool for the West to weaken China by trying to slow down its economic growth.

To fight the impact of the global financial crisis and economic downturn, more than 4 trillion yuan is being spent to stimulate economic growth in China, which was intended to lead to an 8 percent expansion of the economy in 2009. It is reported that 80 percent of this package is for the construction of infrastructure, mostly the building of new highways, railroads, and airports. In other words, the traditional pattern of development that puts GDP growth as the top priority continues at the expense of efforts to curb pollution and carbon emissions.

The situation in the social realm is not satisfactory in China either. Indeed, the Chinese leadership has called for building up a "harmonious society" based on the "people-first" principle, which means putting priority on distributing the benefits of recent decades of speedy economic growth more evenly. The government has set aside billions of dollars in new farm subsidies; increased spending on social security, education, and healthcare; and made public efforts to root out rampant corruption. But it is an uphill task to overcome these longstanding difficulties and ease social tensions. The eruption of violent riots in Tibet in 2008 and Xinjiang in 2009 have reminded Chinese elites of the danger of intensified ethnic and religious tensions in the national minority areas. Instead of reassessing and readjusting policy, however, more attention and money are being allocated to tightening political, social, and informational controls.

In contrast with China, Japan is one of the most advanced "green" countries in the world, taking the lead in areas such as protecting the environment, improving energy efficiency, and developing solar- and wind-generated electricity. The decreasing Japanese population may not bode well for long-term economic growth, but it ensures that Japan will continue to set a good example in terms of keeping its energy consumption under control, keeping its educational level high, and dealing with climate change more successfully than most other countries. In addition, Japan has undertaken initiatives to provide technological assistance and funding to developing countries to assist them in coping with global warming and environmental degradation.

True, Japan's economy has been hit hard by the recent global financial crisis, and its current growth rate is barely above zero. However, Japan's very low interest rate, a high savings rate, a social safety net that covers almost the whole population, and the ethnic homogeneity of its population make its society much less vulnerable to the negative impact of globalization. Japan's immigration policy remains tightly controlled, and many observers regard this as an impediment to the maintenance of its labor force. Yet this policy ensures that Japanese society keeps its inherent cohesion.[28]

Compared with Japan's policy and performance in the realm of sustainable development, the United States does not present an enviable case. America's per capita energy consumption is four times the world average, its per capita water usage is three times the world average, its per capita garbage generation is twice the world average, and its per capita carbon emissions are four times the world average.[29] Despite these statistics, the US government has refused to sign the Kyoto Protocol for curbing global carbon emissions.

One encouraging sign is that the entire American nation now seems determined to move in the right direction to reduce carbon emissions and improve energy efficiency. On November 18, 2008, President-elect Barack Obama proclaimed, "Few challenges facing America—and the world—are more urgent than combating climate change . . . but too often, Washington has failed to show the same kind of leadership. That will change when I take office."[30] The Obama administration is now committed to engaging vigorously with the international community to find solutions and help lead the world toward a new era of global cooperation on climate change.

In a speech on energy policy, Obama remarked on March 19, 2009, "We have a choice to make. We can remain one of the world's leading importers of foreign oil, or we can make the investments that would allow us to become the world's leading exporter of renewable energy. We can let climate change continue to go unchecked, or we can help stop it. We can let the jobs of tomorrow be created abroad, or we can create those jobs right here in America and lay the foundation for lasting prosperity."[31] To be sure, whether such rhetoric and strategic vision can translate into substantive policy changes and practices remains to be seen. But given America's extraordinarily rich natural and human resources, along with its technological know-how and educational advancement, there is cause to anticipate great progress in America's energy and environmental policies, which will make its economic growth more sustainable and balanced.

Soft Power and Smart Power

An additional alternative measurement is "soft power," as well as the relatively new concept of "smart power."[32] Soft power is generally defined as the power to attract, convince, and persuade others through diplomacy, aid, the spread of values, and the force of example. Smart power, in turn, refers to a combination of hard power—to coerce by military or other means—and soft power. The phrase is a relatively recent addition to the diplomatic phrasebook, even if the concept is not. It was coined not long after the American invasion and occupation of Iraq and was presented as a liberal alternative to the aggressive neoconservatism of the Bush administration.

China's soft power has been growing rapidly in the past few years.[33] Frequently mentioned reflections of China's soft power include the apparent attraction of the Chinese model of development (the "Beijing Consensus") for the developing world, the successful hosting of the Olympics and Paralympics in Beijing in 2008, Beijing's moderate and balanced foreign policy, its expressed desire for peaceful settlement of territorial disputes with neighboring countries, its expanded and more active role in international institutions and in UN peacekeeping operations, the establishment of more than 100 Confucius Institutes to promote Chinese language and culture all over the world, and the popularity of China's cultural products.

However, the growth of China's soft power is offset by a number of constraints, including a tainted image in relation to its handling of the Tibetan and Xinjiang issues, problems related to product safety and quality, widespread corruption, the lack of government transparency, and the recent rise of radical nationalistic sentiments among Chinese students and elites.

The Chinese leadership has officially adopted the notion of soft power and has spared no effort to project a better image of China in global affairs. What is unique in such efforts is the overwhelming dependence on the government and the Communist Party to promote soft power. For example, 45 billion yuan was reportedly allocated in early 2009 to China Central Television (CCTV), the *People's Daily*, and the New China News Agency for expanding their publicity and networking. CCTV already has four international channels that broadcast in English, French, and Spanish, as well as Chinese. A new Arabic-language channel was established in July 2009, which is accessible to nearly 300 million people in 22 Arabic-speaking countries, and a Russian-language channel was launched in September 2009.[34]

The promotion of soft power on the part of China is directed mainly at countering what the Chinese see as Western schemes to criticize and demonize China, and at "correcting" the Western media's "distortions." However, what are the political and cultural values the Chinese official media are hoping to project at home and abroad? Are there universal values that China shares with other nations, or should China's value system be essentially different from the so-called Western values like democracy, human rights, rule of law, and the market economy? As China attempts to correct other people's distortions, are there distortions in China about the outside world that need to be corrected as well? What should the role of civil society—which is rather weak and discouraged in China—be in promoting soft power?[35] These are some of the key questions being debated today in China, and they must eventually be answered as China progresses along the road toward global power status.

As both its hard power and soft power are on the rise, China's smart power will certainly grow and be exerted in global affairs. Chinese policymakers have demonstrated a remarkable ability to understand changes in world politics and to use their power to influence others. As was noted by Kishore Mahbubani, a respected Singaporean political commentator,

> Chinese policymakers are better students of history than their American counterparts . . . China has become geopolitically more competent than America: China is aware that the world has changed. China does careful global geopolitical calculations in which it tries to objectively analyze its geopolitical assets and liabilities. It then works out a long-term plan to enhance its assets and minimize its liabilities. Each time a new problem surfaces, China looks for advantage in it, assuming that it must adapt to the world, not shape the world as it wishes.[36]

However, domestic weaknesses and problems in coordinating domestic and foreign policies do constitute constraints on China's ability to exercise "smart power" abroad.

Japan's soft power appears to be holding steady in the world. In recent years, Japan has invested substantial sums in the exercise of soft power to shape hearts and minds abroad. For example, it was reported that former Prime Minister Yasuo Fukuda showed a deep interest in enhancing Japan's cultural influence in the United States and China. During his 24-hour stay in Washington in November 2007, for example, he met with 26 representatives from the field of Japan-related education with the objective of promoting the status of Japanese studies in America and promoting US-Japan cultural exchange. According to news reports, in a conversation the previous month with Gerald Curtis, a professor at Columbia University and a leading Japan scholar, Fukuda expressed true concern over the development of Japan's soft power as a whole, including the strengthening of relations with the United States.[37]

Japan's soft power also lies in its culture, and more prominently in its current popular culture—electronic games, anime, manga, novels, film, fashion, "cosplay" cafes, and other creative cultural products—that are hugely popular in South Korea, the Chinese mainland, Taiwan, Hong Kong SAR, and elsewhere in Asia. It is hard to fathom the extent to which these cultural goods and phenomena can translate into political influence, but they are surely helpful in conveying a positive image of Japan.

On the other hand, Japan's soft power, and for that matter its smart power, is seriously hampered by a number of deficiencies. In the eyes of many international observers, in recent years Japan has lacked a clear strategic direction and a positive vision of its future. As Aurelia George Mulgan explains, "In many ways, Japan now finds itself a ship without a rudder." Internally, a divided Diet and dissent in both the Liberal Democratic Party and the Democratic Party of Japan injected uncertainty into the policy process and obscured Tokyo's foreign policy, at least until the historic elections in August 2009. "With so many internal problems," Mulgan notes, "Japan now can no longer even contemplate extending its influence abroad."[38] Internationally, Japan's unapologetic attitude toward its World War II (and earlier) history has severely impaired its leadership credentials in Asia. In addition, Japan's civil society is still underdeveloped. Full-fledged Japanese think tanks are few, and those concerned with international affairs are not playing a significant role in Japan's foreign policymaking. Therefore, while Japan enjoys a positive international image in some aspects and its economic power remains formidable, it has lacked the capability to generate sufficient smart power. Although Japan's new prime minister, Yukio Hatoyama, has put forward some new ideas like the "spirit of fraternity" and proposals such as the establishment of an "East Asian Community," to what extent these ideas and proposals will increase Japan's smart power remains to be seen. Thus far, many international observers, including many in China, are doubtful that Japan is really moving into a new era.

As for the United States, a public opinion survey done by the Chicago Council on Global Affairs in 2008 showed that America's soft power in Asia greatly exceeds that of China. When looking at the five categories of soft power separately, the United States was ahead of China in four: political, human capital, economic, and diplomatic, China was ahead only in culture.[39]

Despite the decline of US soft power worldwide since the Iraq War and the further damage done by the financial crisis, it now seems to have gained some momentum toward recovery. The election of Barack Obama as the first nonwhite US president and the appointment of Hillary Clinton as secretary of state boosted the US image in Asia. Hopes have been rekindled in America and many other nations that the United States will play a more constructive role in world affairs. These hopes were best reflected by the international responses to the award of the 2009 Nobel Peace Prize to President Obama for his extraordinary efforts to strengthen international diplomacy and cooperation between peoples. However, a lot depends on whether the Obama administration can use its hard and soft power in a smarter manner than was done in the past, whether the United States will be able to lead the world out of the current financial and economic quagmire, and whether Americans will honor their commitment to setting a good example and playing a leading role in making the planet more "green and clean."

CONCLUSION

In looking ahead at the evolving power balance among China, Japan, and the United States over the next few years, the conventional wisdom among politicians and policy analysts in all three countries is that China's power and international influence will continue ascending rapidly, whereas the balance is likely to tilt toward the United States in the US-Japan leg of the equation.

This conventional wisdom is based largely on the traditional measurements of power, in particular economic growth and military capabilities. However, when one adjusts the prism to reflect the dimensions of sustainable development, distribution of social welfare, governance, and soft power or smart power, the picture is vastly different. For example, in the sustainable development dimension, Japan is doing better than the United States, and China is definitely the most vulnerable. If China does not change its mode of production and consumption and continues to rely heavily on its already deteriorating environment and cheap labor, its edge in economic growth will be lost. It might also be fair to point out that the United States currently has the greatest soft power, followed by that of Japan (in Asia at least), and China lags behind. Unlike the case with hard power measurements, it would be difficult for China to catch up with Japan and the United States in terms of soft power.

On the one hand, it will serve the best interests of the United States and Japan to embrace a stronger, more prosperous, and more stable China and to encourage China to move toward a market economy, good governance, and the rule of law. On the other hand, overestimating Chinese power on the part of Japan and the United States runs the risk of overreaction and of being caught in a "security dilemma." US-Japan coordination in hedging against the rise of China may appear plausible and appealing to some interest groups in both countries. To see China as the target of the US-Japan alliance, however, would backfire. Particularly for Japanese policymakers, China's resurgence should not be seen as a zero-sum game in which Japan is on the losing side of the equation.

On the part of China, the regained confidence in its power is helping the country rid itself of the "siege mentality" that characterized the Chinese mindset about the world for a long period, starting with the First Opium War of 1839–1842. Meanwhile, Chinese policymakers and analysts should also avoid overestimating the power and influence that China is obtaining. After all, China's economic, political, and diplomatic successes will continue to depend largely on its successful management of relationships with the United States and Japan. Furthermore, overconfidence about China's strength and growth, along with an underestimation of Japan or the United States, would do a disservice to its long-term interests. Surging Chinese power will inevitably give rise to Chinese nationalism. One real challenge for the Chinese leadership, therefore, is to encourage a healthy sense of patriotism while keeping excessive nationalism at bay.

The most serious threats to China's national security, domestic stability, and economic growth come from within rather than without. China should regard neither the United States nor Japan as the major threat to its security if these two countries do not see China as a major threat. For historical reasons and because of concerns about a possible conflict over Taiwan, Beijing has had strong reservations about the US military presence in the Asia Pacific region and the continuation of the US-Japan alliance. However, at a time when China faces more serious challenges ranging from the global financial crisis to nuclear proliferation and nontraditional security issues, and with the remarkable improvement in cross-strait relations, the maintenance of the US presence in Asia should be accepted not only as a fait accompli, but also as a potentially advantageous point. US participation in Asian affairs and strengthened China-US cooperation in the region, for example in the context of APEC, will benefit both China and Japan. By the same token, Japan's legitimate and reasonable aspirations to become a "normal country" should be recognized as long as it maintains its status as a non-nuclear power. To the extent that the US-Japan alliance serves to reassure Japan and thus keep it away from nuclearization, China should at least acquiesce to it.

While military security and the nonproliferation of nuclear weapons are still important, the China-Japan-US relationship needs a new focus, one that takes up issues such as energy efficiency, climate change, environmental protection, public health, and other nontraditional security issues. In exploring its particular development model, China should avoid repeating the American mistakes of overspending, overconsumption of energy (driving large cars, competing to build the largest skyscrapers, etc.), and the wasteful use of land (building numerous golf courses) and other natural resources. Instead, China should look more to Japan for lessons in protecting the environment, saving water and energy, and economizing on raw materials. On the road toward a "harmonious society," China has a lot to learn from American and Japanese experiences.

[handwritten margin note: China should learn from US mistakes]

A new form of trilateral cooperation can be established by starting with the global challenge of climate change. The three countries should coordinate their positions to make the ongoing negotiations on a global climate change treaty a success and should jointly and faithfully carry out any subsequent UN resolution on the issue. The three governments and NGOs in the three countries should encourage and support efforts to initiate trilateral and multilateral cooperation on alternative energy sources and energy efficiency. Meanwhile, scholars and experts in the three countries can undertake joint research projects to compare their development models and find ways to work together to influence their societies to adopt healthier, more environmentally friendly lifestyles.

In conclusion, refocusing on sustainable development and good governance should pave the way for more comprehensive and effective cooperation that will benefit the three peoples in the 21st century. Only by doing so will the three strongest economic powers in today's world be truly able to avoid the strategic competition and rivalry that characterized the 20th century and brought about so much human tragedy.

NOTES

1. See Morton Abramowitz, Yoichi Funabashi, and Wang Jisi, *China-Japan-US: Managing the Trilateral Relationship* (Washington DC: Brookings Institution and Japan Center for International Exchange, 1998); and Morton Abramowitz, Yoichi Funabashi, and Wang Jisi, *China-Japan-US Relations: Meeting New Challenges* (Washington DC: Brookings Institution and Japan Center for International Exchange, 2002).

2. A bestselling book, *China Is Unhappy*, published in China in March 2009, presents the notion that "with Chinese national strength growing at an unprecedented rate, China should stop self-debasing and come to recognize the fact that it has the power to lead the world, and the necessity to break away from Western influence." The book further argues, "We need a country with an accumulation of history, generations of civilization and a population big enough to carry out such reforms (in the international order). China is doing pretty well in this structure but the structure can't continue. China needs to act as a savior. This is our historical task." Cited in Jane Macartney, "China Is Unhappy:

Censors Take Hands-Off Approach to Bestseller," *Timesonline*, March 26, 2009, http://www.timesonline.co.uk/tol/news/world/asia/china/article5981766.ece.

3. "The Current International Financial Crisis and the Transition of the International System—A Symposium Held by the China Institutes of Contemporary International Relations," in *Xiandai Guoji Guanxi* [Contemporary international relations], no. 4 (2009): 1–42.

4. Ibid., 14–15.

5. "China's National Defense in 2008," white paper released by the Information Office of the State Council of the People's Republic of China, January 2009, http://news.xinhuanet.com/english/2009-01/20/content_10688124.htm.

6. According to a poll conducted by the Horizon Research Consultancy Group from 2000 to 2004, Chinese citizens' feelings toward Russia were more positive than those toward the United States or Japan. Around 30 percent of respondents thought Russia was a friendly country toward China, while less than 5 percent liked Japan. The respondents also viewed Russia as a more powerful country than Japan. See http://www.horizonkey.com/showart.asp?art_id=376&cat_id=6.

7. See, for example, Xinhua News Agency, "Koizumi States China's Development Is Not a Threat But an Opportunity," November 10, 2004.

8. "Japanese Foreign Minister Openly Plays Up the China Threat Theory," *Xin Jing Bao*, December 23, 2005, http://news.thebeijingnews.com/0099/2005/1223/011@149961.htm.

9. "Riben shouxiang Masheng zai Jing yanjiang bochi Zhongguo weixielun" [Japanese Prime Minister Aso rejects China threat theory in Beijing speech], *Chongqing Evening News*, May 1, 2009, http://cqwb.cqnews.net/webnews/htm/2009/5/1/327916.shtml.

10. According to a public opinion survey sponsored by the Japanese government and released in December 2008, two-thirds of Japanese citizens did not feel friendly toward China, the highest percentage since 1978. "Ties with US Shaky, Record-High 28% Say," *Japan Times*, December 7, 2008, http://search.japantimes.co.jp/print/nn20081207a2.html.

11. National Intelligence Council, *Global Trends 2025: A Transformed World* (November 2008), 29, www.dni.gov/nic/NIC_2025_project.html.

12. Ibid., 33–34.

13. Richard N. Haass, "The Age of Nonpolarity: What Will Follow US Dominance," *Foreign Affairs* 87, no. 3 (May/June 2008), http://www.foreignaffairs.com/articles/63397/richard-n-haass/the-age-of-nonpolarity.

14. Fareed Zakaria, *The Post-American World* (New York: McGraw-Hill, 2008).

15. Fareed Zakaria, "Wanted: A New US Grand Strategy," *Washington Post*, December 1, 2008, http://newsweek.washingtonpost.com/postglobal/fareed_zakaria/2008/12/wanted_a_new_grand_strategy_1.html.

16. Zbigniew Brzezinski, "Moving toward a Reconciliation of Civilizations," *China Daily*, January 15, 2009.

17. Robert B. Zoellick and Justin Yifu Lin, "Recovery Rides on the 'G-2,'" *Washington Post*, March 6, 2009, A15.

18. Robert Kagan, "The End of the End of History," *New Republic*, April 23, 2008, http://www.tnr.com/environmentenergy/story.html?id=ee167382-bd16-4b13-beb7-08effe1a6844.

19. Elizabeth C. Economy and Adam Segal, "The G-2 Mirage: Why the United States and China Are Not Ready to Upgrade Ties," *Foreign Affairs* 88, no. 3 (May/June 2009): 20.

20. Calculated based on data from the International Monetary Fund's World Economic Outlook Database (October 2009 edition), http://www.imf.org/external/pubs/ft/weo/2009/02/weodata/index.aspx.

21. Xinhua News Agency, "China's Defense Budget to Grow 14.9 Percent in 2009," *China Daily*, March 14, 2009.

22. "Japan Defense Focus," Japanese Ministry of Defense official website, http://www.mod.go.jp/e/jdf/no12/topics.html.

23. "Scientific Outlook on Development" is a concept initiated by the 16th Central Committee of the Communist Party of China (CPC) in 2003. It stresses a comprehensive, balanced, and sustainable development that is people oriented. With priority on addressing the needs and protecting the rights of the people, the country will grow not only in economic terms but also in political and cultural terms. The growth aims to bridge regional disparities and the urban-rural gap and to preserve natural resources and the environment. This concept forms the core of the policies of the CPC's current leaders, headed by Hu Jintao. At the 17th CPC National Congress in October 2007, it was formally included in the Communist Party Constitution.

24. Kai N. Lee with Lisa Mastny, "World Is Soon Half Urban," *Vital Signs 2007–2008* (Washington DC: World Watch Institute, 2007), 52.

25. "Facts & Figures: China's Basic National Circumstances of Climate Change," *People's Daily*, June 4, 2007, http://english.people.com.cn/200706/04/eng20070604_380718.html.

26. Huang Kangsheng, "Quanqiu biannuan, Zhongguo jiji yingdui" [China actively copes with global warming], *People's Daily* (overseas edition), December 22, 2007, 3.

27. "Zhongguo shouci fabiao luse GDP baogao, wuran sunshi zhan GDP 3.05%," [China releases its first green GDP report, stating pollution causes loss of 3.05% of GDP], *Xinhua News*, September 9, 2006, http://news.xinhuanet.com/fortune/2006-09/07/content_5062240.htm. For further data indicating the impact of environmental degradation on China, see Wang Jisi, "Cong Zhongmeiri liliang duibi kan sanbian guanxi de fazhan qushi" [The trend in China-Japan-US trilateral relations through the prism of power balance], *Guoji Zhengzhi Yanjiu* [International Politics Quarterly], no. 3 (2008): 8–12.

28. In the United States, new immigrants, together with the ethnic and cultural diversity they bring to the country, have caused worries and identity problems, as described by the late Harvard professor Samuel Huntington. See Samuel P. Huntington, *Who Are We? The Challenges to America's National Identity* (New York: Simon & Schuster, 2004). In China, 140 million people, or 15 percent of the total work force, are economic migrants on the move. This scale of social mobility may contribute to the economic boom, but the social and ecological costs are also enormous. Some Chinese commentators have analyzed the reasons why there was no apparent panic in Japan during the 2008–2009 financial crisis, pointing out that Japan's high savings rate, low unemployment rate, and social safety network give Japanese society enough resilience and confidence in coping with the crisis. See, for example, Ding Gang, "Weiji laile, Riben weisha meiluan" [Why Japan is not in chaos when the crisis comes], *Oriental Morning Post*, February 18, 2009, A19; Ma Ting, "Weiji laile, Riben weihe buhuang" [Why Japan has no panic when the crisis comes], *Global Times*, February 20, 2009, 11.

29. Data are from the World Resource Institute's "EarthTrends" database, http://earthtrends.wri.org/searchable_db/index.php?. Estimates on energy consumption are calculated based on 2007 statistics from the International Energy Agency Statistics Division, *Energy Balances of OECD Countries* (2008 edition); per capita water usage on 2000 statistics from the Food and Agricultural Organization of the United Nations (FAO), *AQUASTAT Information System on Water and Agriculture 2005*, and the UN Department of Economic and Social Affairs *World Population Prospects: The 2004 Revision*; and carbon emissions on data from the International Energy Agency, CO_2 *Emissions from Fuel Combustion* (2006 edition).

30. Dave Rochelson, "President-elect Obama Promises 'New Chapter' on Climate Change," from President-elect Obama's official website, http://change.gov/newsroom/entry/president_elect_obama_promises_new_chapter_on_climate_change.

31. Cited from the official White House website, http://www.whitehouse.gov/issues/energy_and_environment.

32. For an early discussion of the concept of "smart power," see "Smart Power: John J. Hamre Talks with Joseph Nye and Richard Armitage," *American Interest* 3, no. 2 (November–December 2007), http://www.the-american-interest.com/article.cfm?piece=346.

33. For a discussion of China's soft power, see Joseph S. Nye and Wang Jisi, "The Rise of China's Soft Power and Its Implications for the United States," in Richard Rosecrance and Gu Guoliang, eds., *Power and Restraint: A Shared Vision for the US-China Relationship* (New York: PublicAffairs, 2009).

34. Michael Bristow, "China Launches Arabic TV Channel," BBC News, July 25, 2009, http://news.bbc.co.uk/2/hi/asia-pacific/8166486.stm.

35. For my own observations on some of these questions, see "China Shouldn't Obsess over Western Media," an interview with Wang Jisi, *Global Times* (English edition), July 27, 2009, http://opinion.globaltimes.cn/chinese-press/2009-07/451265.html.

36. Kishore Mahbubani, "Smart Power, Chinese Style," in *American Interest* 3, no. 4 (March/April 2008), http://www.the-american-interest.com/article-bd.cfm?piece=406.

37. Yoo Jae-woong, "Smart, Soft Powers Key to Promoting National Interests," December 30, 2007, Korea.net, http://www.korea.net/News/news/newsView.asp?serial_no=20071224024&part=111&SearchDay.

38. Aurelia George Mulgan, "Why Japan Can't Lead," *World Policy Journal* 26, no. 2 (Summer 2009): 101–10.

39. The survey concludes that "Asians have great respect for American businesses, popular culture, education, diplomatic efforts, and … political system," and that "importantly and somewhat surprisingly, survey results indicate that China's 'charm offensive' has thus far been ineffective." See *Soft Power in Asia: Results of a 2008 Multinational Survey of Public Opinions* (Chicago: Chicago Council on Global Affairs, 2008), 34.

3 | The China-Japan Relationship, East Asia Community, and the Dynamics of Trilateral Relations

RYOSEI KOKUBUN

LOOKING BACK AT the recent history of Asia, there is one major structural change that stands out. Whereas relations among China, Japan, and the United States throughout the 20th century basically made China a passive target of competition and cooperation by the region's two great powers—Japan and the United States—with the advent of the 21st century, China's extraordinary economic growth and the concomitant expansion of its political and military influence has transformed it into an international power that is playing on the regional and global playing field alongside both Japan and the United States. In fact, Asian affairs over the past decade have been defined by the rise of China. It therefore should come as no surprise that this decade has also seen a precipitous deterioration in China-Japan relations and renewed momentum for the establishment of an "East Asia community"—phenomena that are interlinked and can be partly explained as a reaction to China's growing influence.

This chapter reflects on the history of China-Japan-US relations in order to explore how the rise of China is transforming regional relations in Asia, how it is connected to the effort to build an East Asia community, and what impact the resultant changes in the regional context are likely to have on trilateral relations. It tackles a number of important questions: How badly did China-Japan relations sour over the past decade, and to what extent have they subsequently improved? Can we conclude that, with the recent improvement in bilateral relations, the two countries have evolved beyond the basic issues that had defined postwar China-Japan relations—namely, the issues related to their wartime history and to Taiwan—and have reached a stage that can rightly be termed a "post-postwar China-Japan relationship"? Moreover, what position should China-Japan ties occupy in the context of the proposed East Asia community, how should the United States factor into that equation, and how does the potential emergence of an East Asia community relate to the dynamics of the trilateral China-Japan-US relationship?   *post- postwar C-J 左 右*

THE RISE OF CHINA

In 1949, journalist Jack Belden published a work entitled *China Shakes the World*, which was based on his own reporting at the time of the birth of the People's Republic of China (PRC).[1] Viewed objectively, however, one might ask whether any events have actually occurred in the six decades since the PRC's founding where the world was actually "shaken" by China. To be sure, the world was affected and influenced in various ways by such events as the Cultural Revolution in the 1960s and the Tiananmen Square Incident in 1989. However, can we truly say that the world was "shaken" by these events? Was it not China itself that was shaken? If we look at the bigger picture, 20th-century China was not an independent international power shaking the world but was rather standing on the outside as other actors formed the international system. The primary reason for this was that China during those years maintained a closed national economy based on a socialist system.

This situation changed only after the death of Mao Zedong in 1976. China turned to policies of reform and opening in 1978, under the leadership of Deng Xiaoping. Change came again, beginning in the 1990s, when China started down the path toward a socialist market economy, achieving rapid economic growth and eventually obtaining membership in the global economic system by joining the World Trade Organization in 2001. Since then, China has been greatly affected by the norms of the international economic system. The pace at which China has internationalized its economy in such areas as intellectual property rights has perhaps been slower than one might have expected. Nevertheless, China is definitely being incorporated into the framework of the international regime. From this standpoint, the world is still clearly shaking China. Although the engagement policy of the Clinton era in the latter half of the 1990s still did not fully recognize China as a member of the international system, the notion adopted by the Bush administration at the outset of the 21st century of a "responsible stakeholder" positioned China as one of this system's members.

Today, circumstances continue to change significantly. China has now surpassed Germany to boast the third highest gross domestic product (GDP) in the world, following only the United States and Japan. Moreover, Japanese growth has turned markedly sluggish amidst the global financial crisis, and the likelihood has increased that China will outstrip Japan within one or two years and rise to the number two spot in world economic rankings. China also ranked third worldwide in 2007 in terms of trade; whereas it accounted for less than 1 percent of the total global trade in 1978, this figure had reached about 8 percent by 2007. China's total amount of trade in this period more than doubled, and as a percentage of GDP it grew from 9.7 percent in 1978 to 66.8 percent in 2007, making China a global leader in trade. Moreover, among China's exports, the proportion occupied by industrial products rose to 94.9 percent, while primary products decreased to just 5.1 percent.[2] Needless to say, the direct investment that was introduced into China from abroad has provided the impetus for this growth, and nowadays it is China itself that is rapidly increasing its direct investment overseas.

In sum, despite its internal economic disparities, China can no longer rank itself as a developing country. Moreover, every action China takes today plays a major role in moving the world economy. To be sure, the Chinese yuan cannot yet be considered an international currency and is probably still insufficient to shake the world in terms of international finance. However, China unquestionably represents a huge market and is becoming a serious global presence in trade and investment. When it comes to US government bond holdings, China is now first in the world by a decisive margin and Japan is in second place; this means that China is now the largest overseas shareholder in the United States, and its influence on the financial crisis that originated in the United States has become stronger than ever before. Even though Belden's prediction was greatly amiss, China has, in fact, emerged in the early 21st century as a great power that is truly "shaking the world"—albeit through a market economy rather than through socialism.

The world has recently been confronted by an unparalleled financial crisis, which was set off by the collapse of the American economy. What this crisis has demonstrated is that the world is no longer in a situation that can be handled by only the G7 or G8, which have monopolized economic management in the postwar liberal world. Instead, the G20—which involves countries like the so-called BRICs (Brazil, Russia, India, and China)—has rushed to play the central role in coping with the current crisis. China's presence among the 12 non-G8 countries stands out. This is because a regulated economic system known as "state capitalism"—a half-baked capitalist system premised on major market intervention by the state—is operating effectively there amid the current financial crisis. Moreover, as noted above, China holds a large amount of US government bonds. Accordingly, although there had been a debate until recently about whether or not to add China to the ranks of the G8, with Japan and the United States opposing the idea based on the fact that China is not a democratic country, the new global recession has brought an almost instantaneous shift from the age of the G8 to the age of the G20.

CHANGING RELATIONS AMONG CHINA, JAPAN, AND THE UNITED STATES

Looking back over the past century, international relations in East Asia have been greatly affected by the state of relations among China, Japan, and the United States. In the first half of the 20th century, the pattern of relations was dominated by the rise of Japan and its invasion of China, and then by the response of the United States and its alliance with China. This had as its direct trigger the financial collapse that began in 1929. The start of the tragedy came in 1931, when Japan, beleaguered by its economic difficulties, sought to create a lifeline for itself in Manchuria. Needless to say, the United States supported China, and this subsequently set the stage for the Pacific War between the United States and Japan over power and interests in Mainland China and the Western Pacific.

When Japan was defeated in August 1945, it was occupied by the United States. In the latter half of the 20th century, Japan became an ally of the United States, and it took communist China, which was born in 1949, as a hypothetical enemy that required containment. The resultant structure of postwar East Asia involved a standoff between Japan and the United States on the one hand and communist China on the other. This state of affairs did not change until the China-US rapprochement of the early 1970s, and that shift was in turn based on the theory of power politics, which viewed the Soviet Union as the hypothetical enemy of all three countries. At the time, China accepted the US-Japan alliance, and a relationship of partnership and cooperation was thus formed in opposition to the USSR.

However, the Tiananmen Square Incident of 1989 and the end of the Cold War marked the disappearance of the Soviet Union as a common enemy. A new modus vivendi for China-Japan-US relations was therefore needed.[3] In the 1990s, as China was enjoying rapid economic growth and making strides toward creating a market economy, Japan and the United States adopted a policy of engagement with China. This policy did not view an emerging China as a threat but rather was based on the policy objective of finding ways in which Japan and the United States could incorporate China into the international system. But when President Clinton spent more than a week in China in 1998 without stopping in Japan, concerns in Japan began to rise over "Japan passing" as analysts feared that the new "strategic partnership" between the United States and China would be strengthened at Japan's expense.

Beginning in 2001, the Bush administration initially placed top priority on relations with its allies and therefore emphasized US ties with Japan while putting some distance between the United States and China. But when counterterrorism was thrust to the top of the agenda due to the terrorist attacks on September 11, the United States realized that cooperation with China was necessary. In the Six-Party Talks on North Korea, the United States avoided taking direct responsibility and instead entrusted China with the role of moderator. China was troubled at the time by the separatist tendencies of Taiwan, and the United States, which took no joy in Taiwan's policy of needling China, provided indirect support to China by consistently urging restraint on the part of the Chen Shui-bian government. During this time, trade and investment between the United States and China were continuing to grow, and an economic bloc of sorts was formed between them. It was in the context of such developments that former Deputy Secretary of State Robert Zoellick in 2005 spoke about China's being a "responsible stakeholder in international society," and the United States has not altered that position to this day. One can only conclude that this is essentially further evidence of the strengthening of the strategic partnership between the United States and China.

Both the United States and Japan had major political shake-ups in 2009. In the United States, a new Democratic administration under President Barack Obama came to office in January 2009, with Hillary Clinton serving as secretary of state. It had been during the Democratic administration of President William Clinton in the latter half of the 1990s that the United States and China began forming their strategic partnership, and few expect a significant departure from that policy under President Obama. Despite the many differences between the United States and China, in light of the current financial crisis and the need for ongoing counterterrorism efforts, it appears likely that their bilateral relationship will continue to be stable and that their strategic partnership will grow stronger in the future. The US-Japan alliance is also likely to remain stable in the future and to continue to be the main pillar of Japanese diplomacy. It is highly unlikely that the United States would simply abandon its strongest ally in the Pacific. Japan plays host to critical US military bases and places the greatest emphasis within its diplomatic relations on its alliance with the United States.

Similarly, in Japan's August 2009 election, the Liberal Democratic Party (LDP) tasted a historic defeat, and the Democratic Party of Japan (DPJ) took power under the leadership of Yukio Hatoyama. As this book is being published in the early days of that administration, there are many unknowns when it comes to the sort of foreign policy the DPJ will implement. However, while there may be some modifications in Japan's stance toward the United States, it is highly unlikely that the DPJ will do anything that would fundamentally harm the foundation of the US-Japan alliance, and it is unthinkable that the DPJ, which is expected to place even greater priority than the LDP on Japan's foreign policy toward Asia, would aggressively pursue policies that would worsen Japan's relations with China and South Korea. It is therefore likely that the basic framework for Japanese foreign policy will not change greatly under a DPJ administration.

That being said, the weakest link when it comes to the future stability of the relationship among China, Japan, and the United States is the China-Japan relationship. The ties between Japan and China, which rank second and third in the world respectively in terms of GDP, are extremely important for understanding the situation and direction of not only East Asia but the entire world. At the start of the 21st century, this bilateral relationship was severely tested. When Junichiro Koizumi took office in 2001, bilateral relations became entangled over issues such as the prime minister's visits to the controversial Yasukuni Shrine, and it appeared as though no resolution was possible. The world took note of the difficulties in the China-Japan relationship and expressed great concern about where it was headed.

However, after Shinzo Abe took over as prime minister in September 2006, he promptly visited China, proposing that the new motto for bilateral ties should be a "mutually beneficial strategic relationship." Relations between the two counties in every field began to improve immediately, and reciprocal visits of the two nations' leaders were revived as well with the successive visits of Chinese Premier Wen Jiabao to Japan in April 2007, Japanese Prime Minister Yasuo Fukuda to China in December of the same year, and Chinese President Hu Jintao to Japan in May 2008. During this period, both countries' leaders barely touched on the so-called "historical issues," including the problem of Yasukuni Shrine, or on the Taiwan issue. As a consequence, state-to-state relations improved dramatically. However, no such improvement has occurred in the mutual images held by the peoples of each country. In the case of Japan in particular, far from an increase in positive feelings toward China, the improvement at the state-to-state level has in fact been accompanied by a worsening in public sentiment toward that country.[4]

The Deterioration in China-Japan Relations and the US Response

Relations between Japan and the PRC were normalized in 1972. The Treaty of Peace and Friendship between the two countries was concluded in 1978, and it aimed to strengthen bilateral ties with a focus on economic exchanges. The following year, Japan began providing official development assistance in the form of concessional yen loans to China. In the 1980s, the economic relationship, which centered on bilateral trade, expanded due to China's policies of reform and opening. At the same time, however, even though "China-Japan friendship" served as the premise of bilateral ties from 1972 on, various underlying sources of friction still remained.

To generalize, these problems fell under the rubric of either historical issues involving the acknowledgement of war responsibility or Taiwan-related issues. In the former case, tensions began with the textbook revision issue in 1982, when the Japanese Ministry of Education called for softening a textbook's description of the Japanese army "invading" Northern China by rewriting it as "advancing" instead, and with the official visit by Japanese Prime Minister Yasuhiro Nakasone to Yasukuni Shrine in 1985. In the latter case, Taiwan issues began to come to the fore with the groundbreaking civil aviation agreement between Japan and China in 1974 that marked a thaw in their relations and with the so-called Kokaryo issue, which entailed a legal dispute regarding whether the government in China or Taiwan was the lawful owner of a dormitory for Chinese students studying in Kyoto. To be certain, the problem of the territorial rights to the Senkaku [Diaoyu] Islands has arisen from time to time, and there is no question that this has also been a thorny matter between the two countries. However, the pattern to date has been that whenever China-Japan relations worsen for any reason, that deterioration creates a spillover to the Senkakus rather than the other way around. Moreover, it appears that China has basically been acting on the premise that the Senkakus are currently under Japanese sovereignty.

Despite the various disputes that arose in China-Japan relations through the 1980s, on the whole the bilateral relationship remained relatively stable under the slogan of "China-Japan friendship." In past essays, I have described the state of China-Japan ties during this period as the "1972 framework," which among other things was characterized by the Cold War system that pitted the United States, China, and Japan against the Soviet Union; the Japanese government's aid for China's modernization; the agreement of the war generation not to make war responsibility an issue; and the agreement to overlook disagreements associated with Taiwan.[5] The key point was the formation of an anti-Soviet alliance among the three nations that tacitly acknowledged China as a developing country and agreed to guide it toward the Western camp. As a result, the relationship among China, Japan, and the United States remained stable.

However, following the Tiananmen Square Incident in 1989 and the end of the Cold War, many of the preconditions that had supported China-Japan relations under the 1972 framework began to change, and at the start of the 1990s the two countries entered a stage in which they were groping for a post-1972 framework. Then, in 1992, China switched its economic policy to an all-out market orientation with its motto of establishing a socialist market economy. That brought an increase in direct investment from overseas and triggered rapid economic growth. The sudden "rise" of China also gave rise—primarily in Japan and the United States—to the "China threat" theory and exacerbated the Taiwan problem.

The Japanese emperor visited China in 1992 for the first time ever, and this was tacitly interpreted in Japan as signifying the conclusion to outstanding historical issues, but amid the rapid advance of the market economy, the ruling circle around Jiang Zemin established a policy of strengthening patriotic education. Then, in 1995, at the time of the 50th anniversary of the end of World War II, China further strengthened the study of the war with Japan as a form of patriotic education, and the number of anti-Japanese items in the media began to increase. This was perhaps an attempt to stave off any move to abandon socialism or any challenge to the leadership role of the Chinese Communist Party.

This overlapped precisely with the pro-independence push under President Lee Teng-hui of Taiwan from 1995 to 1996 and China's strong reaction to those moves. President Lee gave positive marks to Japanese colonial rule in Taiwan, but the Chinese Communist Party considered Japan's past colonization of Taiwan to have been nothing less than an "invasion of China" and, indeed, another unreconciled historical issue. This further overlapped with the formulation at that time of new guidelines for the US-Japan Security Treaty, which China sharply criticized for their inclusion of joint measures for handling a future emergency situation involving Taiwan.

As noted above, the "China threat" theory coincided with the economic rise of China, but it was also a response to China's belligerent stance during this timeframe, the first instance of which was the 1995 and 1996 Chinese missile tests over the waters surrounding Taiwan.

Jiang Zemin's visit to Japan in 1998 symbolized the frictions in the China-Japan relationship.[6] During this trip, Jiang repeatedly and publicly raised a number of historical issues. He did so even during a banquet hosted by the Japanese emperor at the Imperial Palace. As noted above, there had been a sense in Japan that these historical issues had finally been settled by the emperor's visit to China in 1992, and this conduct on Jiang's part was received extremely negatively by the Japanese public and media.

For the next several years, perhaps as a result of the Japanese backlash, China tended to refrain from touching on these historical issues. However, matters once again took a turn for the worse after 2001, touched off by the new Prime Minister Junichiro Koizumi's decision to visit Yasukuni Shrine. While campaigning for the leadership of the LDP, Koizumi made a public vow that he would visit the shrine on August 15, the anniversary of the end of World War II. Although prime ministers had visited the shrine secretly in the past, formal visits had ended after Prime Minister Nakasone's visit in 1985. Koizumi himself had never visited Yasukuni Shrine before that time, but he was counting on support from the Japan War-Bereaved Families Association (Nippon Izokukai), a key power base of the LDP, and so he promised publicly to do so.[7] After Koizumi assumed office, he suddenly moved up his visit to August 13, perhaps in order to avoid the chaos that a visit on August 15 might cause. China naturally reacted negatively to this. However, when Koizumi visited China two months later in October 2001, he visited the Anti-Japanese War Museum at the Marco Polo Bridge and stated his "feelings of heartfelt apology and mourning for the people of China who were sacrificed due to (Japan's) aggression" and, in response, Jiang Zemin confirmed that bilateral ties had improved after meeting Koizumi.[8] What clearly had happened behind the scenes was that, when Koizumi made his public vow to pay his first visit to Yasukuni Shrine, the foreign ministry officials of the two countries reached an agreement to try to restore relations by scheduling Koizumi's trip to China shortly thereafter.

What made the Yasukuni problem take a turn for the worse were Koizumi's subsequent visits to the shrine. All of Koizumi's other trips to Yasukuni Shrine were sudden decisions on his part and were carried out without any leeway for foreign ministry officials to prepare in advance for damage control. The Chinese appear to have assumed that since previous Japanese prime ministers had made only a single trip to the shrine during their time in office, including their secret visits, Koizumi would also make a single visit. The general view in Japan was much the same. The second visit, on April 21, 2002, came at the height of a domestic debate within Japan on the creation of a replacement memorial that could be visited instead of Yasukuni Shrine. Moreover, it came at a time when Koizumi had just returned from attending the Boao Forum in Hainan Province, which the Chinese side had strongly urged him to attend. For Koizumi, who had been one of the few national leaders to attend the forum, there may have been a feeling that he had earned enough political capital with the Chinese to temper their opposition to his shrine visits, but from the Chinese perspective, his decision undoubtedly appeared to be a betrayal. Koizumi subsequently made four more visits to Yasukuni (on January 14, 2003; January 1, 2004; September 17, 2005; and August 15, 2006), essentially going once annually right up until he left office, for a total of six visits.

It was amid such circumstances that China-Japan relations confronted a major challenge in 2005, coinciding with the 60th anniversary of the end of World War II. When UN Secretary-General Kofi Annan announced his support for including Japan among the permanent members of the UN Security Council in March of that year, a petition movement arose on the Internet in opposition to a permanent seat for Japan. At the core of the movement was an overseas Chinese organization in California, but the movement was picked up by China's main Internet sites as well, without any of the customary restrictions whatsoever being applied by the Chinese government. Anti-Japanese demonstrations then took place in April 2005, again with no restrictions imposed by the authorities. On the first weekend in April, demonstrations were held in provincial cities like Chengdu; on the second weekend, demonstrations were held in Beijing; and on the third weekend they took place in Shanghai. Then, on April 6, Wang Guangya, China's ambassador to the UN, openly stated his intention to oppose the Annan proposal.[9]

It was only on April 19 that China began in earnest to rein in the anti-Japanese demonstrations. This followed the convening of a meeting to report on the state of China-Japan relations that was chaired by Chinese Foreign Minister Li Zhaoxing, who until then had been forcefully claiming that responsibility for the demonstrations lay with the Japanese side. The meeting was attended by 3,500 cadres from the Central Propaganda Department, the Ministry of Education, and the military.[10] Although the meeting was convened at the direct order of Hu Jintao, there is a deep-seated view that, in the process leading up to this, there was an underlying power struggle between the Hu Jintao faction, which was calling for reconciliation with Japan, and the old Jiang Zemin forces and conservative factions in the Chinese military, which were launching a hard-line campaign against Japan.[11]

Just prior to that meeting, on April 17, Japanese Foreign Minister Nobutaka Machimura made a hasty trip to China and, in addition to requesting that the Chinese authorities deal directly with the situation, he also proposed to convene a China-Japan leaders dialogue at the Asia-Africa Leaders Conference that was scheduled to be held in Indonesia the following week. Based on this proposal, Koizumi and Hu held a meeting on April 23, 2005, at Bandung, at which time they promised to promote dialogue and exchange with a view toward restoring relations. The words were not followed up with action, however, and it seemed as though the Chinese had more or less abandoned any hope for improved ties during the Koizumi era. In fact, the Chinese side ended up taking a hard-line position instead, asserting that there would be no visits between the leaders of the two countries as long as the visits to Yasukuni Shrine continued.

The world's media reacted sensitively toward the antagonism between the two major countries in East Asia. In the South Korean and Hong Kong media, there was of course criticism of Japan's interpretation of history, and it goes without saying that there were many articles sympathetic to China. However, even though major American media outlets like the *Washington Post, New York Times,* and *Los Angeles Times* also called for an improvement in Japan's treatment of historical issues, they appeared to criticize the violent conduct in China even more.[12] Similarly, in England, while the *Financial Times* and the *Times* initially expressed doubts about Japan's position on historical issues, as the situation became more serious they pointed out the danger of a "patriotic" policy for mobilizing the masses in China.[13] The *Economist* more or less consistently supported Japan's elevation to the status of full member of the UN Security Council and strongly criticized China's nationalism, noting its resemblance to Japan in the 1930s.[14]

For its part, the US government was bewildered. At the China-US summit meeting in November 2005, President Bush reportedly asked the Chinese to promote a dialogue on historical issues. The National Security Council's Senior Director for Asian Affairs Michael Green, who accompanied Bush on that trip, stated after he had left the government that although it was problematic for China to claim that Japan was the villain due to historical issues, one way that Japan could have dealt with this was for the Japanese prime minister to have ceased his visits to Yasukuni.[15]

On January 23, 2006, during a press conference with the Japanese media, Deputy Secretary of State Robert Zoellick made his case for joint research by historians from the three countries—China, Japan, and the United States—in order to alleviate tensions. Zoellick made it clear that he himself had raised this proposal at a think tank in the United States in September 2005. However, China immediately rejected such American mediation and stated that historical research should be carried out chiefly by China, Japan, and South Korea.[16] The idea of a historical joint research project among China, Japan, and the United States did not receive a warm reception in Japan either and subsequently faded away.

This was the first and last time that the United States, which had never before intervened in the historical issues between Japan and China, volunteered to mediate, and one must wonder just how much the Bush administration, which was struggling with the Iraq War during this period, was troubled by the disharmony between Japan and China when formulating its Asia policy. Among all of the world leaders, it was Koizumi who had most strongly supported the Bush administration on Iraq, and one can read this situation as indicating that the United States had refrained to the utmost degree from criticizing the visits to Yasukuni in a way that might embarrass Koizumi, instead calling behind the scenes for a restrained attitude from the Chinese side. Of course, from a realist point of view, other than those times when there is a clear common enemy outside the three countries, it is not necessarily disadvantageous to the United States for there to be a certain degree of tension in China-Japan relations. This is because, given the precondition of the US-Japan alliance, favorable conditions are more readily generated for the United States to handle both China and Japan when there is a certain amount of friction between the latter two countries. The fact that the United States was truly hoping for an improvement in China-Japan relations, then, shows just how serious the situation was.

An Improvement in China-Japan Relations

The improvement in China-Japan relations came quite suddenly. In September 2006, Koizumi retired from the scene after his term in office expired, and Shinzo Abe replaced him as the new Japanese prime minister. Although Abe had previously been known as a politician prone to making hard-line statements toward China, such as calling for the revision of history textbooks, he made an electrifying trip to China on October 8–9, 2006, immediately after he assumed office, and effected a rapid improvement in China-Japan ties. In April of the same year, when he was still serving as chief cabinet secretary, Abe had secretly visited Yasukuni Shrine. As a result, during his October trip to China, Abe had to parry questions about whether he had visited the shrine and whether he would or would not do so as prime minister; he refused to make any clear statements on the matter, and the Chinese side did not probe deeply in this regard.[17] In other words, his visit succeeded by leaving the Yasukuni problem vague, and this was a major diplomatic concession on the part of China.

As a result of Abe's China visit, which was called an "ice-breaking trip," China-Japan relations were finally able to escape from the bilateralism represented by the previous "good neighbor" line. Based on a new strategy of seeking a "mutually beneficial strategic relationship," the two countries hammered out a new orientation for China-Japan ties that instead adopted a multilateral orientation, situating the bilateral relationship within the broader contexts of Asia and global affairs. According to the joint press statement issued during Abe's visit, agreement was reached on strengthening cooperation in a variety of fields including the denuclearization of the Korean Peninsula and the promotion of the Six-Party Talks, as well as energy, environmental protection, finance, intellectual property, and joint historical research. The two sides also agreed on the need to further promote dialogue at every level, including among the heads of government and cabinet officials.[18]

These agreements naturally represented a major advance, but the more startling point in the joint press statement was the fact that almost no mention was made of the two major disputes in postwar China-Japan relations, namely historical issues and Taiwan. There were no statements at all that evoked issues related to the colonial period and the war, let alone any mention of the Yasukuni problem. To the contrary, what the statement did include was China's positive assessment of the peaceful development of postwar Japan: "The Japanese side emphasized that Japan, more than 60 years after the War, has been consistently following the path of a peaceful country, and would continue to follow this path. The Chinese positively appreciated this."[19]

Although Taiwan is usually touched upon in some manner or another in bilateral documents issued by China, this document was an extremely rare exception in that the issue was not raised at all. According to this author's own interviews with Japanese foreign policy officials, they had in fact run out of time for negotiations, and the Chinese side ultimately acceded to the Japanese side's resistance to the inclusion of the Taiwan issue. This reportedly was interpreted at the negotiation site as tacitly suggesting "a resolution by the supreme leadership" of China.[20] This accords with the fact that, since the enactment of the Anti-Secession Law of 2005, China has switched to a policy of avoiding to the maximum extent possible any mention of the Taiwan problem and essentially accepting the maintenance of the status quo as long as Taiwan does not take any steps toward independence. As noted above, during this period China was relying on the United States to hold Taiwan's independence movement in check, and China also ended up devoting itself fully to the Six-Party Talks, both of which can be interpreted as being extensions of Hu Jintao's new foreign policy. However, perhaps because of potential criticism in China over the total omission of the Taiwan issue from the joint press statement, a sentence to the effect that both countries would continue to observe the principles of the 1972 China-Japan Joint Communiqué was included in a joint press statement released during Premier Wen Jiabao's April 2007 visit to Japan.[21]

Why did China agree to allow mutual visits of the heads of government when the issue of whether the Japanese prime minister would refrain from visiting Yasukuni Shrine was left so vague, and why did it agree to such major concessions with respect to historical issues and Taiwan? Without question, this was based on a decision by the leadership team surrounding Hu Jintao. In 1984, Hu Jintao worked as the first party secretary of the All-China Youth Federation under the aegis of Party General Secretary Hu Yaobang. He supported the encouragement of China-Japan amity through youth exchanges that were being promoted by Hu Yaobang and, while working as director general, served as the host when China invited 3,000 Japanese youths to visit. At this time, Hu Jintao was apparently in active contact with counterparts on the Japanese side in connection with these exchanges, and he also traveled to Japan himself. As a result, his personal understanding of Japan is probably far greater than that of other Chinese leaders.

However, this fact alone cannot account for Hu's conciliatory line toward Japan. Another important factor in his decision may have been closely related to the power struggle between the leadership group around him and their political enemies, first among whom is Jiang Zemin. The following is what is known at present about this state of affairs.

As noted above, the Chinese foreign minister at the time was Li Zhaoxing, but on April 21, 2005—two days after Li chaired the meeting on Chinese policy toward Japan following the anti-Japan demonstrations—Vice Foreign Minister Dai Bingguo, a close confidant of Hu Jintao, assumed office as the director of the Central Office for Foreign Affairs, a post that is the supreme office responsible for Chinese diplomacy.[22] Foreign Minister Li's visibility on the diplomatic stage decreased from that point on. In other words, one can infer that the intent of the meeting on April 19 was to have Li take responsibility for having repeated hard-line statements toward Japan.

This shift manifested itself in the creation of a strategic dialogue between China and Japan that was launched in May 2005, in the immediate wake of these events. At the first dialogue, Dai represented the Chinese side, while Shotaro Yachi, a Japanese vice-minister for foreign affairs who enjoyed Abe's deep trust, handled the talks for the Japanese side. These talks, which still continue to be held today, began with a flurry of sessions: the second meeting was held in June 2005, the third in October 2005, the fourth in February 2006, the fifth in May 2006, and the sixth in September 2006, immediately after the Abe government took office. The fourth session was held in Yachi's hometown of Niigata, while the fifth session took place at Guiyang, where Dai was born, in order to help solidify the personal relationship of trust between the two. In the end, Abe's trip to China was negotiated through the channel of these two officials, both of whom enjoyed the deep trust of their respective leaders.

When was the decision made to invite Abe to visit China, then? After he left office, Yachi confirmed that the Chinese side first began sounding him out about a possible Abe visit on the evening of September 28, 2006.[23] This was related to the major changes in Chinese politics, including the power grab by Hu Jintao. On September 25, a few days before that meeting, the Xinhua News Agency reported that Chen Liangyu, secretary of the Shanghai Committee, had been arrested for the misappropriation of a social security fund. Chen was a powerful young politician who had been nurtured by Jiang Zemin for the post–Hu Jintao era. In the background of the drama surrounding this arrest, it was reported that Zeng Qinghong, who had previously been a confidant of Jiang Zemin, had switched allegiances to the Hu Jintao side. Whatever the case may be, this arrest held great significance for Hu Jintao in his quest to strengthen his power base, and the request for Abe to visit China was transmitted to the Japanese side just a few days later.[24]

Another point of considerable interest is the fact that Abe's trip to China was set for October 8, 2006. This was also the date of the sixth Plenary Session of the 16th Central Committee of the Chinese Communist Party, and after Hu Jintao officially opened the plenary session that morning, he went to meet Prime Minister Abe in the afternoon. In other words, Hu Jintao, who was focused at the time on consolidating his position of power in internal Chinese politics, may well have selected the date as a way of flaunting—both for domestic and foreign audiences—his successful power grab by resolving one of China's major diplomatic concerns, its relations with Japan, precisely on the date of the sixth Plenary Session.

Although Abe's visit was accomplished through the volition of Hu Jintao against the backdrop of this complex power struggle and through a negotiation process between Japan and China, one further question that must be asked is why the leadership team around Hu Jintao was so committed to improving relations with Japan. This cannot be adequately explained by the personal will of the leader alone. Perhaps the answer to this question lies in the repercussions inside China and around the world from the anti-Japanese demonstrations in 2005. As many observers pointed out at the time, viewed domestically, the anti-Japanese demonstrations acted to a great degree as a safety valve for venting pent-up social dissatisfaction. To frame it conversely, the government's decision to allow the anti-Japanese demonstrations to continue was probably due in no small measure to the realization that they might turn into demonstrations against the Chinese government if they were mishandled.

In addition, there was a tendency at the outset for the world to focus its attention on Japan's approach to historical issues, with the key issue being the Yasukuni Shrine visits, but after the anti-Japanese demonstrations, the criticism of Chinese nationalism became stronger. In particular, the deep concerns harbored by the US government—which subsequently volunteered to act as a mediator in joint historical research—was of considerable importance. It is not hard to imagine the US side directly conveying this concern to the Chinese government. In that sense, China appears to have taken into consideration its own international standing as a "stakeholder" as it reflected on the deterioration of its relationship with Japan.

THE CURRENT STATE OF TRILATERAL RELATIONS

Abe's 2006 visit to China resulted in a dramatic improvement in China-Japan relations. Since then, Japan and China have aimed to stabilize relations through repeated mutual visits by their top leaders. Chinese Premier Wen Jiabao visited Japan in April 2007, Japanese Prime Minister Yasuo Fukuda visited China in December 2007, President Hu Jintao paid a visit to Japan in May 2008, and Prime Minister Taro Aso visited China in order to attend the Asia-Europe Meeting in October 2008. During each of these high-level visits, the issue of visits to Yasukuni Shrine was glossed over without being discussed and the Chinese side positively appraised the peaceful development of postwar Japan without touching on historical issues, while limiting itself to only the minimal necessary mention of the Taiwan problem.

Fortunately, tensions surrounding the Taiwan issue have also settled down in recent years. The March 2008 presidential election in Taiwan was won by Ma Ying-jeou, who favors conciliation with the mainland, and dialogue between Taiwan and the Chinese government has subsequently been promoted in earnest. On the other hand, Chen Shui-bian, the independence-minded former president who was Ma's predecessor, was arrested on corruption charges in late 2008, and the influence of the pro-independence Democratic Progressive Party has since declined abruptly. Relations between China and Taiwan have improved greatly as a consequence, thereby diminishing what had been a key point of dispute in China-US relations. Both the severe financial crisis and this dramatic change in circumstances surrounding Taiwan have played a large role in the recent trend toward stability and cooperation in China-US ties.

Has this also led to greater stability in China-Japan ties? Unfortunately, there are few who would offer an optimistic response to this question. When one examines the image of China held by Japanese citizens, the turn for the better in state-to-state relations has not necessarily translated into a similar improvement in public perceptions. This is because China-Japan relations are not simply a state-to-state issue but have expanded more broadly to become a social issue. In addition, given that China's future rise is inevitable and Japan's power must inevitably contract to some extent, it is highly likely that China-Japan relations will continue to be prone to friction, including psychological conflicts. In that sense, if we add the fact that unforeseen issues will naturally arise between the two countries in the future, it is clear that the continuation of direct exchanges between top leaders at the state level is extremely important for ensuring the overall stability of China-Japan relations. Therefore, the sudden conciliation between Japan and China following Abe's China trip is of great significance—all the more so given that it overturned the common assumption held around the world that the problems in the China-Japan relationship were unsolvable by those two countries alone and that the standoff would continue and expand in the future.

What sort of stance will the United States adopt concerning the direction of China-Japan relations? To start from the conclusion, the Obama administration will likely be more solicitous about stability in China-Japan ties than was the Bush administration. The reason lies in the fact that, unlike in the past, cooperation between China and Japan is increasingly necessary for the United States. Neither the situation in the Middle East nor the fight against terrorism has seen any great improvement, and North Korea's development of nuclear weapons is increasingly a fait accompli. Thus, it is hard not to conclude that the actual situation facing the new administration is more challenging than ever. The worst-case scenario for the United States at this time would be for the Taiwan situation to deteriorate, and it is likely hoping for improved cross-strait relations through the expansion of direct exchanges between China and Taiwan. Moreover, for the United States, which is confronting above all else a deep global recession, Japan and China are the largest overseas holders of US government bonds, and the weight of China, which holds massive amounts of US dollars in both government bonds and foreign currency reserves, is particularly consequential when it comes to the recovery of the US economy. Assuming that this situation will continue for quite some time, the United States cannot help but apply itself to strengthening its ties with China, even as it continues to emphasize its alliance with Japan. In this context, stability in the China-Japan relationship will be in the national interest of the United States as well.

Trilateral Relations and the "East Asia Community"

China-Japan rapprochement is also extremely important when it comes to considering the future of the proposed "East Asia community." The momentum for building such a community grew in the aftermath of the 1997 Asian financial crisis. At the time, Japan floated the notion of an Asian Monetary Fund that would be separate from the US-dominated International Monetary Fund, but this suffered a setback due to opposition from the United States and China. Japan consequently abandoned the Asian Monetary Fund concept, shifting instead to a framework known as the "New Miyazawa Plan" that would provide US$30 billion in funding support for various Asian countries. The United States was economically at its zenith at that time, and it reacted strongly to the idea of economic management under the guidance of Asian countries, which it viewed as a means to exclude the United States. For this reason, it strongly asserted that, in principle, APEC should serve as the primary cooperative framework in the region, which would maintain the leading US role.

Despite this, the Asian financial crisis was an event of sufficient magnitude to make the nations of Asia keenly feel the need for an independent framework of regional cooperation. A new opportunity presented itself in the expansion of the ASEAN framework to involve consultations with

Northeast Asian countries. The leaders of China, Japan, and South Korea were invited to participate in the 1997 ASEAN Summit in Kuala Lumpur, which focused in part on the need for greater regional cooperation, and that meeting provided the impetus for the regularization of ASEAN+3 Summits. In November 1999, a Joint Statement on East Asia Cooperation was issued at the ASEAN+3 Summit, and in addition, a high-level meeting among just China, Japan, and South Korea (involving Zhu Rongji, Keizo Obuchi, and Kim Dae-jung respectively) was held for the first time in history.[25] Then, in 2003, at the fifth summit meeting among the "Plus Three" nations, the leaders issued a Joint Declaration on the Promotion of Tripartite Cooperation among Japan, the People's Republic of China and the Republic of Korea, and concrete cooperative plans were set in motion.[26]

However, following the sixth meeting in November 2004, these trilateral summits were suspended for more than two years. The reason for this was the chaos in China-Japan relations, including the 2005 anti-Japanese demonstrations, China's opposition to a permanent Japanese seat on the UN Security Council, and Prime Minister Koizumi's visits to Yasukuni Shrine, which gave rise to the Chinese refusal to allow head-of-government visits between the two countries. These problems spilled over to relations with South Korea as well, and the atmosphere for holding top-level meetings among the three countries completely soured.

The breakthrough came with the improvement in China-Japan relations following Abe's October 2006 China trip. After China, Prime Minister Abe also visited South Korea. Thus, the long-delayed seventh summit meeting among China, Japan, and South Korea was finally held at the site of the ASEAN+3 Summit, which was convened in the Philippines on January 14, 2007, and an eighth meeting was held at the Singapore ASEAN+3 Summit in November 2007.

Building on that foundation, the first China–Japan–South Korea summit meeting ever to be held separately from a meeting of ASEAN was convened on December 23, 2008, in Fukuoka, Japan. The leaders at that time were Wen Jiabao, Taro Aso, and Lee Myung-bak respectively. It is no exaggeration to say that this was a historic watershed in relations among the three countries. At this meeting—the ninth summit overall among the three countries—an extremely large number of documents were issued reflecting the agreement of all three parties. These included a Joint Statement for Tripartite Partnership, a Joint Statement on the International Finance and Economy, and a Trilateral Joint Announcement on Disaster Management Cooperation. An Action Plan for Promoting Trilateral Cooperation among the People's Republic of China, Japan, and the Republic of Korea was also produced, outlining practical cooperation in various fields. In addition to calling for regular meetings among cabinet officials and high-level bureaucrats of the three countries, these agreements offered concrete proposals aimed at cooperation in an extremely broad variety of fields such as investment, energy, logistics, the environment (e.g., regional air pollution and marine pollution), maritime search and rescue, and health. They also focused on the promotion of youth exchanges, policy dialogue on Africa, and the Six-Party Talks.[27]

Rather than depicting these accords as a symbol of the improvement in relations, it would be more appropriate to say that the necessary cooperation in these areas had been postponed because of the deterioration in state-to-state ties. Globalization and the growing interconnectedness among China, Japan, and South Korea created a sudden increase in the number of specific issues that required the three countries' cooperation and coordination, and thus avenues for dialogue and consultation were urgently needed. Once the diplomatic logjam was removed, these initiatives were all launched in one fell swoop. Whatever the case may be, there is no question that the improvement in relations among the three countries vastly expanded the range of possibilities for cooperation in East Asia, especially broader cooperation that includes the ASEAN countries.

From the beginning, the concept of an "East Asia community" was born amid the development of relations between ASEAN, China, Japan, and South Korea, but Prime Minister Koizumi's remarks in Singapore in January 2002, made during his visit to five countries in Southeast Asia, may have been the initial statement of this concept: "If you took a poll of the world's economists and asked them what region of the world they believe to have the greatest potential in the immediate future, I have no doubt of their answer. They would say East Asia. By cooperating, I believe we can gain the critical mass to advance this potential. Our goal should be the creation of a 'community that acts together and advances together.'"[28]

Since then, various debates have in fact arisen concerning the East Asia community, and China and Japan have played a central role. When China-Japan relations were worsening during the Koizumi era due to the controversy surrounding Yasukuni Shrine and other issues, the discussions lessened significantly. Moreover, the rivalry between Japan and China exhibited itself in the debate surrounding the membership composition of the East Asia Summit that was launched in 2005. To put it simply, Japan, perhaps out of concern about its relationship with the United States and the potential expansion of China's influence, called for the inclusion of Australia and New Zealand, whereas China attempted to limit the framework to the

ASEAN+3 members. Ultimately, the East Asia Summit ended up including not only Australia and New Zealand but also India, but it was the competition between Japan and China rather than the cooperation in East Asia that impressed observers.

As China-Japan ties improved in recent years, and trilateral relations between China, Japan, and South Korea improved greatly as well, the debate over an East Asia community once again picked up steam.[29] Moreover, the United States, which was formerly critical of such regionalism in Asia, has become more positive about the idea. According to a 2008 survey of public intellectuals in nine Asia Pacific countries conducted by the Center for Strategic and International Studies, the combined figures for "strongly favor" and "somewhat favor" an East Asia community exceeded 70 percent even in the United States.[30] To be sure, this is lower than the average in Asian countries (81 percent), but it indicates a major shift from the strong opposition the United States once showed to the Asian Monetary Fund. In addition, while one might find it only natural that the vast majority of respondents in Japan and South Korea would rate the participation of the United States in the East Asia community as "very important" or "somewhat important" (91 percent in Japan and 83 percent in South Korea), the figure in China, too, has reached 80 percent.[31] This change in the figures likely reflects an acknowledgement of the need for joint measures to handle the global financial crisis, which originated in the United States. In other words, China, Japan, and South Korea have recognized the United States as a major stakeholder in the formation of an East Asian order, and the United States, for its part, has become more inclined to allow others to play a more central role in global economic management.

In a sense, it is impossible to separate the debate about the future of an East Asia community from the debate about the trilateral relationship among the United States, Japan, and China, the three countries that now rank first, second, and third in the world in terms of GDP. Of course, the debate over an East Asia community must inevitably address the delicate issue of what the status of America will be therein. As East Asia confronts an increasing number of global issues, including not only the current economic crisis but also growing problems such as the environment, energy, nuclear proliferation, and so on, it is unrealistic to ignore the presence of the United States. In addition, China will likely continue to become stronger and more self-assertive, and since it is impossible for Japan by itself to engage China so that the latter's power is more directed at contributing to the world, America's involvement will be indispensable for this. To look at it from the opposite angle as well, China realizes that its own future growth is dependent upon the success of measures to respond to global issues. Incorporating itself into a regional framework in which the United States regularly participates and working to alleviate the sense of threat felt by others in the region, such as Japan, can go a long way in helping build the cooperation needed to deal with these global issues.

It goes without saying that the road to an East Asia community is not going to be straight or smooth. That is only natural given the differences in historical awareness, political systems, economic development, culture, religion, philosophies, and so on that exist in the region. It indeed took quite some time for these problems to start to be overcome in Europe. These differences are related, in turn, to the very underpinnings of the nation-state. Of course, the elimination of national borders is the ultimate goal in forming a community. This is because a community cannot be formed unless it becomes possible for people, goods, and money to flow freely without regard to national boundaries. However, the majority of East Asia is currently devoting its attention to the establishment and strengthening of the nation-state. Any action aimed at eliminating national boundaries is virtually impossible. So, as the community debate advances, there is a high likelihood that states will stir up nationalistic sentiments for the sake of self-preservation.

The road to an East Asia community will not be easy and it will involve many twists and turns. In particular, it is hard to predict how Japan and the United States will react to the rise of China and the unforeseen incidents that will inevitably come up. But that being said, the framework for an East Asia community is likely to continue to advance—albeit bit by bit—because, as is evidenced by the current financial crisis, the Westphalian nation-state framework is inadequate to address the global issues that will continue to challenge the region and the world.

CONCLUSION

Based on the above analysis, the improvement in China-Japan relations since October 2006 is extremely significant for four reasons. First, the improvement occurred because the historical issues and the issues associated with Taiwan that had been the major points of dispute in postwar China-Japan relations were set aside and a new, future-oriented relationship based on "strategic mutual advantage" was formed. This suggests that we are entering the "post-postwar era" in China-Japan relations. Naturally, there is little hope that all of the outstanding issues between the two countries will be resolved in the near future, and it is more likely that they will serve as the basis for repeated disputes in the future as well. However, in an increasingly interdependent world, if Japan and China, the two major countries in East Asia, continue to be tripped up by problems carried over from the first half of the 20th century, it will not be possible for us to address the mountain of issues that we confront today and whose resolution is our most urgent task. Even though the problems of history and of Taiwan are crucial topics meriting continued debate in the future, these are issues that should be discussed in a forward-looking manner, in a long-term perspective, and in a calm atmosphere. It is not possible to expect any advances or solutions to emerge from an atmosphere such as has existed to date, in which national prestige is placed on the line.

Second, the détente between Japan and China in recent years is a reflection of the will and ability of the two countries to solve the problems of the region on their own. As already noted, the antagonism between Japan and China at the start of the 21st century came as a shock to the world. Although the main focus was on the visits to Yasukuni Shrine, a fierce sense of competition between the two nations was evident in the background. The world's media debated the likelihood that Japan and China would collide in the East China Sea, and from time to time the view was expressed that the capacity to resolve the issue simply did not exist in either country. And indeed, one could hardly say that everything has been resolved or that the rapprochement was complete. There will be many flashpoints in the future as well. But the fact that the two major countries in the region are stepping up to solve the problems of the region along with their neighbors is an extremely important step to consider when contemplating future East Asian cooperation.

Third, the improvement in China-Japan relations has produced a situation that the United States should welcome. The United States currently finds itself facing unprecedented difficulties. On top of the economic worries, there are the regional problems posed by Iraq, Iran, and Afghanistan, the huge issues presented by terrorism on a global scale, the North Korean issue, and finally the rise in anti-US sentiments and the lack of trust in the United States. Given these circumstances, the United States would find itself in an extremely difficult position if feuding were to break out again between Japan and China—the two major powers in Asia, the second and third largest economies in the world, and two nations that are supporting the US economy and the dollar system and that are exhibiting a relatively well-intentioned, cooperative stance toward many of the global issues afflicting the United States. This state of affairs may not be permanent. In particular, it will depend in large part on the outcome of China's rise to great power status, including the future path it pursues in military affairs. However, if we focus on the coming five to ten years, there will probably be no major changes to the status quo unless some major, unforeseen event should occur.

Fourth, one could perhaps claim that China-Japan rapprochement marked the first real step toward an East Asia community. The question of an East Asia community has already been debated at length, but one of the major obstacles has been the fragility of relations between Japan and China, or among China, Japan, and South Korea. The fact that they have begun to assemble through their various summits signifies that one major obstacle to an East Asia community is beginning to crumble. Even the United States, which formerly harbored doubts about the desirability of purely Asian regional institutions, is exhibiting a positive stance toward an East Asia community out of a realistic sense of necessity. In other words, the United States has judged that mutual cooperation among the countries in East Asia will function to its own benefit and to the benefit of each individual nation in the region.

The positive steps discussed here could be negated in one blow by future developments, such as the occurrence of some chance event between Japan and China. The history and the tensions between Japan and China have not been completely resolved, popular sentiment between Japan and China has not improved, and the complex psychological conflicts created by China's rise and Japan's descent in terms of national power have not been dispelled. However, what must be emphasized at a minimum is that the deterioration and subsequent improvement of China-Japan relations in the recent past clearly signals that in any future cooperative system that aims at an East Asia community, the course of China-Japan relations will be a major variable, and the position of the United States in that system will therefore hold great influence. This clearly means that the dynamics of trilateral China-Japan-US relations will continue to be intrinsically entwined with the regional community-building project.

Notes

1. Jack Belden, *China Shakes the World* (New York: Harpers, 1949).

2. "Gaige kaifang sanshizhounian baogao, 2" [Thirty years of reform and opening up: report 2], October 28, 2008, Guojiatongjiju (National Bureau of Statistics) website, http://www.stats.gov.cn/tjfx/ztfx/jnggkf30n/t20081028_402512576.htm.

3. Since the latter half of the 1990s, there has been a boom in studies of relations among China, Japan, and the United States, and a large volume of joint research has sought to gain a better grasp on the future of this triad. See for example, Zhang Yunling, ed., *Zhuanbianzhong de Zhong, Mei, Ri guanxi* [Evolving China-US-Japan relations] (Beijing: Zhongguo Shehuikexue Chubanshe, 1997); Ryosei Kokubun, ed., *Challenges for China-Japan-US Cooperation* (Tokyo: Japan Center for International Exchange, 1998); and Tatsumi Okabe, Seiichiro Takagi, and Ryosei Kokubun, eds., *Nichibeichu anzenhosho kyoryoku wo mezashite* [Toward Japan-US-China security cooperation] (Tokyo: Keiso Shobo, 1999).

4. *Gaiko ni kansuru seron chosa* [Public opinion survey on foreign policy], 2008, Cabinet Office, Government of Japan, http://www8.cao.go.jp/survey/h20/h20-gaiko/images/z10.gif.

5. Ryosei Kokubun, "The Shifting Nature of Japan-China Relations after the Cold War," in Lam Peng Er, ed., *Japan's Relations with China* (London: Routledge, 2006); and Ryosei Kokubun, "Changing Japanese Strategic Thinking toward China," in Gilbert Rozman, ed., *Japanese Strategic Thought toward Asia* (New York: Palgrave Macmillan, 2007).

6. Ryosei Kokubun, "Shiren no jidai no Nicchu kankei: Ko Takumin hounichi kijitsu" [Sino-Japanese relations in a time of testing: a record of Jiang Zemin's visit to Japan], *Hogaku Kenkyu* [Journal of law, politics, and sociology] (Keio University) 73, no. 1 (January 2000).

7. Yomiuri Shimbun Political News Department, ed., *Gaiko wo kenka ni shita otoko—Koizumi gaiko nihyakunichi no shinjitsu* [The man who turned diplomacy into a fight—the reality of 200 days of Koizumi's diplomacy] (Tokyo: Yomiuri Shimbun, 2006), 223.

8. "Statement by Prime Minister Koizumi Following His Visit to the Memorial Museum of Chinese People's War of Resistance against Japan" (in Japanese), October 8, 2001, Ministry of Foreign Affairs of Japan website, http://www.mofa.go.jp/mofaj/kaidan/s_koi/china0110/hatsugen.html; "Visit to the People's Republic of China by Prime Minister Junichiro Koizumi (Overview and Evaluation)," October 8, 2001, Ministry of Foreign Affairs of Japan website, http://www.mofa.go.jp/region/asia-paci/china/pmv0110/overview.html.

9. "Chugoku kugatsu ketsuron ni hanpatsu" [China opposes September timing of decision], *Asahi Shimbun*, April 7, 2005 (evening edition). Afterwards, the United States also came forward to express its intention to oppose the Annan proposal.

10. "Li Zhaoxing zuo Zhongri guanxi xingshi" [Li Zhaoxing reported on the state of China-Japan relations], *Renmin Ribao*, April 20, 2005.

11. Ryosei Kokubun, "Nicchu kankei to kokunai seiji no sogo renkan" [The connection between China-Japan relations and domestic politics], *Hogaku Kenkyu* 81, no. 6 (June 2008); and Yoshikazu Shimizu, *"Chugoku mondai" no uchimaku* [The inside story on the "China problem"] (Tokyo: Chikuma Shobo, 2008), chap. 2 and 3.

12. "A 'Peaceful Rise'?" *Washington Post*, April 23, 2005, A18; "A Rising China," *New York Times*, May 6, 2005; and "Japan's Worst Enemy," *Los Angeles Times*, April 18, 2005, B12.

13. "Japan's Burden," *Financial Times*, April 8, 2005; "Asian Blame Game," *Financial Times*, April 12, 2005; "Japan Says Sorry," *Financial Times*, April 23, 2005; "Unleash the Mob," *Times*, April 11, 2005; and "Shouting Is Not a Policy: China Has to Find More Mature Ways of Making Itself Heard," *Times*, April 19, 2005.

14. "The Genie Escapes; China and Japan," *Economist*, April 16, 2005; "Managing Unrest; China and Japan," *Economist*, April 23, 2005.

15. "Bei seiken 'Yasukuni' ni kenen" [US government concerned about 'Yasukuni'], *Mainichi Shimbun*, January 1, 2006.

16. "Nichibeichu de rekishi kensho wo" [Historical verification by Japan-US-China] and "Bei kokumu fukuchokan Nicchu kaizen ni kitai" [US Deputy Secretary of State expects improved Japan-China relations], *Asahi Shimbun*, January 24–25, 2006; and "Zeerikku Bei kokumu fukuchokan Nicchu kincho kanwa unagasu" [US Deputy Secretary of State Zoellick urges Japan-China détente], *Mainichi Shimbun*, January 24, 2006.

17. "Press Conference by Prime Minister Shinzo Abe Following His Visit to China," October 8, 2006, Prime Minister's Office website, http://www.kantei.go.jp/foreign/abespeech/20 06/10/08chinapress_e.html.

18. "Japan-China Joint Press Statement," October 8, 2006, Ministry of Foreign Affairs of Japan website, http://www.mofa.go.jp/region/asia-paci/china/joint0610.html.

19. Ibid.

20. Interview with Japanese officials within the Ministry of Foreign Affairs, October 2006.

21. "Japan-China Joint Press Statement," April 11, 2007, Ministry of Foreign Affairs of Japan website, http://www.mofa.go.jp/region/asia-paci/china/pv0704/joint.html.

22. *China Directory 2006* (Tokyo: Radiopress, 2005), 31.

23. Shotaro Yachi, "Watashi no nigawarai" [My bitter smile], *Nihon Keizai Shimbun*, March 24, 2008.

24. Zheng Yi, *Shanghai dafengbao: Chen Liangyu daotai yu Shanghai bang de mori* [Shanghai storm: the fall of Chen Liangyu and the end of the Shanghai Gang] (Beijing: Wenhuayishu Chubanshe, 2006); Zi Ping, ed., *Jikui Shanghai bang* [The defeat of the Shanghai Gang] (Hong Kong: Huanqiu Chuban Youxian Gongsi, 2006); and Shi Weijian, *Chen Liangyu chuanqi* [The legend of Chen Liangyu] (Hong Kong: Wenhuayishu Chubanshe, 2007).

25. "Joint Statement on East Asia Cooperation," November 28, 1999, Ministry of Foreign Affairs of Japan website, http://www.mofa.go.jp/region/asia-paci/asean/pmv9911/joint.html.

26. "Joint Declaration on the Promotion of Tripartite Cooperation among Japan, the People's Republic of China, and the Republic of Korea," October 7, 2003, Ministry of Foreign Affairs of Japan website, http://www.mofa.go.jp/region/asia-paci/asean/conference/asean3/joint0310.html.

27. "Action Plan for Promoting Trilateral Cooperation among the People's Republic of China, Japan, and the Republic of Korea," December 13, 2008, Ministry of Foreign Affairs of Japan website, http://www.mofa.go.jp/region/asia-paci/jck/summit0812/action.html.

28. "Japan and ASEAN in East Asia—A Sincere and Open Partnership" (speech by Prime Minister of Japan Junichiro Koizumi), January 14, 2002, Ministry of Foreign Affairs of Japan website, http://www.mofa.go.jp/region/asia-paci/pmv0201/speech.html.

29. See for example, the discussions in the Council on East Asian Community, http://www.ceac.jp/e/index.html.

30. Bates Gill, Michael Green, Kiyoto Tsuji, and William Watts, *Strategic Views on Asian Regionalism: Survey Results and Analysis* (Washington DC: CSIS, 2009), http://www.csis.org/media/csis/pubs/090217_gill_stratviews_web.pdf.

31. Ibid.

TRILATERAL RELATIONS AND REGIONAL SECURITY

4 | China-Japan-US Relations and Northeast Asia's Evolving Security Architecture

Gui Yongtao

THE SECURITY ARCHITECTURE in Northeast Asia has been characterized primarily by the US-centric alliance system since the end of the Cold War. The US alliances with Japan and South Korea, the only formal security institutions currently in effect in this subregion, are key components of the broader "hub-and-spokes" security system that the United States has structured across the Asia Pacific region. Recently, however, some multilateral arrangements, most notably the Six-Party Talks, have emerged to tackle the challenges that the traditional bilateral alliances may not be able to meet effectively. Thus the security architecture in Northeast Asia seems to be evolving toward a more diverse and multilayered framework. This chapter first reviews the respective US, Japanese, and Chinese perspectives on the exiting security architecture; then discusses three major security questions facing Northeast Asia—China's rise, Taiwan, and North Korea—in light of their impacts on the security arrangements in the region; and concludes by offering some policy recommendations on this subject.

PERSPECTIVES ON THE EXISTING SECURITY ARCHITECTURE

US Views

For the United States, the alliance-centered strategy has been a success in that it has helped America maintain its regional primacy and achieve its global objectives. The United States also tends to believe that the existing alliance system is a public good that benefits other countries as well by providing peace and stability for the whole region and alleviating antagonism between regional powers, for instance a potential China-Japan rivalry. Therefore, in the US view, reinforcing the existing alliances should remain the core of its security policy toward Northeast Asia. In the meantime, the United States seems to welcome the development of multilateralism, as it has demonstrated in its commitment to the Six-Party Talks, but considers it as merely complementing rather than supplanting the current alliance framework.

A more controversial move in recent American efforts to expand its network of alliances has been the attempt to form a quadrilateral group including the United States, Japan, Australia, and India.[1] This initiative was for a time embraced and enthusiastically promoted by Japan under the Abe administration but received lukewarm responses from Australia and India. Currently, it seems to have lost momentum due to the leadership shifts in Japan, Australia, and the United States. However, the logic behind this kind of initiative, namely a multilateral coalition based on common values like democracy, may not vanish from US strategic thinking.

Japanese Views

In the case of Japan, its active involvement in the war in Afghanistan and the reconstruction of Iraq, and the consequent domestic movement toward constitutional amendments, indicate a new approach in its alliance strategy. Japan, by playing a proactive rather than reluctant role in the US-Japan alliance, has marched significantly forward on its road to becoming a "normal nation," and at the same time it has effectively met the US demand for reciprocity in a post-9/11 era.[2] The logic underlying Japan's decision to redefine the alliance, unlike that of the United States, is not global but regional; it is seeking to address the threat from North Korea and the fear of a rising China. In addition to the above-mentioned quadrilateral grouping, Japan once attempted to pursue a so-called "values diplomacy" that aimed to build an "arc of freedom and prosperity," and it deepened its military relationship with Taiwan, all of which raised serious concerns in China.

There is also a distrust of the reliability of the US-Japan alliance in Japanese political, policy, and intellectual circles. Some Japanese worry that the United States might withdraw its commitment to protecting Japan due to either a decline in its relative power or growing isolationism. They go so far as to suggest that Japan should develop a small nuclear arsenal to counter the potential threat from China.[3] Although a nuclear Japan may seem unrealistic for the foreseeable future, the very emergence of such opinions in Japan's public discourse still poses serious questions for its neighboring countries as well as for the United States.

Japan's role in the Six-Party Talks has been seriously hampered by the deadlock on the abduction issue. The deeply rooted mistrust of and aversion to North Korea in the Japanese public has made any immediate breakthrough with North Korea infeasible. Japanese policymakers are further shackled by the ongoing turmoil in national politics. Hence Japan for the moment is unlikely to take the initiative in the multilateral framework.

Chinese Views

China is always wary of US hegemony and the US-Japan alliance and is particularly sensitive to the deployment of the ballistic missile defense system and Japan's expanding military role. Looking at the Chinese defense white papers published biannually between 1998 and 2006, one finds that the US-Japan alliance was continuously mentioned as a negative, destabilizing, or complicating factor from 1998 to 2006; the ballistic missile defense system was raised as a concern in 2000 and 2004; and Japan's expanding military role was highlighted as an issue from 2000 to 2006.[4]

At the same time, there does exist in China a degree of ambivalence about the US-Japan alliance. Since the normalization of US-China relations in the early 1970s, the United States has been trying to persuade China that the alliance acts as a "cap on the bottle" that can prevent Japan from growing into a military power. This persuasion seems to have worked to a certain degree so far. Some Chinese analysts recognize the alliance as a constraint on Japan's remilitarization and contend that a sudden collapse of the alliance would cause fundamental changes in the existing security architecture, a situation not necessarily serving China's interests.[5]

The determinant here seems to be Taiwan. Since the United States and Japan redefined their security relationship in the mid-1990s, the question of whether Taiwan is included as a so-called "situation in surrounding areas" has been the most controversial point between China and the US-Japan alliance. When the United States and Japan issued a joint statement in February 2005 after a "2+2" meeting of the US-Japan Security Consultative Committee, explicitly including Taiwan as one of the "common strategic objectives" between the United States and Japan, the Chinese government and media launched another round of criticism of the alliance. Taiwan has thus become China's litmus test of the strategic value of the US-Japan alliance. At the end of 2005, a Chinese analyst published a widely noted essay arguing that the alliance "will act as a propellant of, rather than as a cap on, Japan's military development," and that "as far as China is concerned, the bright side of the US-Japanese alliance seems to be gone."[6] It is also worth noting that in its 2008 defense white paper, China described the US-Japan alliance as one of the "uncertain" factors in the Asia Pacific region.[7] This change toward more neutral wording might be interpreted as partly deriving from the significant easing of tensions across the Taiwan Strait in the past year or so.

Even if we recognize the stabilizing aspect of the US-centric alliance system, the destabilizing aspect of the system and the limitations on its capacity to deal with regional security problems are still undeniable. An alliance is in essence an exclusive arrangement based on a zero-sum-game assumption and a worst-case-scenario calculation. It makes both sides imagine each other as potential enemies. The US-Japan alliance was reinforced in the mid-1990s as a response to the North Korean nuclear crisis and the Taiwan Strait crisis. However, this alliance reinforcement merely strengthened the US stance in a potential crisis; it did nothing to alleviate the tensions, let alone solve the problems. It even exacerbated the security dilemma between China and the US-Japan alliance and deepened China's suspicion over Japan's military role. Above all, it is the Six-Party Talks, not the US-led alliance system, that has been playing a central role in addressing the North Korean nuclear issue.

In contrast to the alliance-centered approach, since 1997 China has been advocating and promoting its "new security concept," which emphasizes dialogue and cooperation among nations. The core of the new concept includes mutual trust, mutual benefit, equity, and coordination.[8] China's commitment to this new concept has been evidenced by its constructive roles in the ASEAN Regional Forum, the Shanghai Cooperation Organization, and the Six-Party Talks. Unlike the alliances, these multilateral arrangements are inclusive and do not assume the existence of an adversary. At the same time, China does not intend to challenge the US-led alliance system since that could only lead to competition rather than cooperation. Thus, from the Chinese point of view, the security architecture in Northeast Asia will evolve through both multilateral and bilateral approaches.

CHINA'S RISE AND STRATEGIC HEDGING

One central question that the current Northeast Asian security architecture must address is how to respond to the rise of China. The various answers to this question, especially for those in the United States, seem to converge at a strategy termed "hedging." This strategy is believed to combine cooperation and competition, two seemingly contradictory policies, toward China's rise. The cooperation dimension of the strategy includes promoting economic and military exchanges between the United States and China, encouraging China's involvement in and contributions to regional and global institutions, and welcoming improved bilateral relations between China and US allies. The competition dimension of the strategy seeks to address the uncertainty about the intentions and capabilities of a rising China by improving the scope and quality of the US-led security framework. The recent enhancement of US security ties with Japan and India, the attempt to form the quadrilateral group, and the improvement of US security relations with Southeast Asian countries are all cases in point.[9]

The first US official document that defined the hedging strategy toward China was the report of the 2006 Quadrennial Defense Review. Based on the assumption that the choices made by "countries at strategic crossroads"—a euphemism for China—"will affect the future strategic position and freedom of action of the United States, its allies, and partners," the report offered the following suggestion: "The United States will attempt to shape these choices in ways that foster cooperation and mutual security interests. At the same time, the United States, its allies and partners must also hedge against the possibility that a major or emerging power could choose a hostile path in the future."[10] This policy was reaffirmed shortly thereafter by the Bush administration in its second national security strategy, which stated, "Our strategy seeks to encourage China to make the right strategic choices for its people, while we hedge against other possibilities."[11] The national defense strategy published in 2008 also followed this line of thinking, maintaining that the Defense Department "will respond to China's expanding military power, and to the uncertainties over how it might be used, through shaping and hedging."[12]

The hedging strategy seeks to keep a balance between the engagement and integration policy and the dissuasion and deterrence policy, both of which have already unfolded and become well known in the past decade of China-US relations. The fact that the two major schools of US thinking on China policy, the "accommodationalists" and the "confrontationalists," can both find niches for themselves in this equilibrium accounts for the durability of the hedging strategy.[13]

The US hedging strategy has significant implications for the evolution of the Northeast Asian security architecture. If the stress is put on the competition side, then the US-led alliances will be enhanced and the security dilemma between this alliance system and China will only deteriorate. If the balance tilts toward the cooperation side, then the United States will be more willing to engage China in various multilateral mechanisms. The hedging strategy can also have a great impact on the China-US-Japan trilateral relationship, since each aspect of the strategy may anchor its Asia policy on either China or Japan. Some US analysts associated the two faces of hedging with two former deputy secretaries of state, Richard Armitage and Robert Zoellick. The Armitage approach emphasized Japan's potential role as a global partner and placed the United States firmly on Japan's side, thereby representing ultimately a skeptical view of China's future role in Asia. In contrast, the Zoellick approach expected China to act as a responsible stakeholder and highlighted shared interests between the United States and China.[14]

Most US analysts believe that the two aspects of the hedging strategy are compatible and complementary and should be integrated into a coherent policy, while at the same time admitting that pursuing such a strategy could encounter difficulties and involve risks in practice. Problems might come from a lack of leadership on US China policy, uncoordinated and mixed messages sent by different parts of the US government, and declining domestic support for the cooperative dimensions of the strategy.[15] Some analysts further pointed out that "hedging is contagious" and could lead to a dangerous arms race as it did during the Cold War.[16]

Japan seems to be pursuing a hedging strategy as well, but Japan hedges in a different way. It engages with China in the economic field and competes with China in the political and military field.[17] Under the Koizumi administration, the Japanese leadership took steps that contributed to a strained China-Japan relationship characterized by "cool politics, warm economics." Shinzo Abe, Koizumi's successor, at one time also advocated a China policy of "separating politics from economics." As part of the quadrilateral grouping efforts, the Abe administration signed a joint declaration on security cooperation with Australia and established a Japan-Australia version of the "2+2" meeting between Japan and the United States.

As a result of the improvement in China-Japan relations during the past several years, China and Japan have revitalized military-to-military exchanges between the People's Liberation Army (PLA) and the Self-Defense Force (SDF). A historic step was taken by the two countries when mutual port calls were carried out between the Chinese PLA Navy and the Japanese Maritime SDF for the first time since the end of World War II. This was underscored by a joint statement signed in May 2008 by President Hu Jintao and Prime Minister Yasuo Fukuda, in which the two sides recognized that they "are not threats to each other."

These positive developments notwithstanding, the mistrust between the two countries still persists. After the earthquake in China's Sichuan Province in May 2008, the Japanese government responded promptly by sending the first foreign relief team to China but then decided to substitute chartered commercial planes for Air SDF transport aircraft to carry relief supplies to the province due to a fear of stirring up Chinese public opinion. When assessing Chinese Minister of Defense Cao Gangchuan's visit to Japan in 2007, the first trip of its kind in more than nine years, the *East Asian Strategic Review*, an annual publication of the Japanese National Institute for Defense Studies, concluded that Cao "did not satisfactorily address" Japanese concerns regarding China's increased defense budget, that his trip "largely failed to advance basic mutual understanding, trust, and friendship as envisioned by Japan," and that "China may likely exploit this superficial exchange as a tool for advertising itself as a peaceful state."[18] Although the views expressed in this report do not necessarily represent the official position of the Japanese government or the Ministry of Defense, they still reflect Japan's deep distrust of China. In fact, in April 2008, the Japanese government reportedly decided to undertake a drastic revision of the National Defense Program Guidelines in response to China's military buildup.[19]

It seems that Japan holds a different view from that of the United States regarding Chinese military modernization and the effectiveness of military-to-military exchanges with China. The United States views China's military modernization as reasonable and far from challenging US military dominance; it sees military-to-military exchanges as an instrument not only of engagement in the responsible stakeholder framework but also of hedging in that it can help to avoid miscalculations in a crisis situation.[20] Japan is understandably more suspicious due to China's geographic proximity and its complex feelings about China's rise. The history issue also exacerbates distrust between the two countries. Other possible causes of the relative sluggishness in Japan's military exchanges with China include the frequent changes of defense ministers due to Japan's domestic political turmoil and the inward-looking orientation of the Japanese defense establishment, which tends to see the exchanges merely as an administrative burden with little impact.[21]

But Japan is also closely watching US military exchanges with China and fears that it might be left behind if ties between the other two keep progressing.[22] In early 2009, momentum was restored to China-Japan exchanges through a visit to Japan by the deputy chief of general staff of the PLA and a visit by Japan's defense minister to China. During the latter visit, the two sides released a press communiqué confirming 10 points of defense exchange, which included continuing mutual visits and dialogues at various levels, holding defense and security consultations in Tokyo within the year, discussing the establishment of a maritime liaison mechanism, exchanging views on international peacekeeping operations, coping with natural disasters, and cracking down on piracy.[23]

CHINESE STRATEGIC VISIONS

Some US analysts also use the term "hedging" to describe China's security policy, which includes its multilateral and bilateral diplomacy in Asia, its cooperation with Russia, and its own military modernization programs.[24] But from the Chinese perspective, these policies are merely defensive responses to the potential of US containment or encirclement of China, as well as a continuation of China's traditional good-neighbor diplomacy. After all, China does not seek any formal bilateral or multilateral alliances as the United States has done in the region.

Chinese analyses of the hedging strategy are mostly negative. Although the concept of hedging may seem a neutral one for the Americans, many Chinese see it as merely a continuation of the concept of strategic competition. When the United States strengthened its alliances and security partnerships with Japan, Australia, India, and the ASEAN countries, or promoted such notions as a "league of democracies," and when Japan advocated building an "arc of freedom and prosperity," the Chinese intuitively felt as if they were being encircled. Although some Chinese analysts may recognize that the US security network in the Asia Pacific region is not solely targeted at China, they still argue that it at least harbors the intention of guarding against China.[25]

In the eyes of some Chinese analysts, the hidden assumption of the hedging strategy remains that China is a potential rival, an assumption that could become a self-fulfilling prophecy, leading to a security dilemma and an arms race. The factors that they believe contribute to the adoption of such a strategy include the structural tension between China as a rising power and the United States as an existing power, the different interests and positions of the two countries on the Taiwan issue, the influence of neo-conservatism and offensive realism in the United States, and the demands of interest groups close to the defense industry.[26] There is even concern in China that hedging implies a containment policy.[27]

That being said, the Chinese people are not preoccupied with the fear of being encircled or hedged against. The above-mentioned new security concept and China's active involvement in regional multilateral institutions are initiatives that China originally took to counter the "China threat theory" but later integrated into its foreign and security strategies.[28]

China attaches special importance to stable relations with the countries that surround it. A case in point is China's successful negotiations of territorial disputes with most of its neighboring countries. Although disputes over the South China Sea and East China Sea remain difficult to tackle, and some recent events in the two areas may have temporarily raised the level of tension, China still clearly insists that these problems be solved through peaceful means, and the Chinese government has been taking pains to prevent these negotiations from being influenced by public opinion.

China is also seeking stability in its relations with the major world powers, characterizing them basically as "strategic partnerships." Being aware of the dual effect of the hedging strategy, some Chinese analysts still argue that the shift from being deemed a potential rival to a stakeholder marks significant progress in China's relationship with the United States, and that the so-called "neither enemy nor friend" relationship, though not ideal, is a relatively realistic and acceptable relationship for both countries under the current circumstances and is likely to continue for the foreseeable future.[29] There seems to be a consensus among Chinese scholars that the existing international system of "one superpower and several big powers" (*yichao duoqiang*) will remain unchanged in the coming decades and that this system has not impeded China's development up to the present, nor will it do so in the future. In this light, China should recognize the status of the United States as a superpower, as well as its interests and role in the Asia Pacific region; the United States should also recognize China's interests and role in the existing international system, as well as its need for development and stability.[30]

In the meantime, there do exist in China pessimistic views on China's relations with other major powers, which contend that "strategic partnership" is no more than a euphemism for "neither enemy nor friend" and that any enemy can be called a strategic partner as long as it is not engaged in an all-out confrontation with China. From this perspective, the major powers will simply compete in the name of cooperation, resulting in less trust and less stability in their relations with each other.[31] More moderate analysts may acknowledge that interdependence and cooperation are still the mainstream of the relations among major powers, but they are wary of the return of traditional realism. Some are particularly concerned about the so-called "hidden agenda" behind the war on terrorism, which means that the United States, by sharpening its weapons and strengthening its alliances, is altering its threat perception and refocusing on some major powers, despite the fact that antiterrorism remains on top of the agenda in all US official documents.[32]

Chinese analysts are also debating where the main sources of threats to China come from. Some argue that while China has traditionally linked external threats directly to internal stability, this linkage between external and internal security has been declining over the past three decades. This argument assumes that, as a result of the rapid growth of China's national strength, foreign influence upon China's domestic politics has gradually waned and that forces promoting independence in Taiwan, Tibet, and Xinjiang are unlikely to achieve their goals. Therefore, when the Chinese people no longer face the danger of the ruin of their country or the overthrow of their government, they will be able to take greater account of external threats and factors when developing their international strategies.[33] Other scholars may share the view that China's domestic stability has become less susceptible to external threats but point out that China's three decades of reform and development have also created many difficult problems that could undermine domestic political stability. In this view, China's grand strategy should be different from that of the United States in the sense that the internal threats China faces are still larger than the external ones.[34]

The extremely complicated situation in China today offers no easy answer to this debate. One recent example is the difficulty in assessing the extent to which the violence in Lhasa in March 2008 and in Urumchi in July 2009 affects the national security of China. The resurgence of an old theme in China's strategic debate, namely that of reorienting toward the western interior regions, shows that problems such as regional disparities in economic development, ethnic and religious conflicts, and relations between the central and local governments are likely to pose new threats to China's stability in its next stage of development.[35]

Regardless of the various arguments in China's strategic debate, the Chinese leadership has on many occasions elaborated on China's strategic choice to pursue peaceful development, sending a clear message to the people at home and abroad. As Hu Jintao's report to the 17th National Congress of the Communist Party of China clearly stated, "Historic changes have occurred in the relations between contemporary China and the rest of the world, resulting in ever closer interconnection between China's future and destiny and those of the world."[36] It seems apparent that co-operation and harmony will remain the theme of Chinese diplomacy. As one Chinese official put it, on the one hand, China must acknowledge that its self-definition as a developing country can hardly be endorsed by other countries and that the international community is increasingly expecting China to shoulder greater responsibility, while on the other hand, the Chinese people must also be clear that their own country's strength and influence have not changed fundamentally and that the heated discussion on China's rise only reflects the growing gap between the perceptions and realities of China's power. Therefore, China should continue to pursue a prudent foreign policy.[37]

TAIWAN AND NORTH KOREA: OPPORTUNITIES AND CHALLENGES

The Taiwan issue and the North Korean nuclear issue are both challenges to and opportunities for the evolution of the security architecture in Northeast Asia. The situation across the Taiwan Strait has shown significant progress since the Kuomintang took power in Taiwan in May 2008, while the recent developments surrounding North Korea indicate that the road ahead will continue to be filled with twists and turns.

Taiwan

China and the United States can be generally satisfied with each other regarding their coordination on the Taiwan issue. The US efforts to moderate the independence movement in Taiwan proved to be partly effective and were appreciated by the Chinese side. The strategic basis of this coordination lies in the "one China" framework and the "status quo" consensus maintained by both sides. Although China and the United States still differ greatly on issues such as Taiwan's political position and the ultimate solution of this issue, the two sides have at least acknowledged the unbearable risks that a drastic change in the "one China" policy or the "status quo" could entail. The lessons that China and the United States have learned in the past are conducive to parallel management of potential Taiwan Strait crises in the future. This proves that the strategic dialogue and defense exchanges between the two countries have produced positive results and that the security dilemma posed by the case of Taiwan is manageable to a certain extent.[38]

It should also be noted that the United States is not shifting its policy on the Taiwan issue, which can be understood as a dual balance approach. In cross-strait relations, the United States maintains a balance between the mainland and Taiwan, and in the internal politics of Taiwan, it also wants to keep a balance between the pro-independence pan-green camp and the more conservative pan-blue camp. Such a dual balance allows the United States to exert greater influence on both the mainland and Taiwan. From the Chinese perspective, this US strategic ambiguity is not enough to prevent the independence forces from moving in a dangerous direction. Mixed messages from the United States might encourage adventurism by the Taiwan independence forces, which could spur a new crisis in the future. And in the short and medium terms, tenacious problems such as US arms sales to Taiwan, a possible upgrading of the US-Taiwan relationship, and the international role of Taiwan will keep haunting China-US relations and regional security. Moreover, there is a lingering wariness in China that accepting the status quo could perpetuate the separation of Taiwan from the mainland.

These differences, however, should not become reasons for competition between China and the United States. On the contrary, the two sides should continue their strategic dialogue to ameliorate the security dilemma, alleviate mutual misapprehension, and avoid spirals of tension over the Taiwan Strait. The two sides should also seize the current opportunity to institutionalize bilateral coordination in coping with the Taiwan issue.

Japan's involvement in Taiwan has deepened in the past decade. As mentioned above, by introducing the concept of the "situation in surrounding areas" into its security agreement with the United States, Japan has committed itself to providing rear area support to the United States in a conflict scenario involving the Taiwan Strait. Although the Japanese government often reiterates its official policy of "one China," the relationship between Japan and Taiwan, especially in the military field, has always been a serious concern to China. This relationship includes dispatching high-ranking retired officers or officers in active service as representatives and military attachés, conducting high-level military dialogue, and cooperating covertly in military exercises and intelligence sharing. Although the military relationship between Japan and Taiwan will not match that between the United States and Taiwan for the foreseeable future, some Chinese observers still caution that a US-Japan-Taiwan quasi-alliance is stealthily being built.[39] The defense cooperation between Japan and Taiwan is also viewed in China as one of the main obstacles to enhancing China-Japan military mutual trust.[40]

Fears of a reunified China dominating Asia, sympathies for Taiwan among the public, and the influence of an anti-China and pro–Taiwan independence force in Japan's domestic politics underlie the Japanese government's reluctance to clarify its position on this issue. However, Japanese policymakers and analysts should rethink their Taiwan policies in light of the recent overall improvement in China-Japan and China-US relations. An encouraging step in this direction was Japanese Prime Minister Yasuo Fukuda's statement concerning the Taiwan issue during his visit to China in December 2007. In his talks with Chinese Premier Wen Jiabao, Fukuda said that Japan would give no support to the claims of "two Chinas"; "one China, one Taiwan"; or "Taiwan independence" or to Taiwanese authorities' attempts to join the United Nations and to seek UN membership through a referendum. Compared with the US statement that called the planned referendum provocative and said that the United States would oppose it, Japan's "no support" stance could perhaps be regarded as not being straightforward enough and falling short of China's expectations.[41] Nevertheless, the Japanese statement of these "four nos" was publicly appreciated by the Chinese government as "complete and clear." Chinese scholars also acknowledged that Japan had taken an appropriate step forward, which would facilitate the continuing development and improvement of China-Japan relations.[42] With the anti-Chinese and pro–Taiwan independence elements in Japan losing momentum for the time being, Japan should be able to regain its composure and acknowledge that the major threat to regional security is not the rise of China but the adventurism in Taiwan and thus restrain itself from sending the wrong messages to Taiwan independence forces in the future.

The Taiwan authority is currently proposing an Economic Cooperation Framework Agreement with the mainland. Beijing has responded with a very positive attitude and has stressed that this issue should not be politicized. With the leaderships in both Taipei and Beijing being pragmatic and focusing on the economic rather than the political aspects of their relationship, the three governments of China, the United States, and Japan can expect more stability across the Taiwan Strait. By carefully coordinating with Beijing, Washington and Tokyo will be able to manage their relations with Taipei without irritating the mainland. It therefore becomes possible to play a positive-sum game over the Taiwan issue. Needless to say, it is ultimately the Chinese people on both sides of the Taiwan Strait who must find a solution by themselves. A favorable external environment, however, is also indispensable. In addition to institutionalizing China-US bilateral coordination, the three governments should seek ways to establish a trilateral dialogue in order to further reduce the risks involved in coping with future uncertainties in Taiwan.

North Korea

The central questions of the North Korean nuclear issue are whether and how the goal of denuclearization can be achieved. For the United States, the threat is not the nuclear weapons allegedly possessed by North Korea but possible nuclear proliferation by North Korea. Should the United States compromise on its goal of denuclearization as it did in the Indian nuclear case, China and Japan would find themselves in serious straits. Up until now, US officials in charge of the negotiations have repeatedly clarified that the goal is complete denuclearization, not just the declaration of existing nuclear programs, and that the Six-Party Talks will not stop halfway. But suspicions remain since they admit at the same time that the process will be extraordinarily difficult and cannot be completed in one phase. This incrementalist approach to denuclearization faces criticism at home and abroad. Conservatives in the United States do not believe that North Korea will ever make concessions, and they tend to exaggerate the maneuvering power of North Korea. Liberals, for their part, are also loath to make deals with the regime in Pyongyang.[43]

Meanwhile, in Japan, some conservative politicians have been blaming the Six-Party Talks for the failure to prevent North Korea from going nuclear and for not effectively addressing the abduction issue. They attribute these failures to the lack of consensus among the other five countries involved in the talks, which North Korea can exploit. But the Japanese government recognizes the validity of the Six-Party framework and is likely to shift gradually to a more pragmatic policy toward North Korea. One difficulty, however, is that without some progress on the abduction issue, the Japanese public will not allow their government to give economic or energy assistance to North Korea, which may undermine multilateral initiatives that should include Japan.

China's position on the issue is twofold: denuclearization and stability. Although North Korea's nuclear weapons may not pose a direct threat to China, a nuclear-armed North Korea still causes grave concern for Beijing since it could trigger a chain effect in the region with South Korea, Japan, and even Taiwan pursuing their own nuclear capabilities—the scenario China would least like to see. In fact, China's security interests have already been compromised as a result of this issue. In the past few years, in response to North Korea's missile tests and its nuclear tests, the United States and Japan have accelerated their joint research and deployment of a ballistic missile defense system, a move that has the potential to neutralize China's deterrent capability and weaken China's leverage over the Taiwan issue. In the meantime, any kind of non-peaceful solution to the issue is also not in China's interest because it might create a refugee crisis and other problems that could destabilize the Chinese provinces bordering North Korea. Hence, China will continue its effort to promote the Six-Party process and develop it into a multilateral security mechanism in Northeast Asia.

It should be noted, however, that simultaneously attaining the twin objectives of denuclearization and stability is no easy task. There is a view in China that the two objectives may not be compatible because North Korea has never truly intended to give up its nuclear weapons. According to this argument, the Six-Party Talks may not be the sole option and the issue of North Korea should not be allowed to drag on indefinitely.[44] In spite of their different priorities, China, the United States, and Japan share a common interest in the denuclearization of the Korean Peninsula, as well as a common recognition of the Six-Party process as an appropriate framework for addressing this complex issue. If the emphasis is placed on moving ahead peacefully from one phase to the next rather than on forcing North Korea to give up its nuclear programs once and for all, the three countries should be able to sustain their cooperation in this multilateral process.

FROM BILATERAL COORDINATION TO TRILATERAL STRATEGIC DIALOGUE

The security architecture in Northeast Asia may evolve to include three types of security arrangements—bilateralism, trilateralism, and multilateralism. Bilateralism is likely to remain the point of departure for security cooperation; trilateralism is a goal to be pursued in the near and medium-term future; and multilateralism should, in the long run, lay the foundation for a new security architecture. It is the problems facing the countries in the region—not the power distribution among them—that require such a multilayered, parallel evolution of regional security frameworks.

In a post–Cold War and post-9/11 era, security threats may come not from any particular country but from problems on which countries lack communication and coordination. Both the United States and Japan have realized in recent years that the rise of China is not necessarily a threat but possibly an opportunity. Although the hedging strategy still denotes some insecurity and wariness on the parts of the United States and Japan in terms of their perceptions of China, the positive course of their recent relations with China demonstrates that there has been significant progress in various types of bilateral coordination. As mentioned above, the coordination between China and the United States over the Taiwan issue did not challenge the security interests of any party involved. In fact, it benefited all parties. Here, the key to success lies in a problem-driven rather than power-centric approach to security affairs. If emphasis were to be put on power competition with China, the United States and Japan would naturally view Taiwan as a military asset to counterbalance China's geopolitical influence, which could only be detrimental for their relations with China as well as for stability across the region.

It is true that the US-Japan alliance may still create difficulties for China as long as it remains central to the competition aspect of the hedging strategy. But if stable bilateral relations between China on the one hand and the United States and Japan on the other can be consolidated and further developed, the negative ramifications of the alliance will be limited. Recent incidents such as the China-US spat in the South China Sea in March 2009 and the December 2008 China-Japan encounter near the Diaoyu [Senkaku] Islands could serve as justification for the reinforcement of the US-Japan alliance if they are viewed through a power-centric prism. But these events could also be seen as opportunities to develop more effective communication and preventive measures in order to avoid the further escalation of tensions. Admittedly, the current lack of confidence between China and both Japan and the United States is reflected in the state of the bilateral military-to-military exchanges and security dialogues underway. But it is for this very reason that confidence-building measures should be pursued through further military consultation and cooperation.[45]

Without bilateral coordination, any trilateral or multilateral mechanism will be infeasible. However, bilateral coordination itself can also cause problems because this will inevitably arouse the suspicions of third parties. Historically, China has been worried about the US-Japan alliance, while Japan has been worried about a US-China strategic partnership. Whenever Washington joins hands with Beijing without consulting Tokyo, the Japanese people experience a bitter sense of being "bypassed" or even "betrayed" by their American ally. The perceived rise of China's standing in US policy toward Asia has recently become a serious concern in Japan, and this drove the Japanese government to lobby strongly for Japan to be the initial stop on Hillary Clinton's first overseas trip as secretary of state and for Prime Minister Taro Aso to be the first foreign leader hosted by President Barack Obama. Although the message from the US side seems to be that the US-Japan and US-China relationships are not zero-sum, the Japanese remain uneasy.[46]

It is against this backdrop that Beijing, Washington, and Tokyo should commence a trilateral strategic dialogue to dispel the skepticism and reduce the uncertainty among them. In fact, not only are policy analysts in all three countries actively promoting the idea of a trilateral strategic dialogue, either in the form of meetings among senior officials or summits, but the three governments are also starting to incorporate this idea into their diplomatic agenda.[47] It is reported that the first official trilateral talks among China, the United States, and Japan were scheduled for Washington DC in late July 2009, but these were later shelved for fear of unnecessarily angering North Korea. The plans were for this trilateral meeting to be chaired by the director general of the Department of Policy Planning from China's Ministry of Foreign Affairs, the director of policy planning from the US State Department, and the deputy vice-minister for foreign policy from Japan's Ministry of Foreign Affairs. The topics would include the overall Asian situation and global issues such as the financial crisis, climate change, and energy.[48]

The scheduling and subsequent postponement of the talks point to both the imperatives and obstacles in implementing trilateralism in the region. It can be said that the easing of tension across the Taiwan Strait has partly removed one of the major obstacles toward establishing a trilateral dialogue but that the escalation of the North Korea situation has forced policymakers to be cautious in launching such a dialogue. Even if the North Korea nuclear issue per se were not to be included in the planned talks, the very emergence of such a trilateral meeting at a delicate time would be widely viewed as further isolating Pyongyang. This could be counterproductive to the goal of alleviating tensions with North Korea. In the meantime, hardliners in US and Japanese domestic politics are gaining ground due to North Korea's recent nuclear and missile tests, creating a situation that could encourage a divergence rather than a convergence of opinions among China, the United States, and Japan. Therefore, apart from the improvement of bilateral relations between the three countries, another precondition for holding trilateral talks is the de-escalation of regional tensions.

It might be wise to start such trilateral discussions with a focus on less sensitive issues such as the global economic slowdown, climate change, and energy. These global issues undoubtedly top the list of common concerns for the three countries. Moreover, enhancing policy coordination among the world's three largest economies on these issues will serve the interests of other countries as well. This being said, global issues may be only the starting point rather than the long-term focus of trilateral dialogue, because addressing global economic and environmental issues requires the involvement of a wider range of countries, such as the G20 countries.

Hence, in the long term trilateral dialogue should focus on hard security issues, especially those relating to China's military modernization and the US-Japan alliance. Through trilateral interaction, China should aim to convince the United States and Japan that its military modernization has an inherent rationale and is not necessarily targeted at Taiwan. Meanwhile the United States and Japan should explain to China that their newly advanced military cooperation in the counterterrorism campaign will not be used to contain China. Enhancing military transparency, thus, might be one of the major aims of such a dialogue. To achieve this goal, it is advisable that the confidence-building measures currently being discussed and developed through bilateral military-to-military exchanges be expanded to the trilateral level and that the three sides conduct studies of joint crisis management. One point that should be made, though, is that any steps aimed at promoting military transparency must be symmetrical and balanced, meaning that China's efforts in this respect must be reciprocated by the United States and Japan with corresponding measures.

Given the sensitivity of the Taiwan issue and the North Korean nuclear issue, it might be prudent not to explicitly include these as topics in the trilateral dialogue. After all, these two issues are, by their nature, the internal affairs of the Chinese people and Korean people respectively. In any case, China will not allow the trilateral talks to directly discuss Taiwan, nor will North or South Korea allow the talks to discuss North Korea's nuclear capacity. However, if military transparency and mutual trust can be advanced through trilateral dialogue, the risks of miscommunication and miscalculation will be reduced. This would allow some sort of parallel management or coordination, though not direct discussion and cooperation, to be nurtured among the three countries with regard to their policies on Taiwan and North Korea.

As for the form of the trilateral strategic dialogue, the proposed director general–level talks among ministries of foreign affairs could serve as a preparatory and necessary step toward regular higher-level talks (ministe-rial or vice ministerial level). Since hard security issues should be the focus of this dialogue in the long run, it would be necessary to involve defense ministry officials as well. Officials from ministries related to nontraditional security issues such as finance, the environment, and energy can also be participants if the three governments deem that necessary. But the scope of the dialogue should not be expanded so much as to obscure its main purpose. Accordingly, foreign ministries alone or together with defense ministries should be the lead agencies in this dialogue.

We have known that the foreign ministries of the three countries are all interested in launching a trilateral dialogue. However, a deep attachment to the alliance with the United States and dissatisfaction with China's lack of military transparency seem to be restraining people in the Japanese defense establishment from endorsing this proposal.[49] This probably explains why the defense ministries did not take part in the preparations for the post-poned trilateral talks. The fundamental questions, however, are whether Japan can or is willing to play an independent strategic or security role in the way that China and the United States do and whether China and the United States are ready to see Japan play such a role.[50]

Also, North and South Korea may oppose such trilateral security co-ordination.[51] Neither North nor South Korea will endorse the concept or practice of a "concert of powers" in Northeast Asia. Therefore, Beijing, Washington, and Tokyo should define their coordination by the problems that such coordination will tackle, not by the powers of its participants. In addition, it should be made clear that trilateral coordination will only take the form of a dialogue and will not supplant the role of existing bilateral alliances. Thus, Japan need not worry about the decline of its position vis-à-vis China.

Meanwhile, both the United States and China have expressed posi-tive attitudes regarding the creation of a multilateral peace and security mechanism. Japan, however, may have some reservations, fearing that a multilateral framework would enhance China's relative power and weaken the US-Japan alliance. Countries outside Northeast Asia, like Canada and Australia, have also shown interest in participating in such a framework. One difficulty is that each country has certain issues that it does not want to include in such a discussion. For China, it might be Taiwan; for Japan and Russia, it might be territorial disputes. Although a future multilateral peace and security mechanism may not grow out of the Six-Party Talks, the Six-Party process does help to cultivate a habit of multilateralism among the relevant countries. Nonetheless, in light of the vicissitudes that the process has experienced, it is premature at the current stage to discuss building a new multilateral security architecture in Northeast Asia.

Therefore, a more realistic option at present is to pursue the establishment of a trilateral strategic dialogue on the basis of enhanced bilateral coordination. For the first time since the end of the Cold War, the three bilateral relationships between China, the United States, and Japan are all in fine shape. This provides a historic opportunity for the three countries to jointly explore the possibilities of building a new type of trilateral relationship. Regularizing and institutionalizing trilateral strategic dialogue will be an important step leading to improved trilateral relations characterized by confidence and cooperation. And, in the future, this trilateral process will certainly add momentum to the trend toward multilateral security cooperation.

NOTES

1. Emma Chanlett-Avery and Bruce Vaughn, "Emerging Trends in the Security Architecture in Asia: Bilateral and Multilateral Ties Among the United States, Japan, Australia, and India," CRS Report no. RL34312 (January 7, 2008).

2. Gerald Curtis, "The US in East Asia: Not Architecture, But Action," *Global Asia* 2, no. 2 (2007): 45–46.

3. Masahiro Matsumura, "The Japanese State Identity as a Grand Strategic Imperative" (working paper, Brookings Institution, Center for Northeast Asian Policy Studies, Washington DC, 2008), 2 and 17, www.brookings.edu/papers/2008/05_japan_matsumura.aspx.

4. People's Republic of China (PRC) State Council Information Office, *Zhongguo de guofang* [China's defense] (1998–2006), www.scio.gov.cn/zfbps/.

5. Yu Tiejun, "Dongya de junshi tongmeng" [Military alliances in East Asia], in *Dongya heping yu anquan* [Peace and security in East Asia], ed. Yan Xuetong and Jin Dexiang (Beijing: Shishi Chubanshe, 2005), 352–63.

6. Wu Xinbo, "The End of the Silver Lining: A Chinese View of the US-Japan Alliance," *Washington Quarterly* 29, no 1 (2005): 119–20.

7. PRC State Council Information Office, *Zhongguo de guofang* [China's defense] (2008).

8. Ding Kuisong, "East Asia: Evolving Security Concepts," in *Dongya anquan hezuo* [Security cooperation in East Asia], ed. Yan Xuetong and Zhou Fangyin (Beijing: Peking University, 2004), 147–9.

9. Evan S. Medeiros, "Strategic Hedging and the Future of Asia-Pacific Stability," *Washington Quarterly* 29, no. 1 (2005–2006): 148–53.

10. US Department of Defense, *Quadrennial Defense Review Report*, February 6, 2006, 27–28.

11. White House, *The National Security Strategy of the United States of America*, March 16, 2006, 42.

12. US Department of Defense, *National Defense Strategy*, June 2008, 10.

13. David M. Lampton, "The Paradigm Lost: The Demise of 'Weak China,'" *National Interest* 81 (Fall 2005): 76.

14. James J. Przystup and Phillip C. Saunders, "Vision of Order: Japan and China in US Strategy," Strategic Forum 220 (June 2006): 1–3, www.ndu.edu/inss/Press/NDUPress_STRFOR.htm.

15. Ibid., 161.

16. Ashton B. Carter and William J. Perry, "China on the March," *National Interest* 88 (March/April 2007): 16.

17. Richard J. Samuels, *Security Japan: Tokyo's Grand Strategy and the Future of East Asia* (Ithaca: Cornell University, 2007): 198–205.

18. *East Asian Strategic Review 2008* (Tokyo: National Institute for Defense Studies, 2008): 95–96, www.nids.go.jp/english/dissemination/east-asian/e2008.html.

19. "Chugoku no taito ni taiou, seifu ga 'boei taikou' bappon kaitei e" [Government moves toward a drastic revision of its defense guidelines in response to the rise of China], *Yomiuri Shimbun*, April 20, 2008.

20. Carter and Perry, "China on the March," 22.

21. The author wishes to thank Professor Yasuhiro Matsuda for sharing his views and explanation of this issue.

22. Japanese Self-Defense Force officers expressed this concern in a conversation with the author, February 24, 2009, Beijing.

23. The press communiqué is available in Japanese at www.mod.go.jp/j/news/youjin/2009/03/20.html.

24. Medeiros, "Strategic Hedging," 154–7.

25. Xia Liping, "Zhongmeiri zhanlue guanxi: zhengqu gongying he bimian anquan kunjing" [China-US-Japan strategic relations: seeking common benefits and avoiding a security dilemma], *Shijie Jingji yu Zhengzhi* [World economics and politics] 9 (2007): 35.

26. Wu Xinbo, "Shixi bushi zhengfu duihua anquan zhengce de hexin gainian" [An analysis of the core concepts of the Bush administration's security policy toward China], *Meiguo Yanjiu* [American studies quarterly] 21, no. 4 (2007): 19.

27. Yang Jiemian, "Guoji guanxi zhuanxingqi Zhongmei guanxi de xintedian" [New features of China-US relations in the transitional international system], *Shijie Jingji yu Zhengzhi* [World economics and politics] 12 (2007): 46.

28. David Shambaugh, "China Engages Asia: Reshaping the Regional Order," *International Security* 29, no. 3 (Winter 2004–2005): 64–99; Evan S. Medeiros and Taylor M. Fravel, "China's New Diplomacy," *Foreign Affairs* 82, no. 6 (2003): 22–35.

29. Cui Liru, "Zhongguo heping jueqi yu guoji zhixu yanbian" [China's peaceful rise and the evolution of international order], *Xiandai Guoji Guanxi* [Contemporary international relations] 1 (2008): 4.

30. Tao Wenzhao, "Zhongmei liangguo keyi bimian zhanlue tanpai" [China and the United States Can Avoid a Strategic Showdown], *Heping yu Fazhan* [Peace and Development], no. 4 (November 2008): 4.

31. Yan Xuetong, "Shijie geju zouxiang ji Zhongguo de jiyu" [The trend of world structure and China's opportunity], *Dangdai Yatai* [Journal of contemporary Asia-Pacific studies] 5 (2008): 10–11.

32. Yang Yi, "Quanqiuhua beijingxia de diyuan zhengzhi yu guoji fankong douzheng de qianjing" [Geopolitics in the context of globalization and prospects for the international fight against terrorism], *Shijie Jingji yu Zhengzhi* [World economics and politics] 1 (2008): 59–64.

33. Wang Jisi, "Zhongguo guoji zhanlue yanjiu de shijiao zhuanhuan" [The change of vision in China's international strategy studies], in *Zhongguo guoji zhanlue pinglun 2008* [China international strategy review 2008] (Beijing: Shijie Zhishi Chubanshe, 2008), 2.

34. Ye Zicheng, "Guanyu Zhongguo guoji zhanlue yanjiu siwei dingshi de yixie sikao" [Some thoughts on the patterns of thinking in China's study of international strategy], in *Zhongguo guoji zhanlue pinglun 2008*, 15–16.

35. Yuan Peng, "Zhongguo diyuan zhanlue ying sikao de jidui guanxi" [Some relationships that should be considered in China's geopolitical strategy], *Xiandai Guoji Guanxi*, [Contemporary international relations] 5 (2008): 24.

36. Hu Jintao, "Report to the 17th National Congress of the Communist Party of China," October 15, 2007, www.china.org.cn/English/congress/229611/htm.

37. Qiu Yuanping, "Guanyu woguo guoji zhanlue yanjiu de ruogan kanfa" [Some views on the study of international strategy of our country], *Guoji Zhanlue Yanjiu Jianbao* [International and strategic studies report] 21 (September 25, 2008): 5–6.

38. The author wishes to thank Professor Taylor Fravel for his suggestion that such wording as "parallel management" or "coordination" rather than "cooperation" should be used in defining the relationship between Chinese and US policies concerning the Taiwan issue.

39. Wu Jinan, "Ritai junshi hudong de xianzhuang, beijing ji weilai zoushi" [The present situation, backgrounds, and future trend in the Japan-Taiwan military interaction], *Xiandai Guoji Guanxi* [Contemporary international relations] 9 (2006): 56.

40. Li Xiushi, "Zhongri guanxi zhong de Taiwan wenti" [The Taiwan issue in the China-Japan relationship], *Riben Xuekan* [Journal of Japanese studies] 4 (2008): 37.

41. Reuters, "US Opposes 'Provocative' Taiwan Referendum Bid: Rice," December 21, 2007, www.reuters.com.

42. Xinhua News Service, "Japan PM States Four 'No's on Taiwan Issue," *China Daily*, December 27, 2007, www.chinadaily.com.cn/china/2007-12/29/content_6357662.htm.

43. Winston Lord and Leslie H. Gelb, "Yielding to North Korea Too Often," *Washington Post*, April 26, 2008, A17.

44. Zhang Haibin, "Dongbeiya jushi xianzhuang he qushi yantaohui zongshu" [Summary of the symposium on the current situation and trends in Northeast Asia], *Guoji Zhanlue Yanjiu Jianbao* [International and strategic studies report] 16 (April 25, 2008): 4; Bonnie Glaser, Scott Snyder, and John S. Park, "Chinese Debates on North Korea," PacNet 11 (2008), www.csis.org/publication/pacnet-11-chinese-debates-north-korea.

45. The author is indebted to Professor Seiichiro Takagi for his views on this aspect of the problem.

46. Toshiyuki Ito, "Gaiko, Nichibeichu kawaru 'kyori'" [Diplomacy: The changing distance between Japan, China, and the United States], *Yomiuri Shimbun*, January 7, 2009.

47. Zhang Tuosheng, "2009 nian zhongguo guoji zhanlue huanjing ji duiwai zhengce zhanwang" [Prospects for China's international strategic environment and foreign policy in 2009], *Guoji Zhanlue Yanjiu Jianbao* [International and strategic studies report] 28 (January 19, 2009); Brad Glosserman and Bonnie Glaser, "And Now to Trilateralism," PacNet 24 (May 1, 2007), http://csis.org/publication/pacnet-24-may-1-2007-and-now-tri-lateralism; PHP Research Institute, *Nihon no taichu sogo senryaku* [Japan's comprehensive China strategy] (Tokyo: PHP, 2007), http://research.php.co.jp/research/foreign_policy/policy/post_27.php.

48. Ershiyi Shiji Jingji Baodao [21st century business homepage], August 5, 2009, http://www.21cbh.com/HTML/2009-8-5/HTML_C5UU3O4ND3JU.html.

49. Based on the author's conversations with participants in a series of unofficial US-China-Japan trilateral meetings organized by the Brookings Institution, the Center for Strategic and International Studies, the School of International Studies of Peking University, and the Keizai Koho Center, 2005–2006.

50. Yoshihide Soeya, "Japan's Relations with China," in *The Golden Age of the US-China-Japan Triangle 1972–1989*, ed. Ezra F. Vogel, Yuan Ming, and Akihiko Tanaka (Cambridge, MA: Harvard University, 2002), 210–26.

51. Glosserman and Glaser, "And Now to Trilateralism."

5 | Prospects for Trilateral Security Cooperation

ANDREW L. OROS

SECURITY COOPERATION AMONG China, Japan, and the United States lags behind other forms of cooperation, both in terms of discussions and action. Indeed, one might well question why anyone would expect trilateral security cooperation given the apparent rivalry, suspicion, and at times animosity among the three states. Although in the economic realm the three states are major trading and financial partners, and the volume of people-to-people exchanges (both for business and for tourism) is at an all-time high, one is as likely to characterize the security relationship among the three states as rife with tensions and suspicions as one is to see a basis for institutionalized cooperation. However, the presence of a degree of perceived security threats among the three parties can serve as a vehicle for cooperation as well as for concern. Indeed, when one looks at other regions and time periods, institutionalized cooperation among adversaries has been evident and arguably successful in limiting the escalation of tensions inherent in a security dilemma.[1]

In addition, in the case of the China-Japan-US triangle, each state is increasingly aware of mutual security threats that provide a basis for at least limited security cooperation or coordination on mutual concerns. As noted by Wang and others in this volume, China's power in the international system is expected to continue to rise, contributing to an increasingly multipolar world in the coming decades. As such, now is the time to build on positive bilateral cooperative actions that have taken place in the past several years in order to create a more solid trilateral and broader multilateral cooperative security environment that can meet future security challenges in the region and elsewhere.

This chapter focuses on the theoretical justification for, and recent developments toward, institutionalized security cooperation among China, Japan, and the United States—the largest actors in the region and critical states to any future regionwide cooperative mechanism. It examines the two principal challenges to enhanced trilateral security cooperation: (1) the need to balance rivalries with shared concerns and (2) the need to manage different perceptions of security and security threats, different military capabilities, and varying degrees of political will to face perceived threats among the three actors. Despite these challenges, some progress has been made in recent years toward, if not true trilateralism, at least enhanced bilateralism that has led to increased formal cooperation among the three parties. Still, some describe even the limited cooperation of recent years not as the result of cooperative intent but rather as a "hedging" strategy—essentially, simultaneously balancing and cooperating.[2]

As we examine the possibilities for future security cooperation among China, Japan, and the United States, it is important that arguments for trilateral cooperation not be rooted in sugarcoated optimism. International relations scholarship has long noted a fundamental tension between rising states and status quo powers that cannot be avoided.[3] This tension can be constructively addressed, however, and must be. Nonetheless, at this stage efforts toward trilateral security cooperation should be modest, and there are a number of short-term and medium-term measures that are worth exploring. Given the already difficult security environment in East Asia, and the growing tensions that in some ways have been generated by actions of all three states, even modest progress toward greater dialogue, coordination, and perhaps a pathway to future institutionalized cooperation in the security realm should certainly be a component of future efforts at trilateralism in the relationship. In the medium term, such steps may lead to a higher degree of trilateral coordination and cooperation in the security arena. Beyond symbolism, increased trilateralism—in particular, through greater dialogue, parallel actions, increased transparency, and limited jointly coordinated actions—can play a concrete role in addressing both security concerns among the three actors and, importantly, mutual security concerns.

Existing Trilateral Security Ties: Moving from De Facto to Explicit Mechanisms

Apart from formal, institutional trilateral security cooperation, "trilateralism" can be (and should be) understood in another way: as reflecting the fact that developments in each of the three bilateral security dyads (China-Japan, China-US, and Japan-US) inherently impact the other two dyads. Thus, even without formalized trilateral cooperation, the existing security relationship can be considered "trilateral," or at least interconnected. As such, important policy actions taken by the leaders of each state should be considered more explicitly to have implications for the others. As a result, more venues for substantive, regular dialogue about this interactive relationship should be pursued. Each state faces unique challenges to achieving a higher degree of dialogue and coordination in the near term—such domestic political considerations are discussed later in this chapter—but still greater efforts should be expected.

Two examples of this trilateral interrelationship have been particularly evident in recent years. As the Pentagon and Japan's Ministry of Defense focus more on the "China threat," new efforts at bilateral interaction with China's military establishment have been developed—but not in coordination with each other. For example, both Japan and the United States have hosted and sent senior defense officials to and from China and had their naval forces exchange port calls with China. To some extent, Japan has been alienated by US efforts to engage with China in military matters without prior consultation with its ally, feeding a long-standing Japanese fear of "Japan passing"—that the United States would bypass Japan in its relations with East Asia. At a different level, the deepening of operational cooperation and capabilities of the US-Japan alliance has caused concern among some in China's defense establishment. In particular, Japanese statements that appear to commit Japan more openly to assisting in the protection of Taiwan and US-Japan cooperation on missile defense in the region have raised suspicion (and even condemnation) in China. These two sets of examples both point to areas where greater thinking trilaterally—how the actions of one pair can affect the policy and perceptions of the third party—and more trilateral dialogue as a result of this thinking could benefit the broader security environment.[4]

Institutionalized trilateralism is another matter, however. Unlike in the economic or other spheres, there would appear to be little realistic possibility for joint trilateral military actions of any sort in the near future; in the medium term it may be possible—and should be encouraged—to develop a limited, coordinated military response to a common threat or to a mutually identified area in need of humanitarian or disaster relief. (It also may be possible to work trilaterally on so-called "new" or "nontraditional" security issues—energy security or climate change would be good candidates—but these areas of trilateral cooperation would not primarily draw on the military establishments of the three states and therefore are beyond the focus of this chapter.)

The payoff from achieving greater security cooperation among China, Japan, and the United States appears clear. Three primary arguments rise to the forefront. First, the three states rank as the three largest economies in the world, face numerous shared security challenges (in addition to concerns that are *not* shared), and together possess substantial capabilities to address these challenges. In principle, the three states are capable of addressing many of their shared security concerns, including areas as diverse as sea lane protection, energy security, terrorism, weapons proliferation, and humanitarian emergencies. A second reason to pursue an institutionalized trilateral approach in the security realm is that, given the large amount of collective resources, it arguably could be more efficient for the three states to work together trilaterally than to try to involve a larger number of states in a more complex negotiation or operation. This is particularly the case in East Asia, where the only existing formal security forums involve dozens of states—with the notable exception of the Six-Party Talks related to the security situation in North Korea. Questions of interoperability, habits of cooperation, and agreement on strategic approaches, among other issues, are all easier to manage among three than among many. A third reason to pursue true trilateralism is that some of the security issues faced by each of the three states are in fact created by another of the states among the three. It is therefore logical that the three states would work together directly to resolve these security issues (or that two states work together to resolve the issue bilaterally) rather than engage in broader balancing behavior. In particular, concerns on the part of China about the deepening of the US-Japan military alliance would seem particularly well suited to direct discussion among the three actors rather than to involvement—by either side—of still more actors (e.g., South Korea, Australia, India, or Russia) due to a perceived need to engage in further balancing or capability enhancements.

Recent developments regionally and in each of the three states make discussion of trilateral security cooperation appropriate and even necessary for future regional stability. China's military is modernizing and expanding its capability at a rapid pace and increasingly venturing beyond its traditional limits.[5] For example, it is developing an aircraft carrier and naval basing agreements abroad as part of a true "blue water" navy and increasing outer-space capabilities. It has also deployed warships off the coast of Somalia as part of international antipiracy operations. The United States continues to be deeply involved in providing security in the region and has embarked on a global process of reconceptualizing foreign basing and the use of new military technology in its force structure, in addition to substantially increasing its military spending in recent years. It has stressed in recent policy documents the need to engage in cooperative relations with China in light of its growing military capabilities.[6] Finally, surprising to some, Japan has begun to shed its long-standing aversion to active discussion of military issues at home and abroad; it has also steadily been modernizing its forces and eliminating inefficiencies and has begun to participate in bilateral and multilateral military activities overseas.[7]

Thus, these three states have emerged as the current drivers of the security debate in East Asia today—though certainly other actors (in particular South Korea and Russia, but also Australia and even India) remain relevant and at times decisive. While strictly trilateral security cooperation (i.e., among only China, Japan, and the United States) poses some drawbacks and also faces practical obstacles—both of which are examined below—addressing important regional and global security issues trilaterally should form a part of security planning for East Asia in the coming years.

ALTERING DECADES OF INGRAINED HABITS

Trilateral or broad multilateral coordination of security issues in East Asia would constitute a marked shift from past security practice in the region. Security ties in East Asia historically have taken the form of bilateral alliances or less formal bilateral cooperation.[8] Most prominent among the bilateral alliances is the longstanding US-Japan relationship that has underpinned security in the region for almost six decades and has only deepened in recent years.[9] The United States has also long maintained a bilateral alliance with South Korea. China, for its part, developed bilateral security ties in the postwar period with the Soviet Union and with North Korea, though these were less formalized and have waned over time, in contrast to the strengthening bilateral ties between the United States and its East Asian allies. During the Cold War period, many states in East Asia (including China) were preoccupied with internal politics and domestic security issues, which distracted them from participating in broader, regionwide security concerns.

Since the end of the Cold War, bilateral security cooperation has been supplemented by new efforts at multilateral security cooperation, including the expansion of bilateral mechanisms to new actors (enhanced bilateralism[10]), the creation of new trilateral or small-n multilateral cooperation[11] (whether institutionalized or not), and the deepening of an existing (or creation of a new) regionwide institution for security such as the ASEAN Regional Forum (ARF).[12] Such cooperation—in particular through the ARF, Asia Pacific Economic Cooperation (APEC), the Proliferation Security Initiative (PSI), and the Shanghai Cooperation Organization (SCO)—involves a large number of actors and a much larger region.

To date, strictly trilateral (i.e., three-actor) security cooperation has been minimal. The Six-Party Talks are the closest example of sustained trilateral discussion on security-related topics in that they have involved extensive informal discussions among China, Japan, and the United States, though by design the official talks also involve three other parties (North Korea, South Korea, and Russia). Some expect that the Six-Party model will—or should—be adapted to more formal trilateral cooperation in the near future, a proposal that, according to public statements and informal discussions raised at Track 2 dialogues, is reportedly being considered by the three national governments as well. There are several officials in the Obama administration in the United States known to favor this approach.

OBSTACLES TO TRILATERAL SECURITY COOPERATION

The pursuit of true trilateralism also faces several drawbacks, which partly explain the limited development of trilateral security cooperation to date. First, true trilateralism among China, Japan, and the United States has the potential to alienate other actors in the region. Such actors may display an aversion to a perceived "concert of powers" in East Asia. These actors are many: North and South Korea, the ASEAN states, Australia, India, and Russia would all have reason to feel slighted if not properly consulted about important security issues in the region.

Another limit to China-Japan-US trilateralism is that, to date, there may not be enough of a "shared set" of common security challenges mutually perceived by the three states. The nonoverlapping participation in the PSI on the part of Japan and the United States and in the SCO on the part of China is one example of how the three states have perceived even superficially common security challenges (such as terrorism) differently and therefore have pursued different sorts of solutions. This example also exposes the depth of the challenge in that the United States sees its interests undermined to a degree by the SCO. Regional institution building and cooperation therefore are not necessarily a universally perceived good.

Finally, although there may be some areas in which the pursuit of common security objectives trilaterally is efficient with respect to resources, it is easy to imagine other areas where this would not be the most efficient way to pursue common interests. In some areas, it may be that bilateral confidence building and defense exchanges are easier to manage politically and logistically. In other areas (e.g., search and rescue or counterterrorism), other regional (or global) actors may have valuable and relevant resources to contribute.

Given both the inherent challenges to and the factors that argue against trilateral security cooperation, the near- to medium-term options for such cooperation among China, Japan, and the United States are fairly limited. The security framework we are most likely to see emerge in the region is what Gui calls in this volume a "multilayered security architecture," which will be constituted by a wide range of institutions and relationships, beginning with what might be referred to as "expanded trilateralism within larger forums."

COOPERATIVE POSSIBILITIES UNDER NEW AND OLD NOTIONS OF SECURITY

The very idea of security has evolved greatly since the end of the Cold War, and in particular after the numerous international terrorist incidents that have plagued this post–Cold War period. Such a shift is evident when one compares both the defense white papers of each of the three states and their academic and military discourse over security issues over time. All three states have demonstrated a clear shift in their perceptions of the sources of threat and the necessary responses to it. The three states also share a degree of similarity in identifying among these threats international terrorism, environmental challenges, the global spread of disease, and both conventional and nuclear weapons proliferation. All three thus perceive both nontraditional as well as traditional security threats.

On the surface at least, this would suggest a strong basis for trilateral security cooperation since many of these new issues involve cross-border challenges. Indeed one finds such cooperation emerging to a degree in areas such as energy security, pollution control, and the illegal movement of people. However, such cooperation has been limited and traditional military actors have not been the primary drivers or participants in such cooperation. Moreover, recent forms of cooperation on nontraditional security issues have not yet been institutionalized trilaterally. Rather, as with traditional security issues, they have either taken the form of "enhanced bilateralism," large-n multilateralism, or the Six-Party model. For example, China has been invited to join planning and discussion between Japan and the United States in select areas (enhanced bilateralism) and all three states have joined with more than 20 others to decry international terrorism as part of the ARF (large-n multilateralism).

So-called new security issues have not replaced the traditional security concerns of the three states, however, and in traditional security areas, the primary security concern for these states is often one or both of the others. Both Japan and the United States acknowledge—to varying degrees—their concerns with growing Chinese military might in official public documents, with open public intellectual discourse frequently labeling China as a military threat. China, as well, publicly and privately characterizes both US and Japanese military power as threatening to Chinese interests. In particular, as noted by Matsuda in this volume, the Taiwan issue poses clear limits to trilateral security cooperation. Despite marked progress on this issue recently—due largely to improved Taiwan-China political ties—it remains one of the most dangerous flashpoints in trilateral relations as well as in the broader regional security environment. These realities set clear limits on the potential for trilateral security cooperation in the near future, though they also suggest a path forward to help ameliorate the existing security dilemma that the three states face in their military relationships.[13] Thus, even in traditional security areas there is logic for institutionalized, trilateral security initiatives—but the logic to support such action is different from the logic to support trilateral cooperation on nontraditional security issues. Since state attention paid to new security issues has not been led to date by the militaries or civilian defense institutions of China, Japan, or the United States, and since traditional security issues continue to be the principal challenge to each state, this chapter focuses attention on steps that may be taken to increase trilateral action on traditional security concerns.

In the area of military security, trilateral cooperation may take three general forms, as summarized in table 1.

Table 1. Three general forms of security cooperation

Type of Cooperation	Example
Military-to-military cooperation on military matters	Antipiracy or counterterrorism actions
Military-to-military cooperation on nonmilitary matters	Disaster relief activities in third countries
Political cooperation on military matters	Six-Party Talks; increased military transparency; arms/threat reduction

The first and most direct form of security cooperation involves the military institutions of each state cooperating on a military matter. Given the security rivalries and animosities among the three actors, the scope of possible cooperation is quite limited. At this stage, coordinated military action over a state-based threat (such as North Korea, for example) seems quite unlikely but may be possible in relation to a different sort of mutually perceived security threat, such as the protection of sea lanes, counterterrorism, or antipiracy measures.[14] Such cooperation would likely make only a modest contribution (if any) to the security issue at hand as compared with individual actions by each state but would have the benefit of exposing military personnel to the practices of the other states, perhaps lessening suspicions over time. It also would require the creation of standardized practices to allow the military forces to coordinate action, necessitating officer-level interaction as well as interaction among civilian-level military planners. These benefits are worth pursuing.

Seemingly easier may be military-to-military cooperation on a nonmilitary matter, most likely disaster or humanitarian relief.[15] Similar to the first mode of cooperation, this mode also offers the benefits of bringing military forces together and requiring working-level coordination. The scope of cooperation is much more limited, however—essentially to a time of crisis. This poses problems of its own, since time would be short and stakes may be high in most instances. Widespread public outcry in China over Chinese leaders' initial request for Japanese Self-Defense Force disaster assistance in the aftermath of the Chengdu earthquake in Sichuan Province in May 2008 exposes the sensitivities that even assistance at a time of need can evoke—though sensitivities were likely heightened in that case due to the relief being offered on the soil of one of the states rather than to a third country.[16] (Nonmilitary disaster relief rescue and medical teams were dispatched almost immediately after the earthquake at the request of the Chinese, however, without provoking such an outcry.[17]) Such efforts would still have the benefit of requiring planning that would bring officers and civilian bureaucrats together and would perhaps even include military personnel in training exercises.

At this stage of the China-Japan-US relationship, it is likely to be a third form of security cooperation—political cooperation on military matters—that will bear the most fruit in the short term. Cooperation among the three states over the Six-Party Talks is perhaps the best example to date of security cooperation among the three parties, though strictly speaking it is not "trilateral" cooperation. Further efforts at increased military transparency and formal dialogue over perceived threats should be pursued at this level. One example of a possible formal dialogue would be a meeting on the future of nuclear weapons in the region. This area may, like many security issues, need to be pursued initially as a series of bilateral meetings (US-Japan and US-China), but from the start, leaders in all three states should keep in mind the essentially trilateral nature of the issue: if Japan perceives that the United States is moving toward too great of a reduction in nuclear deterrence vis-à-vis China, it may react negatively; if China perceives that the United States and Japan are developing too great of a joint military capability (in particular in regard to missile defense), it may escalate a nuclear arms race in the region; if all three parties are unsuccessful in coordinated deterrence of further North Korean nuclear weapons development, a series of unhelpful military dynamics may result.[18] For all of these reasons and others, while dialogue on this one issue may begin bilaterally, the goal should be to move toward a truly trilateral dialogue on the issue in the future. Other military security issues similarly might begin with coordinated bilateral dialogue, with an eye to expanding to a trilateral dialogue in the future, building on positive developments in this area in recent years.

POSITIVE DEVELOPMENTS IN BILATERAL SECURITY COOPERATION

At the bilateral level, relations between the three states have improved significantly when contrasted with the beginning of the 21st century. Japan-US security ties have deepened considerably, as witnessed by both formal agreements and three joint statements made in 2005–2006 that outlined an ambitious future agenda.[19] At the same time, the United States and China held their first "strategic dialogue" in August 2005.[20] Then, in June 2006, a high-level Chinese military delegation was invited to observe the

US "Valiant Shield" naval exercises for the first time (together with oft-invited Japanese observers and observers from seven other states), which was reported in the Chinese state media as a "positive step" for military ties between the two countries.[21] China had already invited US observers to Chinese military exercises in 2003 and 2005.

The United States and China also have held a series of historic joint military exercises, beginning in 2006 with joint naval exercises in the eastern and western Pacific. Multilateral naval exercises including China, the United States, and six other states were held in March 2007. Admiral Timothy Keating, commander of US forces in the Pacific, visited China for five days in May 2007—only six weeks after assuming that position—coinciding with a port call by US ships to China. In early November 2007, US Secretary of Defense Robert Gates visited China as well, at which time agreements to strengthen officer exchanges and to establish an official military hotline were reached. Admiral Keating visited China again in January 2008, and a fifth US-China strategic dialogue also was held that month—this despite the hiccup of an abrupt cancellation by China of a planned port visit by the USS Kitty Hawk carrier battle group to Hong Kong in late November 2007 (a decision ultimately reversed by the Chinese Foreign Ministry but too late for the battle group, which had diverted to Japan) and two US minesweepers also being denied access to the port to take shelter from a storm.[22] A port call by several US naval vessels to China took place again in April 2008, but the bilateral relationship suffered another hiccup when China suspended high-level military contacts in response to the US announcement of new military equipment sales to Taiwan in October 2008.

The December 2008 Chinese deployment of a flotilla of small warships to the Gulf of Aden to aid in international efforts to combat Somali piracy and the change of administration in the United States have led to new plans for high-level exchanges. A first meeting between President Obama and President Hu took place in London in April 2009, leading to the announcement of a new series of "strategic and economic dialogues" between the United States and China to take place later in the year, as well as a US presidential visit to China. US Admiral Gary Roughead, chief of US naval operations, also visited China at the time of the 60th anniversary celebrations of the People's Liberation Army in April 2009.

Japan-China security ties also have improved since the end of the Koizumi period in 2006, and have included a November 2007 visit by a Chinese missile destroyer to the port of Tokyo (becoming the first Chinese warship to make a port call to Japan) and, in return, a port call by a Japanese

Marine Self-Defense Force destroyer to Zhanjiang in June 2008.[23] In addition, Chinese Air Force General Xu Qiliang met with Japanese Defense Minister Yoshimasa Hayashi in Tokyo in September 2008 (the first such visit since 2001), and in March 2009 Japan's Defense Minister Yasukazu Hamada met with his counterpart, Liang Guanglie, in Beijing.[24]

In both bilateral dyads (US-China and Japan-China), military officer exchanges have taken place in recent years, and there are discussions about increasing their frequency. Still, the fact that such exchanges and visits make headline news in each state underscores, ironically, the challenge ahead in routinizing security cooperation trilaterally. A more likely first step is to work toward greater institutionalization, or at least regularization, on a bilateral level—again, with an eye toward future trilateral coordination. As represented in table 2, there is still a long way to go before even limited security cooperation becomes routine.

Table 2. Bilateral security cooperation

Type of Cooperation	US-Japan	Japan-China	China-US
Institutionalized cooperation			
Formal military alliance	√	X	X
Joint military exercises	√	X	disaster relief
Substantive discussion of mutual security concerns	√	very limited	very limited
Functional cooperation			
Coordinated response to security concerns in East Asia	√	X	X
Coordinated response to security concerns globally	very limited	nascent*	nascent*
Coordinated disaster relief in East Asia	√	X	X
Coordinated disaster relief globally	political only	X	X
Confidence building / threat reduction			
Military officer exchanges	√	recent	recent
Civilian defense exchanges	√	recent	recent
Negotiated arms reduction	n/a	X	X
Direct military-to-military crisis channel (hotline)	√	X	recent

* Initial discussions have taken place regarding coordinated antipiracy operations in the Gulf of Aden.

Even the vaunted Japan-US security alliance is still lacking fully institutionalized and functional security cooperation—in part due to constitutional and legal constraints on the Japanese side—though significant progress has been made on this front in recent years. By contrast, only first steps are being taken in US-China and China-Japan security cooperation.

Next Steps Forward: Possibilities and Probabilities of Future Trilateral Security Cooperation

Where to go from here? On the surface it does not seem to be an especially promising time to embark on new cooperative activities. Each state is facing serious domestic and economic challenges related to the global economic recession. The United States and Japan are undergoing fundamental political shifts, while China continues to need to balance a desire for policy change with political realities on the ground. Such factors should not be used as an excuse for inaction but rather as an opportunity to jump-start an era of new patterns of cooperation. Even in the short term, one can imagine realistic, if modest, policy options that could be pursued to move leaders in each country toward developing new habits of thinking in a trilateral manner. After examining the domestic realities in each country, this section will offer six such short-term steps and will also explore the sort of institutionalized trilateral security cooperation that may be possible in the medium to long term and how these three countries can begin to work toward those goals as well.

Facing New Domestic Political Realities Together

As leaders in each country work to face their own unique set of challenges, an important starting point is to appreciate that most important policy decisions each state makes will affect the other two states directly. Moreover, the largest challenge each state currently faces—the ramifications of the global economic recession—will require coordination among all three states to solve: the United States as the economic leader and also as the root cause of the financial element of the crisis, and Japan and China both as major exporters to the American market and also as the largest holders of foreign currency reserves in the world, reserves that are critical to support the sort of budget deficits the United States plans to accrue to address the crisis. Of course this is not a traditional security issue, but if handled poorly, it could spill over into security concerns. In particular, leaders in each state must continue to work hard to diffuse any potential nationalist flare-ups as a result of ongoing economic challenges. Already, in the United States, "buy American" legislation was proposed as part of the first round of the financial bailout—prompting varying levels of public outcry from America's largest trading partners—and local government "buy American" regulations remain a concern. One can recall similar outbreaks in both China and Japan in recent years, fueled in part by careless actions by national leaders.

United States

In the United States, the Obama administration faces multiple challenges simultaneously, among them the economic crisis, two ongoing wars in Iraq and Afghanistan, growing instability in Pakistan, threats from North Korea, and several ambitious domestic policy priorities promised in the presidential campaign. The early visit of Secretary of State Hillary Clinton to East Asia (including both China and Japan on the same trip) was a promising first step and signaled that the administration considers its Asian partners as potential contributors to a turnaround in several important policy areas. An early visit means early consultation and an early opportunity to develop personal relationships to weather the crises that are to come. Secretary Clinton reportedly worked to reassure Japan that the United States well understands its sensitivity regarding the abduction issue with North Korea, but also stressed the need for Japan to play a role as a responsible stakeholder in *all* of the security issues China, Japan, and the United States face vis-à-vis North Korea. Secretary Clinton also reportedly expressed support for new Chinese actions to combat piracy off the coast of Africa, rightly stressing the positive opportunities this offers for increased trilateral security cooperation in the future. The American promise of engagement with Asia by way of the new US-China Strategic and Economic Dialogue, which includes Secretary Clinton as well as Treasury Secretary Timothy Geithner, was a welcome follow-up.

The United States must build on these first steps of early coordination, conveying to both China and Japan that it intends not only to remain firmly rooted in East Asia but to pay the region greater attention beyond the crisis issue of North Korea. The United States must not let this important trilateral relationship get lost among other pressing crises. It must work to reverse the tendency of recent years to leave East Asia alone to face the coming challenges. Such a reengagement with the region should be emphasized in policy rhetoric, through regular consultation and visits (including to the APEC Leaders' Summit), as well as through concrete action.

Japan

With the surprising and commanding victory of the opposition Democratic Party of Japan in the Upper House elections in July 2007, Japan entered a phase of what could be called "divided government" for the first time in generations. Domestic politics appear likely to remain volatile in the medium term, making it difficult for strong political leadership to emerge and undercutting the government's capacity to make bold foreign policy decisions.

The broader trend of Japan assuming more "normal" security responsibilities at home and abroad is another domestic political reality that must be treated carefully in the trilateral relationship. As a new generation comes to power in Japan, the shadow of the past will continue to diminish. While the United States and China must remain vigilant in guarding against wholesale revisionism of Japan's past actions, they must also understand that now, well over 60 years after the end of hostilities in the long Pacific War, historical issues simply are not as vivid to many in Japan. There is an important support role for both China and the United States to play as Japan comes to terms with its history (for example, through the recent bilateral history project undertaken by Japan and China). Fundamentally, however, this is not a trilateral process but rather the culmination of a long, solitary process that Japan has been undertaking to discover and to create its new role in the world.[25] There are many potential benefits to the region of a new, more confident, and more engaged Japan. This Japan should be welcomed. To the extent that discussions and rhetoric in Japan depart from norms acceptable to China and the United States, these issues should be addressed, but the first instinct should be to see Japan as a partner in this process and to address concerns through regular dialogue.

As a related illustration (one of many that could be cited), Japan's decision (legislated in May 2008) to abandon long-standing limits on the military use of outer space should be understood as part of this broader evolution of Japan's security identity. Given recent American and Chinese activities in outer space, such a Japanese response is understandable—and, indeed, an example of the interconnectedness of policy developments in the three states. Still, Japan should be expected to continue to explain its policy goals vis-à-vis outer space and to work to avoid a new space race that could lead to offensive weapons based in outer space in the coming decade.

China

China may well face the greatest medium-term domestic political challenges as a result of the global economic recession. Unemployment has risen much more sharply in China than in Japan or the United States and poses a risk of political unrest if not adequately addressed in the long term (though it should be noted that short-term responses have been impressive). As many as 10 percent of an estimated 130 million migrant workers are thought to not be earning enough to cover their basic subsistence needs.[26] Chinese analysts have argued that China needs to maintain a 10 percent growth rate to tackle these growing challenges, but such growth does not look likely in the short term.[27]

Still, as noted in the previous sections, China is by no means the only state among the three to be seriously affected politically by the growing economic recession. Just as leaders in the United States and Japan each could point to "justifiable" reasons to sideline quick attention to growing trilateral coordination with its partners, in China's case too this excuse should not be accepted. China has worked hard to develop a new reputation as a regional and even global stakeholder in recent years. It must not let this reputation slide. Its close neighbors face challenges perhaps more daunting than China itself. Together with Japan, China should help lead the way forward.

Six Steps to Encourage in the Short Term

Despite the serious domestic political challenges each state faces, the security environment in East Asia cannot be put on hold while leaders focus inward. States outside of the three will continue to pose security threats and challenges; nonstate actors will continue to play a role, whether positive (e.g., NGOs) or negative (e.g., terrorists); and regional dynamics will continue to change. The very notion of security—from a hard military definition to a broader conceptualization—will continue to evolve. Given that the region (and the world) continues to face serious traditional security threats, however, a renewed and expanded focus on these traditional security concerns must be a priority for the China-Japan-US trilateral relationship in the coming decade. Short-term steps that should be pursued by each state include the following six items:

1. Greater trilateral discussion of military issues, beginning with common threats but including areas of concern among the three parties—e.g., territorial disputes (Japan-China), encirclement (China-US), proliferation (US-China), and a potential regional arms race (China-Japan-US)

Both common threats and areas of concern among the parties should be part of a regular trilateral dialogue, building on an annual heads-of-state meeting (and the related working-level meetings) that also should be achieved. While some areas of concern among the parties are more bilateral in nature, there is still value in including such issues in a trilateral dialogue to promote openness and transparency. The Six-Party Talks demonstrate a useful first step in terms of discussing and coordinating a response to a common threat, but progress has been slow—halting at times—and the end result is still quite uncertain. Progress on increased bilateral discussion of areas of concern among the parties also should be noted, and efforts should be made to initiate trilateral discussion of such issues where appropriate.

2. Decreased politicization of military concerns—in particular, increased restraint from contributing to nationalist outbreaks at home by talking up military and security concerns publicly rather than addressing them directly through dialogue

More regularized interaction among policymakers and politicians of each state should allow them to engage in greater private dialogue on areas of concern, rather than forcing them to resort to the use of public media to express their concerns. Recent China-Japan public dialogues to develop a mutual understanding of history provide one positive example—though they also illustrate how far there is to go in terms of making such dialogue a habitual method of addressing concerns and in achieving acceptable outcomes on both sides. Security concerns of each party should be taken seriously and addressed constructively.

3. Increased transparency in military spending, equipment development, and strategy

Greater openness in this area should also help allay public fears that can lead to nationalist outbreaks. On the US-Japan side, more explication on how alliance decisions are expected to affect the security relationship with China would be welcome. On the Japan side, more open discussion of military strategy and what sort of political institutional development is desired would be welcome. Such discussions should be included in the regular dialogues suggested in earlier points. China's recent practice of issuing biennial defense white papers should be noted positively in terms of increasing transparency, though progress toward annual white papers and greater details as to how certain numbers and decisions were reached would be welcome.

4. Regularization of port calls and of exchanges of military officers and civilian officials

Regularized port calls build confidence between nations and foster greater transparency and people-to-people contacts. They also serve to build confidence among the general public and offer the media opportunities to discuss the evolving security relationship among the three states. Exchanges of military officers and civilian officials allow even deeper people-to-people contacts to develop and offer another level of transparency. At the moment, such exchanges are conducted bilaterally—a situation likely to continue into the medium term. Over time, however, routinized trilateral exchange opportunities should be considered to allow more personnel the chance to consider security issues trilaterally rather than simply through a bilateral (and unilateral) lens.

5. Regularization and expansion of military exercise observation and joint conduct

There has been notable bilateral progress in this area in recent years. China has observed US military exercises and Japan-US multilateral exercises, and the United States has observed Chinese exercises. There have even been limited China-US joint search-and-rescue naval exercises, with two land-based exercises planned for 2010 in each country, to be built around a simulated natural disaster.[28] Observation and joint conduct, while quite different on some levels, each serves to build confidence, transparency, and person-to-person contact across states and military services and, in the latter case, can also create potential new response capabilities. While it may be premature to move very far in the short term toward trilateral action, it should be on the medium-term planning agenda.

6. Movement toward coordinated action on military-provided disaster or humanitarian relief in response to a regional crisis

Nascent China-US joint exercises in this area are a welcome first step but are taking place only bilaterally. While Japan faces constraints posed by its interpretation of its constitution as limiting the exercise of its right of "collective self-defense," its military has contributed to humanitarian and disaster relief operations in multiple locations abroad in the past decade. Moreover, beyond joint exercises, greater planning and discussion must take place overall, which also could be pursued under some of the other steps suggested above—namely, leader meetings, working-level dialogues, and greater transparency in capabilities, deployments, and strategy. The process of building a trilateral response team, training that team, and deploying it would not only build bonds among the three states but also send important signals regarding international cooperation to states worldwide.

Among these six items, some can be undertaken unilaterally or pursued bilaterally through negotiation. The ideal, however, would be to pursue these points in an explicitly trilateral fashion. If so, progress on these areas—including the act of agenda-setting itself—should help to encourage new habits of thinking. It should instill in each party an inclination to see the security issues they face in an explicitly trilateral manner, even if trilateral institutions to manage the challenges are presently lacking.

Institutionalized Security Trilateralism in the Medium Term

Beyond the six steps above, a more ambitious agenda for future cooperation also should be considered. A matrix of possibilities and probabilities of future trilateral security cooperation can be constructed by pulling together the domestic political challenges currently faced by each state, the areas that might realistically be considered for security cooperation given the traditional security concerns of each state, and the likely views of actors apart from the governments of China, Japan, and the United States.

Table 3. Possibilities and probabilities of future trilateral security cooperation

Possible Cooperation	Probability	Explanation
Institutionalized cooperation		
Creation of trilateral security institution	Very low	Objections of South Korea, Russia, others
Regular meeting of a trilateral security forum	Low	Rivalry between Japan and China
Three-leader meeting in new multilateral forum	Low	Little impetus for a new institution
Three-leader meeting within Six-Party framework	Low	Objections of South Korea and Russia
Three-leader meeting within APEC	Medium	May result from economic cooperation
Functional cooperation		
Coordinated antipiracy measures in East Asia	Medium	Possible starting point for cooperation
Coordinated antipiracy measures globally	Low	Japan's prohibitive constitution; China's limited capabilities
Coordinated disaster relief in East Asia	Low	Japan-China rivalry; slowness of coordination limits response time
Coordinated disaster relief globally	Very low	Political obstacles in each country; slowness of response time
Coordinated response to a regional threat	Medium	Possible for North Korea or elsewhere, despite objections from other regional actors

As summarized in table 3, there are no areas of strong probability for future institutionalized cooperation, but some possibilities for the medium term (i.e., the next 5 to 10 years) do exist. Three of the most likely candidates for trilateral security cooperation are

- institutionalized trilateral cooperation through a new, routine, three-leader meeting at the annual APEC summit;
- functional trilateral cooperation through coordinated antipiracy measures; and
- a coordinated response to a mutually perceived regional security threat (such as North Korea).

More numerous in table 3 are areas where the probability of true trilateralism is low for a variety of reasons: objections from other states in the region, continued rivalry between Japan and China for regional leadership, limited capabilities of one of the states (e.g., military capabilities on the part of China, or institutional and legal limitations on the part of Japan), or domestic political obstacles. Over time, however, some of these limitations are likely to erode. Other states may come to accept greater China-Japan-US trilateral coordination if this is in conjunction with other regional cooperation; rivalry between Japan and China may recede as greater patterns of partnership develop; and capabilities will certainly increase in each state—militarily and politically and institutionally. Even domestic political obstacles may recede if the mass public in each state experiences (and appreciates) the benefits of greater coordination on a limited level in the short term.

CONCLUSION

Moves toward greater trilateral security cooperation among China, Japan, and the United States are likely to develop in tandem with greater trilateral cooperation in other issue areas. As security issues continue to become more enmeshed with economic, environmental, and social issues—and as the three states become more accustomed to cooperating formally in those areas—there is some reason to expect spillover into greater security cooperation as well. Moreover, and separately, there are clear incentives for greater cooperation on traditional security issues as a way to help ameliorate the security dilemma that exacerbates an already challenged set of relationships among the three states.

Thus, trilateral security cooperation should begin to be institutionalized in some ways in the short term, with an eye to greater institutionalization as seems practical in the future. Such institutionalized trilateral cooperation should lead to an annual meeting of government leaders alongside an existing forum (such as APEC) to discuss important security issues trilaterally, annual trilateral military exchanges (an exchange of visits of senior officials or of operational-level military officers), and regular joint observation of military exercises. In addition, some sort of institutionalized transparency would be welcome. Related to this, the three states might initiate an institutionalized form of trilateral scholarly exchange on military issues (or on broader security issues that include traditional military issues).

Such small steps, at least initially, are unlikely to negatively affect long-term bilateral strategies pursued by each actor. Rather, they are more likely to reassure each actor of cooperative intentions by enabling person-to-person trust building and institutional transparency. Regionally, even such small steps would need to be balanced with additional outreach to other regional actors to ensure that such actors do not feel excluded from important decision making. Taken up in this way, trilateralism should serve to enhance existing large-n multilateral efforts rather than supplant them. Similarly, trust building and institutionalized, habituated cooperation in the noneconomic realm among the three largest economies in the world can only serve to enhance global cooperative efforts—both through the cooperative efforts of the three actors (such as in energy security, containing extraregional conflicts, or reducing small-arms proliferation) and by demonstrating to other actors in the global system the benefits of institutionalized cooperation despite existing rivalry.

Institutionalized trilateral security cooperation faces numerous challenges and substantial uncertainty in terms of implementation. It is unlikely to surpass cooperation in other areas. And it should not be included on the agenda out of idealistic aspirations to bypass legitimate security concerns each state holds vis-à-vis the others. Nevertheless, such cooperation has the potential to deepen ties among the three states and to enable better futures for each state in the years to come. As such, trilateral security cooperation should be placed on the agenda at upcoming meetings of the three states.

NOTES

1. On the broad concept of a security dilemma, see Robert Jervis, "Cooperation under the Security Dilemma," *World Politics* 30, no. 2 (January 1978): 167–214. US-USSR cooperation during periods of the Cold War—in particular the period of détente in the 1970s—that allowed for negotiated arms limitations and direct "hotlines" between the two heads of state is one example; French-German dialogue after World War II over both broad historical issues as well as military planning under NATO is another.

2. This term is now widely adopted in policy as well as academic circles. For two recent applications, see Thomas J. Christensen, "Fostering Stability or Creating a Monster? The Rise of China and US Policy toward East Asia," *International Security* 31, no. 1 (Summer 2006): 81–126; and Evan S. Medeiros, "Strategic Hedging and the Future of Asia-Pacific Stability," *Washington Quarterly* 29, no. 1 (2005–2006): 145–67.

3. One classic example of this genre is Robert Gilpin, *War and Change in World Politics* (Cambridge, UK: Cambridge University, 1981); also influential, especially on the mass level, is Paul Kennedy, *The Rise and Fall of Great Powers* (New York: Random House, 1987).

4. Of course it is also possible—indeed certainly the case to some degree—that some actors within each state were quite aware of how one state's actions would be perceived in the other states and that this was part of the reason for the action in the first place—e.g., that US movement toward greater cooperation with China would spur the Japanese to work more closely with the United States, or that Japanese movement toward greater cooperation with the United States in its alliance would spur the Chinese to tone down hostile rhetoric.

5. Taylor M. Fravel, "China's Search for Military Power," *Washington Quarterly* 31: 3 (Summer 2008): 125–41; Bates Gill, *Rising Star: China's New Security Diplomacy* (Washington DC: Brookings Institution, 2007); David Shambaugh, *Modernizing China's Military: Progress, Problems, Prospects* (Berkeley: University of California, 2004); US Department of Defense, *Military Power of the People's Republic of China 2007*, http://www.defenselink.mil/pubs/pdfs/070523-China-Military-Power-final.pdf.

6. US Department of Defense, *Quadrennial Defense Review Report 2006*, http://www.defenselink.mil/qdr/report/Report20060203.pdf.

7. Andrew L. Oros, *Normalizing Japan: Politics, Identity, and the Evolution of Security Practice* (Stanford: Stanford University, 2008); Richard Samuels, *Securing Japan: Tokyo's Grand Strategy and the Future of East Asia* (Ithaca: Cornell University, 2007); Yuki Tatsumi and Andrew L. Oros, ed., *Japan's New Defense Establishment: Institutions, Capabilities, and Implications* (Washington DC: Stimson Center, 2007).

8. See chapters by Kent Calder and Bruce Cumings for expansion on this point in Kent Calder and Francis Fukuyama, ed., *East Asian Multilateralism: Prospects for Regional Stability* (Baltimore: Johns Hopkins University, 2008).

9. Andrew L. Oros, "The United States and 'Alliance' Role in Japan's New Defense Establishment," in *Japan's New Defense Establishment*.

10. Others have used the phrase "expanded bilateralism" to connote the same idea—adding new actors to existing bilateral mechanisms. For example, see Ken Jimbo, "From 'Double Track' to 'Convergence': Japanese Defense Policy and an Emerging Security Architecture in the Asia-Pacific Region," in *Japan's New Defense Establishment*; and Brian L. Jobs, "Multilateralism in the Asia-Pacific Region," in *Bilateralism in a Multilateral Era: The Future of the San Francisco Alliance System in the Asia-Pacific*, ed. William Tow, Russell Trood, and Toshiya Hoshino (Tokyo: Japan Institute of International Affairs, 1999).

11. The recent Six-Party Talks among China, Japan, North Korea, South Korea, Russia, and the United States are exemplary of this option of "small-*n* multilateralism"—i.e., multilateralism that features a limited number of participants. Aurelia George Mulgan appropriately coins the term "modest minilateralism" to refer to the current state of Japan's efforts in the region; see Mulgan, "Breaking the Mould: Japan's Subtle Shift from Exclusive Bilateralism to Modest Minilateralism," *Contemporary Southeast Asia: A Journal of International and Strategic Affairs* 30: 1 (April 2008): 52–72.

12. Several chapters within Calder and Fukuyama, ed., *East Asian Multilateralism*, provide different views of the various forms multilateralism in East Asia might take.

13. See Thomas J. Christensen, "China, the US-Japan Alliance, and the Security Dilemma in East Asia," *International Security* 23, no. 4 (1999): 49–80, on the application of the concept to East Asia.

14. In the case of antipiracy, such actions may also involve the coast guards of each state, which by some definitions may not be strictly "military" but can still usefully be grouped into this category. Indeed, in the case of Japan, the Japanese Coast Guard increasingly is playing a role typically played by the navies of other states. See Richard Samuels, "'New Fighting Power!' Japan's Growing Maritime Capabilities and East Asian Security," *International Security* 32: 3 (Winter 2007–2008): 84–112.

15. In principle, the three militaries also could cooperate over a nontraditional security issue such as planning for the managing of a refugee exodus or joint planning for the adverse consequences of global climate change, but such cooperation would face the additional hurdle of drawing the militaries of each state into these issues—ones not traditionally handled by military forces in any of the three countries.

16. Leo Lewis, "Battered China Asks Old Enemy Japan for Military Help as Flood Threat Rises," *Times Online*, May 29, 2008, http://www.timesonline.co.uk/tol/news/world/asia/article4020002.ece; Leo Lewis, "Internet Backlash Forces Japan to Shelve Plans to Send Relief Planes to China," *Times Online*, May 30, 2008, http://www.timesonline.co.uk/tol/news/world/asia/article4031720.ece?pgnum=4.

17. Ministry of Foreign Affairs of Japan, "Dispatch of Japan Disaster Relief Medical Team to the Earthquake Disaster in Sichuan Province and Return of Japan Disaster Relief Rescue Team to Japan," May 20, 2008, http://www.mofa.go.jp/announce/announce/2008/5/1180154_1010.html.

18. For a recent discussion of the differing Japanese perspectives on this issue, see Ken Jimbo, "Japanese Perceptions of Nuclear 'Twin Commitments' Under the Obama Administration," PacNet 9A (February 28, 2009), http://csis.org/publication/pacnet-9a-february-26-2009-japanese-perceptions-nuclear-twin-commitments-under-obama-adm.

19. These statements were proclaimed by the Security Consultative Committee and endorsed by President George W. Bush and Prime Minister Junichiro Koizumi in February 2005, October 2005, and May 2006.

20. Center for Contemporary Conflict, US Navy, http://www.ccc.nps.navy.mil/events/recent/ChinaConferenceAug05_rpt.asp.

21. The 10-person delegation included 3 generals as well as officials from the foreign ministry. See Agence France-Presse, "Chinese Military Says Seeing US Wargames 'Positive' for Ties," *Defense News*, June 21, 2006, http://www.defensenews.com/story.php?F=1885497&C-assiapac.

22. For a full chronology of exchanges in 2007 and 2008, see Kerry Dumbaugh, "China-US Relations: Current Issues and Implications for US Policy," CRS Report for Congress, no. RL33877 (October 9, 2008).

23. Emma Chanlett-Avery, Kerry Dumbaugh, and William H. Cooper, "Sino-Japanese Relations: Issues for US Policy," CRS Report for Congress, no. 7-5700-R40093 (December 19, 2008).

24. "Hamada, Liang Mull Defense Issues," *Japan Times*, March 21, 2009, http://search. japantimes.co.jp/cgi-bin/nn20090321a9.html.

25. See Oros, *Normalizing Japan*, and Samuels, *Securing Japan*, for two accounts of this current process.

26. Ariana Eunjung Cha, "In China, Despair Mounting Among Migrant Workers," *Washington Post*, March 4, 2009, A10, http://www.washingtonpost.com/wp-yn/content/ article/2009/03/03/AR2009030303287.html.

27. Andrew Batson, "China Fourth-Quarter GDP Confirms a Major Slowdown," *Wall Street Journal Online*, January 22, 2009, http://online.wsj.com/article/SB123259051859504907. html#printMode. Growth in the fourth quarter of 2008 was reported as 6.8 percent, down from an annual growth rate of 13 percent in 2007.

28. Al Pessin, "US, China Agree to Joint Military Exercises," *Voice of America*, July 16, 2008, http://www.voanews.com/english/archive/2008-07/2008-07-16-voa64.cfm?rend.

Managing Challenges to Trilateral Relations

6 Taiwan in the China-Japan-US Triangle

Yasuhiro Matsuda

IN MARCH 2008, Taiwan voted the ruling party out of office for the second time in its history, electing the Kuomintang (KMT) candidate, Ma Ying-jeou, as president. This election was significant not only as a sign that democratization has become more fully consolidated in Taiwan but also, and more importantly, as a shift that could potentially alter Taiwan's role in China-Japan-US relations. President Ma, early in his term, resumed dialogue with Mainland China and opened direct flights to and from Mainland China, welcoming tourists from the mainland to Taiwan. Ma is also seeking to maintain the status quo over the Taiwan Strait by adhering to a vague "one China" stance that differs in important aspects from that held by the People's Republic of China (PRC). This represents a stark contrast with his predecessor, Chen Shui-bian, who was known for his pro-independence stance.

Before discussing the implications of this change in the diplomatic arena, it is useful first to examine behavioral patterns among the major powers in East Asia. This allows for a new analytical lens through which one can understand regional diplomatic relations more fully. With that idea in mind, this chapter aims to achieve three goals. First, it identifies the current strategic structure in the region, explaining emerging trends that have resulted from structural shifts and discussing the behavioral patterns that each actor exhibits. Second, the chapter examines three of the complex triangular relationships among these actors, each of which comprises different political dynamics: China-Taiwan-US, Japan-Taiwan-US, and

China-Japan-Taiwan. These three triangles have a direct impact on the fourth, the China-Japan-US triangle. Indeed, in China, the Taiwan issue is perceived as the most uncertain and the most serious problem facing China-Japan-US relations.[1] This chapter will thus conclude by examining the implications of these various triangular relationships in terms of Taiwan's future position in the China-Japan-US relationship.

STRUCTURAL CHANGE AND EMERGING TRENDS

The Cold War Legacy

East Asia is a region where state sovereignty is alive and thriving. It is unlike parts of Africa, in which state governance appears not to be functioning, or in some cases is even nonexistent. It also differs from much of Western Europe, where integration since the end of World War II has been built on the pooling of sovereignty. In comparison, the states in East Asia are clearly more powerful and their citizens in fact expect their national governments to play a leading role. Initial steps have been taken toward regional integration, but this emphasis on state sovereignty will not easily fade away. East Asia's diversity also presents many obstacles to integration. Despite ever-deepening relationships of trade and investment, there are gaping differences among states in terms of polity, economic development, culture, and religion.

Moreover, the structural legacy of the Cold War era stands firm in East Asia. It is hard, for example, to find even a clue as to how the problems on the Korean Peninsula and in the Taiwan Strait might finally be settled. The civil wars and partitioning that took place during the Cold War have been left unresolved. Many regional powers occupy contested lands and have disputed borders with neighboring countries. Meanwhile, a sizable portion of the citizenry in the region still harbor strong memories of their wartime experiences and of colonial governance, and they have continued to make their voices heard in politics.

This partly explains the fragile relationships among states and ethnic groups in the region. For instance, Japan's relationships with China and South Korea deteriorated in large part due to one act by a political leader. Junichiro Koizumi, during his tenure as prime minister, annually visited Yasukuni Shrine, where Japan's war dead, including those who fought in World War II, are enshrined. China and South Korea strongly objected every time Prime Minister Koizumi paid a visit, and diplomatic relations soured. Of course, while Koizumi's visit was the trigger, this reaction was not unrelated to the emergence in China of nationalistic sentiments, a trend that is often associated with emerging powers.

The Rise of China and the Evolving Taiwanese Identity

Although antagonistic episodes continue to be a feature of the regional strategic landscape, there can be no doubt that globalization and the resultant rise of East Asia as an economic powerhouse have produced significant positive shifts. More specifically, there are two major forces that have emerged that are having a substantial impact, particularly on the situation across the Taiwan Strait.

One is the rise of China. For both Japan and Taiwan, the scale of their trade with China is now as large as that with the United States. Taiwan's trade with China nearly reached US$100 billion in 2008 and China is now Taiwan's largest trading partner, largest export market, and second largest import partner (see fig. 1).[2] This reflects the growing importance of cross-strait trade for both economies. Meanwhile, China's role in international politics has expanded. This is perhaps best seen in the continuous growth in Chinese defense expenditures, which have shown double-digit growth for the past 20 years in a row, starting in 1989.

Figure 1. Taiwan's Trade with China, Japan, and the US, 1972–2008 (US$ billions)

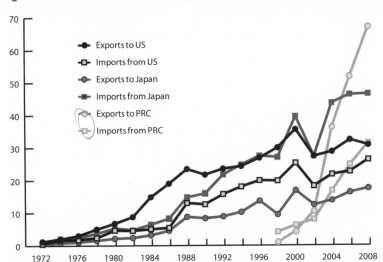

SOURCE: Council for Economic Planning and Development (CEPD), Government of Taiwan, "Commodity Trade with Major Trading Partners," *Taiwan Statistical Data Book 2009* (Taipei: CEPD, 2009), 222, 226.

The second force is the expansion of national identity in Taiwan. In the March 2008 presidential election, Hong Kong–born Ma Ying-jeou, the former mayor of Taipei, defeated Frank Hsieh, the Taiwan-born former premier. Despite what one might think, the election of Ma, a mainlander, did not necessarily suggest that the strength of national identity in Taiwan had weakened. Rather, it was Ma's election strategy of embracing Taiwan's national identity that helped him avoid being labeled as being less than patriotic toward Taiwan—like the communists—and thus propelled him to victory over Hsieh.

For instance, in February 2006, Ma had clearly stated that the path to either unification or independence should depend on the will of the Taiwanese people themselves.[3] In addition, he did not raise any objection when the then-ruling Democratic Progressive Party (DPP) announced that a referendum would be held in Taiwan on the question of whether to join the United Nations under the name "Taiwan." To the contrary, Ma Ying-jeou's KMT also made a similar proposal, which sought Taiwan's "return to the UN" under a "suitable name with dignity."[4] Ma's strategy allowed voters to select their president on the basis of the ruling party's track record and the perceived prospects for a new opposition party administration. Clearly Ma's campaign strategy was successful, as the DPP, which was criticized for its failed economic policy and corruption, was pushed to the opposition side.

If we take a look at figures 2 and 3, we can easily see that the Taiwanese identity did not weaken and that at the same time, pro-unification

Figure 2. Self-identification of Taiwan residents, 1992–2008 (percent)

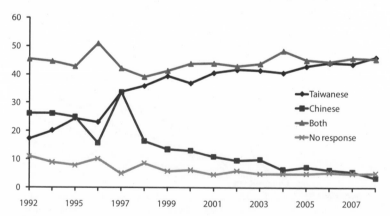

SOURCE: "Changes in the Taiwanese/Chinese Identity of Taiwanese as Tracked in Surveys by the Election Study Center, NCCU (1992–2008)," Election Study Center, National Chengchi University, http://esc.nccu.edu.tw/eng/data/data03-2.htm.

Figure 3. Taiwanese hopes for the future status of Taiwan, 1994–2008 (percent)

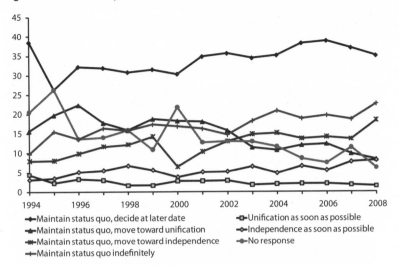

SOURCE: "Changes in the Unification-Independence Stances of Taiwanese as Tracked in Surveys by Election Study Center, NCCU (1994–2008)," Election Study Center, National Chengchi University, http://esc.nccu.edu.tw/eng/data/data03-3.htm.

sentiments did not increase during the 2008 presidential campaign. In fact, it is possible that the Taiwanese identity was enhanced in part by the visit of the chairman of the Association for Relations Across the Taiwan Straits, Chen Yunlin, to Taipei in November 2008. In other words, this suggests that Taiwan's leader is now judged and elected based on his or her ability and performance as viewed through the filter of Taiwanese identity.

A Region of Status Quo Powers

Today, there is a striking contrast between the rapidly changing relationship between the PRC and Taiwan and the fact that the East Asian region is apparently becoming more risk-averse and prone to favoring the status quo. This amounts to a major change in direction, given that "maximalist" politicians were more predominant until several years ago. For instance, China under Jiang Zemin sought to alter Japanese understanding of the past in its favor and also to draw Taiwan onto a course toward unification. Similarly, in the first days of the administration of President George W. Bush, the United States tried to pressure China to accept US demands on trade, human rights, Taiwan, and other issues. And Prime Minister Koizumi's Japan argued that his visit to Yasukuni Shrine would be a purely domestic issue and therefore China was in no position to interfere. For his part, Chen Shui-bian also had a penchant for substantial change, as shown by his effort to create a new constitution, trying to utilize the growing sense of Taiwanese identity as political capital.

These maximalists no longer stand on center stage. China has refashioned its policy toward Japan and Taiwan, improving its overall relationship with the former and opting to maintain the status quo with the latter—i.e., taking a counter-independence stance rather than actively promoting unification. As for the United States, its China policy took on a more cooperative attitude, especially in the wake of the terrorist attacks on September 11, 2001. In Japan, the three prime ministers since Koizumi have avoided visiting Yasukuni Shrine. And, finally, Taiwan elected the pro–status quo Ma administration.

The heated debates and frictions seen across the region in the first years of the 21st century are today on the wane. In this light, a new political pattern has emerged: the major powers appear to be risk-averse and do not hold high hopes of significantly changing East Asia to the advantage of one particular country. This is a major shift from a period of maximalists to an era of minimalists. Especially in the wake of the global financial crisis that began in 2008, the major countries in the region have lost any willingness to permit relations among themselves to deteriorate.

THE US-CHINA RELATIONSHIP AND TAIWAN

The United States: A Dual Strategy of Engagement and Hedging

The current US strategy on China is characterized by its dual approaches of engagement and hedging.[5] On the one hand, the United States is using engagement to encourage China to proceed down a road that is rules-based and thus more predictable. On the other hand, Washington is asking Beijing to shift from being a "free rider," benefiting from the existing international system without paying its dues as a full member of that system, to being a "responsible stakeholder," which implies being an active member that contributes to peace and security in the international community.[6]

At the same time, the United States maintains a hedging strategy in case China chooses not to take the path of a responsible stakeholder. This takes into consideration possible worst-case scenarios in which military power may have to be employed as an option. The hedging side of the strategy also entails the ongoing US military transformation efforts and the strengthening of the US-Japan alliance.

Yet for the Bush administration, East Asia ranked low in terms of strategic significance—or at least lower than in the past—due to the administration's priority on the "global war on terror" and economic issues, both of which constitute major issues at election time. From the US point of view, East Asia appears easier to deal with than areas afflicted by suicide terrorism. At the same time, China has become an increasingly important partner for the United States in regional security. This is especially true since North Korea conducted its nuclear tests in 2006 and 2009.[7] The United States may come to see China as a strategic partner in the future if China continues to focus on its economic growth and shoulders some of the burden for maintaining regional stability. The Obama administration appears to be following in its predecessor's footsteps in this regard and it is unlikely that it will drastically change the basic tone of its China policy.

China: A "Responsible Power" and a Hedging Policy toward Taiwan and the United States

China's basic foreign policy attitude was once articulated by Deng Xiaoping using the proverb, "Keep a low profile, and strive for achievements" (*taoguang yanghue, you suo zuowei*). This attitude remains largely unchanged to this day, but under President Hu Jintao, China has become more willing to be a "responsible power" in international politics. Although China's true intentions are debatable, it is clear that Chinese foreign policy is taking a different approach than in the past.

As a "responsible power," China can enjoy a more influential voice and greater prestige in the international arena. However, this does not signal that other major regional powers can take comfort. There are at least a couple of reasons for concern. One is China's rapid military modernization. Like Washington, Beijing has adopted a strategy of hedging, in this case against Taiwan and the United States. The central idea is to put China in a position to forestall what it views as Taiwan's "secessionism" and simultaneously thwart any potential US interference with a Chinese use of force against Taiwan, or at least to be able to respond effectively to such an intervention by the United States.

If Taiwan were to declare independence, there would be no alternative for China but to engage in a military conflict with Taiwan and the United States, so China perceives that it must take hedging measures to prepare for that worst-case scenario.[8] As part of that hedging policy, China first increased its arsenal of short-range ballistic missiles (SRBMs), which target Taiwan, building up from 200 at the beginning of this century to somewhere between 990 and 1,070 as of November 2007.[9] China's intention was to neutralize a Taiwanese missile defense system before Taiwan could fully deploy one. Within Taiwan's Legislative Yuan, which is led by a coalition of the KMT and the People First Party, attitudes toward the missile defense system have become extremely liberal, and some of the legislators have begun to strongly oppose the system. China's strategy was thus very successful since it has, to some extent, stopped or delayed Taiwan's introduction of a full-fledged missile defense system. Although Taipei decided in 2007 to purchase Patriot PAC-3 missiles, which were mainly developed for missile defense systems, their strategic importance has been greatly reduced by the massive Chinese deployment of SRBMs.

A second concern is that China is trying to enhance its area denial capability against the US and Taiwanese militaries, in part by upgrading its naval and space combat capabilities. China currently deploys 57 submarines, including Kilo-class submarines imported from Russia.[10] These submarines can be used to blockade Taiwan. As demonstrated by its 2007 anti-satellite test, China is also developing space war technology in order to damage US satellite networks, which are key to network-centric warfare.[11] Although there is still a military gap between China and Taiwan, the trends show that the gap is narrowing rapidly.[12]

Another reason for concern is instability in China's domestic politics. The leadership of the Chinese Communist Party (CCP) did not launch a new round of political reform at the CCP's 17th National Congress in 2007. Compared with the speed of economic development, that of political change remains sluggish. Due in part to lopsided economic growth, there remains little hope of improving the various forms of inequality in society or of addressing the frustrations held by ethnic minorities. The communist leadership may have to confront a historic political turning point in the not-so-distant future, when continued economic growth suddenly comes to a halt and demands rise for political accountability. Such a risk is certainly much higher in China than in Japan or the United States.[13]

Taiwan: Solid Democratic Practice and Open Economic Policy toward China

Taiwan has come to enjoy a more positive international reputation thanks to its market-oriented economy and political democratization. In particular, Taiwan has been emphasizing the fact that it shares the same values as the major advanced industrial democracies since its democratic transition.[14] Today, if a crisis erupted in the strait that involved military force, the United

States would find it difficult not to help Taiwan, given its position as one of the region's functioning democracies, although helping Taiwan may not necessarily constitute a vital interest. To be sure, the United States would have to take into consideration the Taiwan Relations Act and the possible implications for its alliances in the case of nonintervention.

But Taiwan under President Chen took an adventurist position vis-à-vis China, much to the chagrin of the United States. Taipei's actions were based on the assumption that the United States would never fail to rescue a democratic Taiwan. The DPP, the then-ruling party, continued to espouse this presumption during the presidential election campaigns, intending to mobilize Taiwanese nationalism. Maybe this calculation was valid. But Taipei's policy—which could be deemed brinksmanship—inevitably invited scathing criticism from the United States. Chen Shui-bian did not seem to fully take into account the growing importance of China in US foreign policy on Asia or in the policy of the rest of the world.

Nevertheless, the economic side of the cross-strait relationship has improved more steadily. The gradual opening of economic relations with Mainland China began with the era of President Chiang Ching-kuo, and the subsequent administrations under Lee Teng-hui and Chen Shui-bian continued that approach. Taipei's policy change on the political front was in part affected by the increasingly cooperative economic relationship across the strait.

US-China Cooperation and the Remaining Source of Confrontation

The United States and China both generally welcome Taiwan's open economic policy with the mainland. In the latter days of the Chen Shui-bian administration, the United States thought that it was Taiwan rather than China that was seeking to upset the status quo. Indeed, Taiwan appeared to generate more trouble than peace. In response, the United States and China both adopted a policy of "managing" the Taiwan issue based on similar grounds. This meant that China, for its part, would not demand unification in a rushed, confrontational manner, while the United States would put pressure on Taiwan not to hold a national referendum on independence-related questions.

Ironically, the birth of the Ma Ying-jeou administration has rendered this policy largely irrelevant. The rise of a conservative government in Taipei was what Beijing wanted to see happen. But the United States will have to come to grips with its concern about whether Ma may perhaps lean a little too far toward the mainland in the US eyes. It remains to be seen how

Washington would respond if the communist leadership in Beijing began to use its economic leverage against Taipei to dissuade it from purchasing arms from the United States.

Of course, it is instructive to remember that the greatest source of friction in the US-China relationship has been the possibility of a Chinese use of force against Taiwan. With this question left unclear, the present strategic environment is likely to tilt toward China's advantage, and at a more accelerated rate than today. This assessment is predicated on other assumptions: that Taiwan will relax efforts to enhance its defense capability and that China will continue its military modernization regardless of Taiwan's policy choice on defense.[15] This kind of strategic scenario would work in China's favor, but at the same time it would generate concern on the part of the United States. In short, strategic competition between China and the United States is here to stay.

US-Japan Relations and Taiwan

The United States: Japan as a Central Partner in Regional Strategy

The United States regards Japan as a central partner in the Asia Pacific region and, more specifically, as the linchpin of its security strategy for the Far East, including Taiwan. Put differently, the US dual strategy of engagement and hedging toward China is hardly effective without the geopolitical position Japan holds. Japan itself has been a major regional power, helping China open its doors to the world and providing an enormous amount of aid for decades via its official development assistance policy.[16] In terms of security in the Far East, the presence of US troops in Japan is indispensable and, in this sense, Japan's contributions are essential in enabling the United States to carry out its China policy.

From the US standpoint, Japan has been an ally not only because it shares common political values such as democracy and human rights but also because citizens of both countries feel an affinity for each other. Likewise, Taiwan is viewed as a friend that has been successful in introducing a market-based economy, improving human rights conditions, and bringing about democratization. In short, through the US lens, not only do Japan and Taiwan appear to be strategically important friends that cannot be neglected—especially when a military threat from China looms large—but they also share basic values with the United States. President Bush's statement in the early months of his presidency, in which he vowed to do "whatever it takes" to defend Taiwan, was based on this premise.

US military support for Taiwan was greatly enhanced during the Clinton and Bush eras. The level of weapons systems being sold to Taiwan was upgraded, and defense talks and strategic dialogues became frequent and institutionalized.[17] The large scale of US arms sales to Taiwan has required that a number of Taiwanese military personnel go to US military training sites and schools in order to master the operation of new weapons systems. Naturally, US exchanges and communications with Taiwan have become more frequent than those with countries that are not allies, such as China.

Japan: The United States as an Ally of Vital Importance

Japan sees the alliance with the United States as one of vital importance both for its own citizens and for the neighboring region. Reliance on the United States for national security derives from the fact that Japan has constitutionally prohibited the use of force abroad and has chosen not to acquire an offensive capability or nuclear weapons. However, the alliance is not confined to the two states. Since it also aims to take responsibility for peace and security in the East Asian region, Japan may by default be drawn into problems not of its making. This includes a possible confrontation with China, if China were to use military might against Taiwan and the United States decided to intervene. That scenario certainly is a major security concern for Japan.

This could also work the other way around. Should cross-strait issues be addressed peacefully, or if political problems regarding Taiwan should become too small to be of concern, it is not difficult to envision China and the United States moving closer to one another. Hence, Japan may be relegated to the position of a secondary player in America's Asia policy as it increasingly views China as being more important. In this sense, it is unlikely that Japan's fears of being "passed by"—as it experienced with President Richard M. Nixon's 1972 visit to China—will be dispelled for the foreseeable future.

This is a dilemma that continues to shape Japanese policy on regional security. In principle, Japan wants to see the problems surrounding Taiwan settled peacefully in the long run, but it tends to favor the status quo in the short run. In other words, the Japanese basically welcome the decreased risk of military conflict under Ma Ying-jeou's new mainland policies, but on the other hand, they are increasingly afraid that the power balance in the region could tip further toward Mainland China as a result.

Taiwan: Constructing a China Policy against the Backdrop of the US-Japan Alliance

Conventionally, Taiwan's policy toward China has been to rely on, at least in part, the US-Japan alliance. It has had few other viable options but to craft a policy based on balance-of-power principles. This is in a sense inevitable because of geography, namely Taiwan's small territorial scale and its vicinity to China, an adversarial state. Though varying in degree, this has been consistent since the Lee administration.

In other words, Taiwan is not in a position to pick and choose which country it would like to work with as it seeks to balance against China. By contrast, the United States can opt to forge a partnership with Japan, Taiwan, or both but, *ceteris paribus*, these two parties can hardly do the same. Taiwan remains less likely to be able to draw the US-Japan alliance into its own security affairs at will. This is particularly true if US policy regards China as a "responsible stakeholder" and Taiwan as creating more problems than it solves.

It is instructive to remember that the raison d'être of the US-Japan alliance in the post–Cold War era is primarily to preserve the capacity to respond to the risks created by the unpredictable or nontransparent nature of regional security. The alliance is not defined as a balancing force against "an increasing threat from China" but is based on the psychology of "bandwagoning" with the United States. That is, both the United States and Japan feel more secure with an alliance than without one. Thus, the implication for Taiwan is that it may have to make its messages to the alliance subtler if it wants to continue to keep the alliance on its side.

Japan-US Cooperation and Sources of Discord

Japan and the United States share many strategic goals on both sides of the strait. On February 19, 2005, the Joint Statement of the US-Japan Security Consultative Committee (also known as the 2+2 Meeting) outlined 12 common strategic objectives of the two countries in the region, 3 of which relate to the Taiwan issue: (1) "develop a cooperative relationship with China, welcoming the country to play a responsible and constructive role regionally as well as globally"; (2) "encourage the peaceful resolution of issues concerning the Taiwan Strait through dialogue"; and (3) "encourage China to improve the transparency of its military affairs."[18] In addition, the two countries agreed to maintain and strengthen their alliance, and their defense forces are pursuing greater operational integration through their daily activities and joint exercises.[19]

The fact that the strait is a shared interest has been reinforced by the responses of the United States and Japan when cross-strait relations have become relatively strained, for example when there were proposals in Taiwan for referendums on Taiwan's national defense or its status in the UN. Both the United States and Japan have tended to send basically the same messages to dissuade China and Taiwan from unilaterally changing the status quo.

There are also sources of discord, however. Japan is geographically situated in East Asia, while the United States projects its power from far afield. Each country thus assesses differently the geopolitical implications of China's rise and Taiwan's tilt toward China. Japan tends to be more concerned about the path China might take. Upon the election of Ma Ying-jeou, there was some debate in Japan about the possibility that Japan may become marginalized if a conservative government in Taiwan builds closer ties with Mainland China. In short, differences in geographic proximity to China and in history generate the potential for discord between Japan and the United States.

The biggest difference between Japan and the United States is that Japan's policy toward Taiwan is characterized by its passivity.[20] Japan is not actively engaged in PRC-Taiwan relations in the way that the United States is, for example through such means as arms sales to Taiwan or taking responsibility for Taiwan's national security. Rather, its constitution and established practices make it difficult for Japan to be an active player in PRC-Taiwan relations, instead compelling it to take a backseat to US actions. It is therefore reasonable to think that Japan has made and will make the decision to take independent action only when its national interest or dignity is threatened by China, and will not pursue closer relations with Taiwan per se.

CHINA-JAPAN RELATIONS AND TAIWAN

Japan: A Strategic Relationship with China, Closer Ties with Taiwan

Japan and China, through the 1972 Joint Declaration and 1978 Peace and Friendship Treaty, have generally maintained their status as good, friendly neighbors. Yet Japan in reality is pursuing its own dual strategy of engagement and hedging. The engagement aspect derives from the concept of a "mutually beneficial relationship based on common strategic interests," as articulated in 2006 by then Prime Minister Shinzo Abe. His successors, Yasuo Fukuda, Taro Aso, and Yukio Hatoyama, inherited this strategy. This relationship has become the basis for cooperation in addressing issues of mutual concern, such as the joint development of natural gas and oil reserves in the exclusive economic zones in the East China Sea.

The hedging aspect of the strategy has, probably deliberately, been left undefined. While it is clear that it is intent on enhancing Japan's alliance with the United States, Japan's cabinet has publicly declared that China does not constitute a threat to Japan.[21] However, the US-Japan alliance has been redefined to counter major uncertainties that can destabilize peace and security in the region. Those "uncertainties" are yet to be defined, and whether China will be included in that definition or not is up to the choices made by Beijing.

Meanwhile, there are a variety of factors that have led to a friendly relationship between Japan and Taiwan. One is geographic proximity. Another has been the rise of pro-Japan political figures in Taiwan, like Lee Teng-hui. Even President Ma Ying-jeou, who was typically seen as an "anti-Japanese politician," hammered out a new policy concept known as the "Taiwan-Japan special partnership" in 2008, and he has tried to manage the Senkaku (Diaoyu) dispute, which could potentially pit Taiwan against Japan in a low-key way. Still another is a political environment that has been conducive to Japan and Taiwan becoming closer, created in large part by the strains in the China-Japan relationship that emerged during the Koizumi administration and by Taiwan's adoption of "pragmatic diplomacy" following its democratization. Moreover, in the background of these trends lays the general movement toward integration throughout East Asia.

As things stand, the Taiwan issue remains one of the main obstacles to stronger China-Japan relations, along with history issues associated with the war.[22] Many observers, in fact, believe that stronger Japan-Taiwan ties are proof of Tokyo's active efforts at balancing vis-à-vis Beijing.[23] These observers point to Taipei's unmistakably friendly gestures toward Tokyo, as well as to the strong pro-Taiwan stances of some conservative political leaders in Japan. However, there is no solid evidence to support this contention that balancing is a genuine component of Japan's strategy.

China: Great Power Diplomacy, Diplomacy toward Neighbors, and Checks on Japan

China has set out four major pillars of its foreign policy: the establishment of good relations with the great powers, the maintenance of stable relations with neighboring countries, the improvement of relations with Third World countries, and the strengthening of its multilateral approach to diplomacy. In this light, Japan is theoretically an important priority. But the record of China-Japan relations over the past decade shows that China did not or could not put its principles into practice, at least until Prime Minister Koizumi stepped down. There is a robust nationalism in China, often directed against Japan, which has factored negatively in Beijing's diplomatic relationship with Tokyo. This has occasionally been fueled by influential figures in Japan, whose comments on political issues involving Taiwan have angered Chinese nationalists. But overall, the Chinese generally believe that it was Koizumi's visit to Yasukuni Shrine that definitively set the China-Japan relationship on a political collision course.

The fact that bilateral ties quickly improved after Koizumi's departure demonstrates that China's Japan policy is back on track. Now, China is trying to win Japan's support in various ways by behaving like a "responsible power." For instance, Beijing has played a central role in the Six-Party framework to address North Korean nuclear disarmament; it has also encouraged Pyongyang to come forward on issues of concern to Tokyo, in particular North Korea's abduction of Japanese nationals.

Yet, China's cooperative attitude can only go so far. It remains uneasy about what to do regarding Japan's general position in the international community. It is unclear if China might support Japan's bid to be a new permanent member of the UN Security Council. Part of the reason is that, on the domestic front, China faces political pressure from public views that are antagonistic toward Japan in general. Thus, it remains to be seen whether Beijing can consistently implement a rational strategy toward Japan.

Finally, it is also important to note that China makes an effort to place checks on Japan. This comes from the belief that Japan should accept China's interpretation of pre–World War II history and its position on the Taiwan issue. It takes little effort to find examples of this. In the late 1990s, China applied pressure on Japan to take Taiwan out of the "coverage" of the US-Japan alliance.[24] Beijing hoped to create a fissure between the allies, thus preventing the two countries from forging a more robust force in East Asia. This approach is less likely to be seen today, perhaps because China is realizing that it is increasingly futile. Beijing also appears to have fewer concerns with the Japan-Taiwan relationship due to the KMT's rise to power in Taipei.

Taiwan: Capitalizing on a Tense China-Japan Relationship

Taiwan's approach has oscillated with the shifting currents of the China-Japan relationship. Taipei under Lee Teng-hui explicitly began to lean toward the US-Japan security framework. That was due, on the one hand, to Taiwan's improving ties with Japan and, on the other, to a maturing US-Japan alliance. Under Chen Shui-bian, it appeared that Taipei was even trying to construct a more tangible security partnership with Tokyo, making it a trilateral US-Japan-Taiwan security relationship. Yet Japan was not in favor of this idea. While Tokyo was forthcoming in terms of exchanges of information and opinions, it stopped short of entering into a more concrete deal with Taiwan. In the end, Taiwan's trilateralism never proceeded beyond unofficial meetings and conferences.[25]

Today, Taiwan's approach requires a new direction. Both cross-strait and China-Japan relations have improved in the post-Koizumi/Jiang/Chen period. Taiwan will have to help create a win-win game rather than one in which any two states balance against each other. However, it is still unclear how the Ma Ying-jeou administration views China-Japan relations.

China-Japan Cooperation and Sources of Confrontation

When all is said and done, it is economics that forms the hub of China-Japan cooperation. Japan is supportive of closer economic ties across the Taiwan Strait. This is more so at the private-sector level than at the governmental level. In fact, there are more than a few instances in which Japanese companies based in Taiwan have formed partnerships with Taiwanese counterparts in order to create joint ventures in Mainland China. China has welcomed this trend as well.

Yet this does not necessarily address the sources of confrontation. As mentioned above, Beijing suspects that in the past Tokyo got closer to Taipei as a way of creating a counterbalance to a rising China. Taipei seemed to be playing this game as well. Meanwhile, Washington has repeatedly urged Tokyo to be more proactive about security issues in order to strengthen the alliance. In this light, Japan has been a "reactive balancer" in its Taiwan policy, responding out of necessity to the demands of China, Taiwan, and the United States in different ways.[26]

In short, the relationship between Japan and Taiwan has been more or less characterized as a positive one and continues to be so. This should hold true irrespective of China's policy choices. China's diplomatic posture vis-à-vis this relationship is highly likely to depend on its international position. In this sense, China's course of action has been as winding as that of Taiwan. With the birth of the conservative government in Taipei, the cross-strait relationship has taken a major turn. Beijing feels more secure about Tokyo's relations with Taipei as a result. The fact that President Hu Jintao did not care to discuss the Taiwan issue during his May 2008 visit to Japan attests to this changed political mood and thus to the change in China's political behavior.

Conclusion

There are four general conclusions that can be drawn from this analysis of Taiwan's position in the China-Japan-US triangle. First, the United States continues to play a hegemonic role on East Asian security issues as well as on economic issues. As long as China's use of force against Taiwan remains a possibility—however distant—the United States and Japan will continue to strengthen their alliance relationship in order to hedge against that. Similarly, US-Taiwan defense cooperation is likely to continue unless China moderates its rapid military development.[27]

Second, the United States may choose whether or not to work with China depending on the given crisis it needs to address. For instance, in a situation where China's threat to use force looms large, the United States might choose to intervene along with Japanese assistance. In this case, China would be pitted against the United States and Japan. But in the reverse scenario, in which Taipei's policies end up disrupting the status quo, Beijing—and even Washington—may respond by launching policies of trying to control Taiwan. Yet, if the crisis were to escalate to the point where Chinese use of force against Taiwan seemed credible, a regional realignment would likely occur, with China pitted against Taiwan and the United States and against the US-Japan alliance.

Third, economics brings all of the major actors—China, Japan, the United States, and Taiwan—together. All winners in economic globalization, they strongly agree on the desire to maintain the status quo, avoid overt political confrontation, and pursue continuous economic growth. This logic has also been evident during the economic crisis that began in late 2008. These economies cannot afford to confront each other since they are too interdependent. In recent years, that trend has been further re-inforced by the start of direct flights between Taiwan and Mainland China, which resulted from ongoing strait-related dialogues. In general, given the adversarial relationship between the two, it would seem inconceivable that Taiwan would rely on China for its economic growth or would agree to direct flights to and from China, and, understandably, many in Taiwan in fact still have strong reservations about it. Nonetheless, as long as China strives to be a rule-abiding state, at least in the economic realm, it is also inconceivable that Taiwan would opt out of this opportunity.

Finally, the three conclusions described here help us understand the shape of Taiwan's political future. As a general trend, Taiwan is likely to play a lesser role in regional security and politics. This is mainly because the other players—China, Japan, and the United States—command a more influential position than that of Taiwan. The United States is determined to maintain a predominant position in the region, which means that Japan also continues to benefit from US policy. China, for its part, is rapidly rising to "great power" status. In other words, the Ma Ying-jeou administration is likely to relegate concerns about security and crisis management to a lower priority, while economic interests play an ever-greater role in the competition among the four actors. In the 1990s, the democratization of Taiwan represented a significant counterweight to the military threat from China. But as China's rising power has led Beijing to shift its political behavior closer to the norms of the international community, Taiwan has become increasingly marginalized. Nonetheless, considering the prospects for the continued emergence of a more robust national identity in Taiwan, political unification over the strait is unlikely to be realized anytime soon.

In short, the overarching political and security framework in East Asia, in which the four parties are set to compete, has not undergone a dramatic restructuring over the last decade. The majority of actors prefer the status quo in order to advance their economic interests. Real prospects for any use of force are minimal, although each actor still actively espouses a hedging strategy.

However, the region's balance of power is no doubt tilting toward China. As a major regional power, China is continuing its military modernization, regardless of how Taiwan responds. If power is the ultimate arbiter in international relations, the changing power balance may in the medium and long run cause security dilemmas. In the short term, Taiwan's policy toward Mainland China may change the cross-strait relationship and thus have an impact on the trilateral relationship.[28] Eventually, however, all the relevant players in East Asia will be affected by what type of country China, the most important "uncertain state" in this region, aims to become.[29] In this sense, the future relations of China, Japan, Taiwan, and the United States depend most of all on the course of China's political development.

Notes

1. Guo Zhenyuan, "Zhong, Mei, Ri guanxi zhong de Taiwan yinsu" [Taiwan factor in China-US-Japan relations], in *Zhuanbian zhong de Zhong, Mei, Ri guanxi* [Changing China-US-Japan relations], ed. Zhang Yunling (Beijing: Zhongguo Shehui Kexue Chubanshe, 1997), 274, 299–301.

2. Republic of China (Taiwan), Directorate General of Budget, Accounting and Statistics, *Statistical Yearbook of the Republic of China* (2009), http://eng.stat.gov.tw/lp.asp?ctNode=2274&CtUnit=1072&BaseDSD=36, accessed October 9, 2009.

3. "Taiwan de wushi daolu" [Taiwan's pragmatic way], *Liberty Times*, February 14, 2006.

4. "Potianhuang, guomindang: Taiwan jiushi Zhonghuaminguo" [Outrageous! KMT: Taiwan is Republic of China], *China Times*, June 29, 2007.

5. David Lampton and Richard Daniel Ewing, *US-China Relations in a Post–September 11th World* (Washington DC: Nixon Center, 2002), 4–10.

6. Robert B. Zoellick, "Whither China: From Membership to Responsibility?" (remarks at the Annual Gala of the National Committee on United States–China Relations, New York, September 21, 2005), http://www.ncuscr.org/articlesandspeeches/Zoellick.htm.

7. US policy toward North Korea changed significantly during the Bush administration. It started with non-engagement, or even the promotion of regime change in the country. In 2007, however, the administration returned to the Clinton administration's original engagement policy toward North Korea.

8. Liu Jianfei and Lin Xiaoguang, *Ershiyi shiji chuqi de Zhong, Mei, Ri zhanlue guanxi* [China-Japan-US strategic relations in the early 21st century] (Beijing: Zhonggong Zhongyang Dangxiao Chubanshe, 2002), 180.

9. US Department of Defense, "Annual Report to Congress: Military Power of the People's Republic of China 2008," 2, 24, http://www.defenselink.mil/pubs/pdfs/China_Military_Report_08.pdf.

10. Ibid., 2, 4, 23, 42–43.

11. Ibid., 19.

12. Michael Swaine and Oriana Skylar Mastro, "Assessing the Threat," in *Assessing the Threat: The Chinese Military and Taiwan's Security*, ed. Michael Swaine, Andrew Yang, Evan Medeiros, and Oriana Skylar Mastro (Washington DC: Carnegie Endowment for International Peace, 2007), 346–7.

13. See Yasuhiro Matsuda, "Domestic Political Determinants of China's External Behavior" (paper presented at the 9th National Institute for Defense Studies International Symposium on Security Affairs, Tokyo, February 1, 2007), 56–57, http://www.nids.go.jp/english/dissemination/other/symposium/e2006.html.

14. Guo Zhenyuan, "Zhong, Mei, Ri guanxi zhong de Taiwan yinsu," 285–6.

15. US Department of Defense, "Annual Report to Congress."

16. Official development assistance to China began in 1979. Since then, approximately ¥3.1 trillion in loan aid, ¥145.7 billion in grant aid, and ¥144.6 billion in technical assistance have been contributed. Ministry of Foreign Affairs of Japan, "Overview of Official

Development Assistance (ODA) to China," June 2005, http://www.mofa.go.jp/policy/oda/region/e_asia/china/index.html.

17. Michael S. Chase, "US-Taiwan Security Cooperation: Enhancing an Unofficial Relationship," in *Dangerous Strait: The US-Taiwan-China Crisis*, ed. Nancy Bernkopf Tucker (New York: Columbia University, 2005), 174–7.

18. Ministry of Foreign Affairs of Japan, "Joint Statement: US-Japan Security Consultative Committee," February 19, 2005, http://www.mofa.go.jp/region/n-america/us/security/scc/joint0502.html.

19. Ministry of Foreign Affairs of Japan, "Security Consultative Committee Document, US-Japan Alliance: Transformation and Realignment for the Future," October 29, 2005, http://www.mofa.go.jp/region/n-america/us/security/scc/doc0510.html.

20. See Yasuhiro Matsuda, "Taiwan mondai no shintenkai" [New developments on the Taiwan issue], in *Kiro ni tatsu Nicchu kankei: kako to no taiwa, mirai e no mosaku* [China-Japan relations at the crossroads: dialogue with the past, and a search for the future], ed. Ryoko Iechika, Yasuhiro Matsuda, and Duan Ruicong (Kyoto: Koyo Shobo, 2007), 237.

21. See Yasuhiro Matsuda, "Japanese Assessments of China's Military Development," *Asian Perspective* 31, no. 3 (October 2007): 187–8, www.asianperspective.org/articles/v31n3-g.pdf.

22. Yoichi Funabashi, "Where Does Japan Fit in the China-Japan-US Relationship," in *New Dimensions of China-Japan-US Relations* (New York: Japan Center for International Exchange, 1999), 82; Ren Xiao and Hu Yonghao et al., *Zhong, Mei, Ri sanbian guanxi* [The China-Japan-US triangular relationship] (Hangzhou: Zhejiang Renmin Chubanshe, 2002), 253–5.

23. Xiu Chunping, "Zhong Ri guanxi zhong de Taiwan wenti" [Taiwan issue in China-Japan relations], *Taiwan Yanjiu: Chuanyue Kan*, no. 76 (December 2005): 49–52. Xiu's arguments are as follows: first, the attitude of the Japanese government toward handling administrative matters related to Taiwan is now distinctly different from its previous attitude; second, official relations between Taiwan and Japan are rapidly improving; and third, military exchanges between Taiwan and Japan are developing. Also, the phrase "military exchanges between Taiwan and Japan" in Chinese articles generally refers to contacts between Japan's retired Self-Defense Force personnel and Taiwan's on-duty military personnel through Track 2 exchanges and not to typical military exchanges (called "defense exchanges" in Japan), such as high-level exchanges, service-to-service exchanges, dispatches of military advisors, and mutual exchanges of students or trainees. Such interpretive stretching is common in China.

24. Yasuhiro Matsuda, "Security Relations between Japan and the PRC in the Post–Cold War Era," in *China-Japan Relations: The Need for Conflict Prevention and Management*, ed. Niklas Swanström and Ryosei Kokubun (Newcastle upon Tyne, UK: Cambridge Scholars Publishing, 2008), 72–78.

25. Philip Yang, "Japanese-Taiwanese Relations and the Role of China and the US," in *Japan-Taiwan Interaction: Implications for the United States*, NBR Analysis 16, no. 1 (October 2005): 102–4.

26. See Yasuhiro Matsuda, "Taiwan mondai no shintenkai," 239.

27. A major US arms sales package to Taiwan, which includes PAC-3 patriot missiles and P-3 anti-submarine aircraft, was sent to the Congress under the Ma Ying-jeou administration. Shirley A. Kan, "Taiwan: Major US Arms Sales Since 1990," *CRS Report for Congress*, no. RL30957, October 8, 2008.

28. Guo Zhenyuan, a prominent Chinese scholar of international politics, argues that if China, the United States, or Japan makes changes to its Taiwan policies, political relations and/or economic relations may become more important than security relations; in that

case, the Taiwan factor will become less important for the trilateral relationship than in the past. Guo Zhenyuan, "Zhong, Mei, Ri guanxi zhong de Taiwan yinsu," 302. Scott Snyder, an Asia specialist formerly with the United States Institute of Peace, argues that to the extent that cross-strait relations improve, one might expect the Taiwan question to become less important as a subject of dialogue among Beijing, Tokyo, and Washington. Scott Snyder, "Introduction: Prospects for a China-Japan-US Trilateral Dialogue," in *New Dimensions of China-Japan-US Relations*, 18–19.

29. According to balance of threat theory, states tend to be either status quo states, revisionist states, or uncertain states, meaning it is unclear whether they will ultimately adapt to the existing international system or rebel against it.

7 | Explaining Stability in the Senkaku (Diaoyu) Islands Dispute

M. TAYLOR FRAVEL

IN THE MODERN era of state sovereignty, territorial disputes are a leading source of conflict and violence in the international system. States have gone to war more frequently over territory than any other issue.[1] Although territorial disputes are usually bilateral conflicts between two states, they play an important role in trilateral relations among the United States, China, and Japan. China and Japan contest the sovereignty of the Senkaku (Diaoyu) Islands in addition to maritime rights in the East China Sea.[2] The United States is an important actor in the China-Japan disputes, especially the conflict over the Senkaku Islands, because the 1960 alliance treaty obliges it to aid Japan in defending the territory under its administration.[3]

As issues that are prone to elicit violence, territorial disputes are also an obstacle to deepening cooperation among states in other arenas. As territorial disputes bear upon the most vital of national interests—sovereignty—they are held to reflect a state's intentions and ambitions. In trilateral relations, escalation of the Senkaku dispute could pose a severe challenge to future cooperation among the three states by pitting China against Japan and the United States. Even in the absence of armed conflict over the land being disputed, tensions over the Senkaku Islands are likely to limit cooperation in other ways, highlighting mutual concerns about long-term intentions and ambitions.

The potential for the polarization of trilateral relations flows from the structure of the Senkaku dispute. In this conflict, China is what international relations scholars would term the "challenger" or "dissatisfied" actor. This does not mean that China overall is a revisionist actor in the international system. What it does mean is that China seeks to change the status quo in this particular dispute. Although China claims sovereignty over the Senkakus, it does not exercise effective authority over the islands, which Japan has administered since 1972.[4] Conversely, Japan is the "defender" in the dispute because it controls all of the territory in question.

Despite the potential for armed conflict, the dynamics of the Senkaku dispute present a puzzle for scholars of territorial disputes and policymakers in the region. Although China and Japan have formally contested the Senkaku Islands since 1970, neither side has used force. Indeed, given the strategic and economic value attached to the islands and periods of tension in the broader China-Japan relationship, the absence of armed conflict or even tense military confrontations is nothing short of remarkable. At the same time, the two sides have yet to engage in any serious effort to resolve the dispute. Instead, both sides have adopted what could be best described as a delaying strategy that defers settlement to the future.[5]

Within the study of international relations, scholarship on territorial disputes provides little guidance about the sources of delay in these conflicts. Instead, scholars have focused their attention on decisions to either escalate and use force or compromise and settle these disputes, as these choices are the most consequential ones that leaders can make.[6] To explore why leaders adopt a delaying strategy instead, this chapter examines the sources of stability in the Senkaku dispute. In particular, it seeks to identify those factors linked with the absence of escalation as well as the absence of compromise. I find that the US-Japan alliance has deterred China from using force in the conflict, while active dispute management by both China and Japan has limited the potential for escalation. At the same time, paradoxically, the perceived value of the islands and the limited benefits to be gained through compromise create strong incentives to avoid efforts to settle the dispute.

The chapter begins with a discussion of the role of the Senkaku Island dispute in the trilateral relationship. It then examines four factors that could explain the absence of the use of force by either China or Japan and discusses in detail the concept of active dispute management. The third section examines three factors that could explain the absence of negotiations and settlement efforts, before concluding with a discussion of the implications of the analysis and the future trajectory of the dispute.

TERRITORIAL DISPUTES IN THE TRILATERAL RELATIONSHIP

A territorial dispute is a conflict between two or more states over the owner-ship and control of a piece of land. In the study of international relations, these conflicts include disputes over land borders as well as islands and other maritime features, such as coral reefs that lie above the high-tide line.[7] By contrast, a maritime sovereignty dispute is a conflict over exclusive rights to bodies of water, especially exclusive economic zones (EEZs) as defined by the UN Convention on the Law of the Sea (UNCLOS). Apart from internal waters, however, states do not enjoy full sovereign rights in maritime areas under their jurisdiction, as they must permit vessels from other countries freedom of passage and transit. Maritime sovereignty thus is weaker than territorial sovereignty. As a result, maritime conflicts are less volatile than territorial disputes and, specifically, less likely to block or prevent cooperation among the United States, China, and Japan.

China and Japan hold conflicting claims over the sovereignty of the Senkaku Islands. Japan asserts that the islands were determined to be unoc-cupied and *terra nullius* ("as empty land") in 1885 and formally incorporated into Japan in 1895. China claims discovery of the islands under the Ming dynasty and asserts that they were ceded to Japan along with Taiwan in the 1895 Treaty of Shimonoseki and thus returned to China at the end of World War II. From 1945 to 1972, however, the United States administered the islands directly as part of the Ryukyu Islands (which included Okinawa) and used one of the islets as a bombing range. With the conclusion of the Okinawa Reversion Agreement, the islands have been administered by Japan since May 1972. China (People's Republic of China) issued its first formal claim to the islands in December 1970, after Taiwan (in the name of the Republic of China) and Japan both issued claims in bids to ensure access to nearby petroleum resources.[8]

China and Japan are also involved in two maritime sovereignty disputes. The first concerns the extent of maritime rights in the area known as the East China Sea. Japan claims that the median line between the Chinese and Japanese coasts should demarcate maritime rights in these waters. China, by contrast, asserts that the continental shelf principle should be applied instead. The area under dispute is large and comprises 160,000 square kilometers of water.[9] This dispute is distinct from the conflict over the Senkakus, which concerns just sovereignty over the islands and not maritime rights (although the islands can be used to claim maritime rights). The second maritime dispute is over Okinotorishima, a coral reef that lies more than 1,740 kilometers to the east of Tokyo. Although China does not claim sovereignty over the reef, it has objected to Japan's position that it can be used to claim a large EEZ in the western Pacific.[10] China asserts that Japan cannot claim an EEZ under UNCLOS in the surrounding waters because Okinotorishima is a rock and not an island.[11]

Finally, China and Japan are involved in territorial disputes with other states in East Asia. Although these disputes fall outside the scope of the trilateral relationship, behavior in these conflicts can influence how China and Japan view each other's intentions in their own disputes. In addition to its long-standing conflict over Taiwan, China today is still engaged in disputes with India and Bhutan over territory along its land border, as well as with various East Asian nations over the Paracel and Spratly Islands in the South China Sea. Although China has disputed a total of 23 areas with its neighbors since 1949, it has settled the majority of these conflicts through peaceful negotiations and compromise settlements.[12] Likewise, Japan participates in territorial disputes with all its immediate neighbors. Since 1945, Japan and Russia have contested the sovereignty of the Northern Territories/ Kurile Islands that the Soviet Union occupied at the end of World War II, and Japan also contests the sovereignty of the Dokdo (Takeshima) Islands, which are under South Korean administration.[13]

Similarly, China and Japan contest maritime sovereignty with their neighbors. Although China resolved part of its maritime sovereignty dispute with Vietnam in 2000, it has yet to determine its maritime boundaries with North Korea and South Korea. The use of a "nine-dotted line" (*jiu duan xian*) to depict Chinese claims in the South China Sea also raises questions about the possibility of extensive Chinese maritime sovereignty claims in the area. Likewise, Japan has yet to reach maritime delimitation agreements with either Korea or Russia.

Although the United States does not contest the sovereignty of any territory with either Japan or China, it is nevertheless an important actor in some of these conflicts through its alliance with Japan. The US role in these conflicts places bilateral disputes within the framework of trilateral relations, as US policy can impact the development of the disputes and thus the prospect for trilateral cooperation. At the risk of oversimplification, US policy toward the Senkaku and other territorial disputes is based on two general principles: (1) neutrality in terms of the ultimate sovereignty of contested areas and (2) peaceful resolution without resort to coercion or armed force.

Since the end of World War II, the United States has been a direct participant in the dispute over the Senkaku Islands. Following the 1951 peace treaty with Japan, the United States administered these islands as part of the Ryukyus until early 1972. When administration of the islands was transferred to Japan in May 1972, the United States underscored that this action had no bearing on the question of disputed sovereignty. Then Secretary of State William Rogers stated, "This [reversion] treaty does not affect the legal status of those islands at all. Whatever the legal situation was prior to the treaty is going to be the legal situation after the treaty comes into effect."[14] Similarly, a State Department document issued at the time noted, "The United States has made no claim to the islands and considers that any conflicting claims to the islands are a matter for resolution by the parties concerned."[15]

Since then, the United States has generally preferred to avoid public comment on the dispute. In 1996, however, as confrontations occurred involving civilian activists from Japan, Hong Kong, and Taiwan who had landed on the disputed islets, the United States repeated its stance, a State Department spokesman confirming that the US position "is that we do not support any individual country's claim to these islands."[16] The State Department repeated this position again in March 2004 when Mainland Chinese activists landed on the islands. In the words of spokesman Adam Ereli, "the United States does not take a position on the question of the ultimate sovereignty of the Senkaku Diaoyu Islands."[17]

Nonetheless, while the United States maintains neutrality regarding the question of sovereignty, it has also clarified that the disputed islands fall within the scope of the 1960 Mutual Security Treaty. According to Article V of the treaty, the United States and Japan agree that "an armed attack against either Party in the territories under the administration of Japan would be dangerous . . . and [each party] declares that it would act to meet the common danger in accordance with its constitutional provisions and processes." When the United States transferred administration of the islands to Japan, it noted that the treaty would now extend to the islands as areas under Japanese administration. Again, the United States has preferred not to stress this commitment in public, but in 1996, partly under pressure from lawmakers in Japan, the United States repeated its position regarding the status of the islands within the alliance. According to Kurt Campbell, then deputy assistant secretary of defense for East Asia, "The 1972 US-Japan agreement on the return of Okinawa to Japan clarifies that the Senkaku Islands fall under Japanese administration."[18] In 2004, State Department spokesman Ereli repeated this position, noting clearly that "Article V of the Mutual Security Treaty applies to the Senkaku Islands."[19] The United States used similar language in a March 2009 statement as tensions increased in the dispute following the discovery of two Chinese maritime survey ships within the Senkakus' territorial waters in December 2008.[20]

THE AVOIDANCE OF ARMED CONFLICT

The dynamics of the Senkaku Islands dispute since the 1970s present a puzzle. At first glance, one might expect that this dispute should be fraught with tension and even violence. Territorial disputes often serve as proxies for broader conflicts of interests, especially between states that might be characterized as enduring or strategic rivals, such as China and Japan.[21] Although the China-Japan economic relationship has continued to deepen since the end of the Cold War, political relations have oscillated between periods of heightened friction and relative calm.[22] At the same time, both sides see the islands as important real estate, endowed with strategic significance and economic value, characteristics that increase a state's willingness to use force in a territorial dispute.[23] China has also used force in other disputes over offshore islands, most notably over the Paracels in 1974 and the Spratlys in 1988 and 1994.[24] Finally, given the history of Japan's occupation of parts of China, one might expect territorial issues to be especially prominent as a source of friction between the two countries and one that leaders might manipulate to mobilize society, perhaps for diversionary ends.[25]

Since 1949, however, China has never used force against Japan over the Senkaku Islands, although it did display its potential to use force once, in 1978, during the peace treaty negotiations.[26] The fact that armed conflict over the islands has been avoided is a major accomplishment and one that deserves detailed examination because, in many ways, it is unexpected. The analysis below focuses mostly on China for several reasons. First—unlike Japan—China, as noted above, has used force in its other territorial disputes since the end of World War II and in half of its offshore island disputes. Second, as the "challenger" in the Senkakus dispute, force remains a viable option for China to regain sovereignty of the islands to improve its otherwise weak position or to compel concessions from Japan.

By contrast, because Japan already occupies and controls the islands, force is not necessary to improve its claim and would only be used to deter or prevent a Chinese attack. Nevertheless, even as the "defender," the use of force for Japan remains a viable option under certain conditions. In particular, because Japan already controls the islands, it may be more willing to use force to arrest or reverse decline in its position in the dispute in the face of increasing Chinese provocations, such as the dispatch of mainland survey ships within the territorial waters of the islands in December 2008. Indeed, reflecting concerns about China's growing military power and naval activities in the East China Sea, Japan's military drafted a contingency plan in November 2004 "to defend the southern remote islands off Kyushu and Okinawa from possible invasion."[27]

Explaining state inaction or the absence of a particular outcome such as the use of force presents a challenge for social scientists. One of the core problems is that patterns of inaction or nonevents are likely to be overdetermined; that is, they are consistent with multiple if not overlapping variables and explanations. As a particular behavior is not observed, it is more challenging to identify those factors that vary with inaction as opposed to using force or offering to compromise. Nevertheless, four reasons help explain the absence of violent conflict in the Senkaku dispute since 1972: deterrence, de facto control, regional rivalry, and active dispute management.

Deterrence

The first and most important reason is deterrence. Put simply, China has lacked the military means to execute a limited-aims operation to seize and defend the islands from any counterattack. Although China did clash with South Vietnam in 1974 and Vietnam in 1988 in other offshore island conflicts, those countries possessed very limited naval power and China was able to achieve victory after short clashes. By contrast, Japan possesses the strongest and most professional navy of any East Asian country.[28] More importantly, however, the US alliance with Japan has arguably deterred China from taking any armed action over the islands. Given Article V, use of force over the Senkakus would run the very real risk of conflict with the United States—conflict that China would prefer to avoid. As discussed below in the section on dispute management, public US statements regarding its commitment under the treaty that were issued during moments of tension in the dispute represent subtle deterrent actions.

De Facto Control

The continuous occupation of the disputed islands by Japan during the period when their sovereignty has been contested is a second reason for the absence of escalation. Continuous occupation by one state in a territorial dispute significantly increases the cost for the other side (in this case China) of using force, as the international community would view any use of force as a clear sign of revisionist behavior. Occupation by one side, in other words, reinforces the status quo bias of the international system. By contrast, although China did use force in the Paracels and the Spratlys, it seized islands and coral reefs that were claimed but not occupied by other states and vacant real estate (with the exception of Pattle Island in the Paracels). In disputes on its land border, China has not seized large amounts of disputed territory through the use of force, especially when contested territory has been occupied by other states. In its 1962 war with India over disputed areas along its southwestern frontier, for example, China won a military victory but then withdrew to the line of actual control that had existed prior to the outbreak of hostilities.[29]

Regional Rivalry

A third reason for the absence of escalation stems from the continuing competition between China and Japan for diplomatic influence within East Asia. For different reasons, both countries likely want to maintain reputations as constructive and benign powers in the region. Escalation or use of force over the Senkakus would tarnish that reputation. In particular, China's current diplomatic strategy revolves around the notions of "peaceful development" and "reassurance."[30] Belligerence over territory would send a signal to most states in the region that a more powerful China might also be more aggressive, thus increasing suspicion and uncertainty about China's long-term intentions.

Active Dispute Management

A fourth and underexamined reason is how both sides have sought to manage the dispute to avoid unwanted spirals of hostility and tension that might culminate in the use of force. Several aspects of dispute management must be stressed, as they have received little attention in analyses of the Senkaku dispute or, for that matter, in the international relations scholarship on territorial disputes. Even if China has been deterred by US power, Japanese control of the disputed islands, or potential reputational costs, the management of tensions in this dispute is also important. All three countries have played a role in the successful management of the dispute, where success is defined as the absence of conflict.

Limited Access Perhaps the leading source of friction in the dispute over the past two decades has been efforts by citizen activists to land on the islands to demonstrate their countries' sovereignty claims. These actions then compel governments to get involved in the dispute, increasing the potential for armed conflict. In the 1990s, several crises over the islands occurred when activist groups from Hong Kong, Taiwan, and Japan journeyed to the disputed rocks. Japanese activists, most notably from the Japan Youth League, frequently visited the islands in the 1990s to maintain a lighthouse on Uotsuri (Diaoyu) Island that was first built in 1978.[31] In response, individuals from Hong Kong, Taiwan, and Mainland China sought to land on the Senkakus to support China's claims. In 1996, a Hong Kong citizen, David Chan, drowned as he attempted to land and plant a flag on one of the islands.[32] A number of other unsuccessful attempts have also been made by groups supporting China's claim, but in 2004, activists from Mainland China successfully landed on the islands.

As a private citizen owns three of the five main islands, the Japanese government was unable (or perhaps just unwilling) to prevent its own citizens from making symbolic visits and increasing the potential for conflict in the dispute. Since 2002, however, the Japanese government has taken a number of steps to enhance its control over the islands and limit access by Japanese citizens, thereby reducing incentives for Chinese patriotic groups to land on the islands in response. First, in April 2002, the Japanese government entered into a lease for the three islands remaining outside of government control. This placed all of the disputed features under the direct control of the Japanese government, and because the government became a leaseholder, it could both prevent the sale of the islands to activists who might seek to make use of them for political goals and block activists from all sides from landing on the islands.[33] Second, just one month after the first successful landing on the islands by Mainland Chinese activists in March 2004, the Japanese government decided to station two Coast Guard vessels near the islands in order to prevent individuals from landing on them in the future.[34] Third, in February 2005, Japan further consolidated control over the islands when it announced that it had assumed control of the lighthouse on Uotsuri that had been built and maintained by the Japan Youth League.

These actions elicited sharp protests in Beijing and Taipei as they were viewed as unilateral assertions of sovereignty over contested territory and consolidation of Japanese control. Nevertheless, they lowered tensions by removing perhaps the greatest irritant in the dispute, the actions of activist citizens. In the past, the rationale for these visits by Japanese activists was the need to maintain the lighthouses and replace their solar-powered batteries. Indeed, according to public news sources, no Japanese activists have successfully landed on the islands since 2003.[35] Although this has not prevented subsequent attempts by Chinese and Taiwanese patriotic groups to land on the islands, the Japanese government has been able to intercept these ships rapidly through the deployment of Coast Guard vessels in surrounding waters.

Similarly, the Chinese government has sought to restrict the activities of its own citizens around the islands. For most of the 1990s, only activists from Hong Kong and Taiwan, not Mainland China, sought to land on the islands in protest. In 2003, however, a mainland-based group, the China Federation for Defending the Diaoyu Islands, began preparations for a voyage to the islands.[36] After several reconnaissance trips, the federation landed seven members on Uotsuri in March 2004.[37] These individuals were detained by the Japanese Coast Guard and deported to China 48 hours later. Although it is not clear what the Chinese government's policy toward such groups was before this landing, since then it has sought to prevent any further landings or maritime excursions to the islands by its citizens from Chinese ports. In July 2004, local officials in Fujian prevented members of the federation from using Chinese fishing vessels for noncommercial purposes such as traveling to the islands.[38] And, following anti-Japan protests in April 2005, the government raided the federation's offices in Beijing in July 2005.[39] In October 2007, four members of the federation who had entered Japanese territorial waters in an attempt to land on the islands were placed under house arrest when they returned to China.[40]

Avoidance of Social Mobilization A second aspect of dispute management that deserves mention is that China has avoided mobilizing the public around the dispute. Indeed, despite its potential to rally people around the flag and its role in past patriotic education campaigns, the Senkakus dispute rarely appears in official newspapers. As figure 1 demonstrates, the total number of articles that refer to "Diaoyu Dao" (Senkaku Islands) in the title that have appeared in the *People's Liberation Army Daily* (Jiefangjun bao) and the *People's Daily* (Renmin ribao) since 1987 is low. In some years, no articles appeared at all. Moreover, as shown in figure 2, the frequency of articles on the Senkakus is roughly one-tenth of those published on the Spratlys and an even smaller fraction of those concerning Taiwan. No clear trend exists in the frequency or timing of articles on the Senkakus either. Analysis of individual news reports suggests that the publication of articles is caused by events linked to the dispute, especially activists' attempts to land on the islands as well as Japan's own administrative actions.

Figure 1. Articles on the Senkaku dispute appearing in major Chinese news-papers, 1987–2005[41]

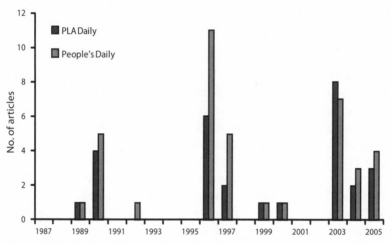

SOURCE: *Jeifangjun Bao* and *Renmin Ribao* online databases.

Interestingly, almost no difference exists in the coverage of the dispute between military and civilian Chinese sources, providing strong evidence against the argument that there are divisions between China's military and civilian leaders over Japan policy. *Liberation Army Daily* coverage of the Senkakus consists almost entirely of articles originally published by Xinhua, the Chinese government's central news agency, or by the *People's Daily*, the newspaper of the Central Committee of the Chinese Communist Party. With just three exceptions, the *Liberation Army Daily* has published no original articles on the dispute, focusing instead on reporting government statements and press conferences. Most of the reporting on the Senkakus is also buried on the inside of the paper, not on the front page. Thus, there appears to be close coordination between the government and People's Liberation Army over the Senkaku dispute, at least in the area of propaganda. Overall, the goal is to minimize attention to the conflict while demonstrating China's "resolute" stance on the question of sovereignty when an event occurs that appears to question or challenge China's claim.

Likewise, since the end of the Cold War, the Chinese government has restricted the number, scope, and duration of protests against Japan over this issue. As Erica Downs and Philip Saunders have demonstrated, the Chinese government understands the double-edged nature of nationalism. Although it has allowed protests to occur during periods of great tension in the dispute, especially in 1990 and 1996, the duration and scope of these

Figure 2. Articles on China's maritime sovereignty disputes appearing in the
PLA Daily, 1987–2005[42]

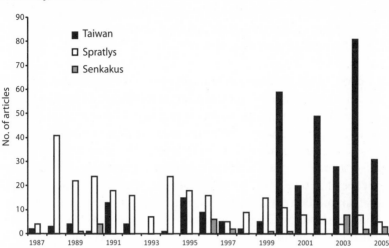

SOURCE: *Jiefangjun Bao* online database.

civil actions were severely limited.[43] Even in April 2005, when anti-Japan
demonstrations occurred throughout major cities in China, the Senkakus
dispute played only a minor role despite its potential utility in mobilizing
support for the demonstrators' goals. Indeed, an incomplete examination
of photographs of the demonstrations reveals no signs, posters, or banners
referring to the Senkaku Islands and only a few banners mentioning the
dispute over maritime rights in the East China Sea.[44]

Japan's Use of the Islands Although it has administered the islands since
1972, Japan has limited their development and use. In particular, Japan has
not erected any military installations on the island that might be viewed as
threatening in Beijing. Such installations would not only constitute a clear
exercise of Japan's sovereignty over the islands but would most likely be
deployed to counter China's growing military power, especially its naval
power. Such installations would further increase the value of sovereignty
over the islands, which in turn could increase the incentives for China, as
the weaker challenger in the dispute, to use force.

Japan's limited use of the islands is important because Chinese sources
distinguish between Japan's administration and occupation of the islands.
In particular, Chinese writings differentiate between Japan's current administration of the islands—sometimes described as "actual control" (*shiji
kongzhi*)—and any potential or future Japanese "occupation" of the islands.

By implication, occupation—described as "*qinzhan*" or "*zhanling*"—appears to refer to any permanent military use of the islands, especially for military assets that could be used in a conflict over Taiwan.[45] Thus, although only by implication, these writers have highlighted what might be viewed as a "red line" for China in its dispute with Japan.

US Policy   A fourth aspect of management of the dispute has been US policy. It is perhaps not a coincidence that the United States has sought to send muted deterrent signals during moments of potential crisis in the dispute. As discussed above, during the events of 1996 that led to efforts by Hong Kong and Taiwanese activists to land on the islands, the Pentagon and Department of State repeated the position that the islands fell under the scope of Article V in the 1960 treaty and stressed the importance of peaceful resolution of the dispute. Similarly, after the first successful landing on the islands by Chinese activists in March 2004, Washington again clarified its commitment. The day after the Chinese activists reached the islands, spokesman Adam Ereli repeated both pillars of US policy: that it remained neutral with respect to the island's ultimate sovereignty but that the islands also fell within the scope of the 1960 treaty and US security commitments to Japan. In both cases, the statements were likely designed to signal the US commitment to a peaceful resolution and to underscore the importance of limiting tensions over the islands.

At the same time, dispute management is a fragile process that requires constant attention. In December 2008, for example, two Chinese government maritime survey vessels entered the territorial waters of the Senkaku Islands.[46] Although China justified its actions in terms of its sovereignty over the islands, Japan viewed the action as provocative, as it marked the first time that Chinese government ships and not civilian vessels had traveled so close to the disputed islands. In response, Japan announced plans in February 2009 to deploy a larger and more capable Coast Guard vessel to the area, a helicopter patrol ship. China responded with alarm to this action, which it viewed as strengthening Japan's control over the island. In March 2009, the US government repeated its treaty commitment to defend territory under Japanese administration. According to a US government spokesperson, "the Treaty of Mutual Cooperation and Security signed by Tokyo and Washington in 1960, which states that it applies to the territories under the administration of Japan, does apply to the island."[47] The reason for China's decision to send survey ships to the Senkakus remains unclear and requires further research. The situation should be monitored closely, however, since it could mark a shift in Chinese policy toward the dispute and, perhaps, the end of the dispute management described above.

THE ABSENCE OF COMPROMISE AND SETTLEMENT EFFORTS

In addition to the absence of escalation, the dynamics of the Senkaku situation present another puzzle, namely the absence of any efforts to compromise and negotiate a settlement of the dispute. Although China has compromised in the majority of its territorial disputes since 1949, it has never entered into talks with Japan regarding the status of the Senkakus.[48] Instead, both China and Japan have preferred what I have described elsewhere as a strategy of delaying and deferring settlement of the dispute.[49] In 1978, Deng Xiaoping described the delaying strategy when he stated, "It does not matter if this question is shelved for some time, say, 10 years. Our generation is not wise enough to find common language on this question. Our next generation will certainly be wiser. They will certainly find a solution acceptable to all."[50]

Similar to the absence of escalation, the absence of cooperation in territorial disputes is also likely to be overdetermined. Why China and Japan have chosen, in essence, to do nothing and defer settlement to some future point in time is difficult to explain with any precision. Nevertheless, three factors have likely played a role in the delay of the dispute.

Shadow of the Future

The first reason why a state might adopt a delaying strategy in a territorial dispute is because the territory at stake is highly valued for economic, strategic, or symbolic reasons. When states bargain over an issue that is seen as highly valued, they have strong incentives to wait and hold out for the best possible deal. When national sovereignty is at stake, these incentives to bargain hard further increase as territorial settlements, once reached, can be hard to reverse through negotiations.[51]

China and Japan both highly value the Senkaku Islands. The islands serve as assets for claiming maritime rights under UNCLOS and thus allow whoever controls the islands to claim a greater proportion of the East China Sea. In addition, ever since the late 1960s, people have come to believe that the East China Sea itself holds large deposits of petroleum, including the natural gas fields in the Xihu Trough that China has been developing since the mid-1990s, which became a point of friction in China-Japan relations after 2003.[52] From a military point of view, the islands could also serve as a listening post or even as a base for anti-ship missiles that could be used to project power over adjacent sea lanes.

For each side, however, the incentives for pursuing delay and avoiding cooperation differ. For Japan, delay only further consolidates a favorable status quo and strengthens its claim under international law by lengthening the period of continuous administration of the islands. By contrast, as China's bargaining power in the dispute remains limited, delay allows it to strengthen its position, which is weak for two reasons. First, it does not occupy any of the territory that it claims. As occupation is "nine-tenths of the law," this is an important source of weakness. Second, it lacks the ability to project military power over the islands to seize and defend them against any Japanese counterattack. Under those circumstances, delay allows China to make the best of a situation in which it has few options while buying time to improve its position. Moreover, the cost of delaying is not high, as China can easily maintain its sovereignty claim through diplomatic statements. China has little incentive to consider any compromise settlement when it might be able to get a better deal in the future.

Costs of Compromise

A second reason for delay is that national leaders view compromise—either by dropping a territorial claim or transferring some or all of the disputed land—as a costly alternative. As Japan already administers the islands, these costs are likely to be higher in Tokyo than in Beijing because it would give up far more than China. In particular, Japanese and Chinese leaders face two costs of compromising, both of which would be seen as high in this dispute.

The first type of cost refers to potential punishment from domestic audiences. Given the underlying political tension in China-Japan relations, along with the politics associated with the history of World War II, a compromise by either side is likely to arouse opposition within each country. Put simply, the leader who offers a compromise will likely be cast as "selling out" his country's territory. He may lose political support within his country at the cost of implementing other policy initiatives or even staying in office.[53] In China, for example, scholars who promoted "new thinking" regarding China's Japan policy were labeled as traitors by other scholars and netizens.[54] In both countries, compromise might also provide an issue around which a coalition of elites could defeat a rival.

A second type of cost concerns the perceptions of the two countries' resolve. Japan and China are the two largest economies in East Asia and possess the two most powerful armed forces in the region. As witnessed in policy toward Southeast Asia over the past decade, the two states are competing for prestige and status in the region. Leaders on both sides may conclude that compromising in this dispute could signal that their country is less resolved to defend their other interests, territorial or otherwise.

Benefits of Compromise

A third reason for delay is that the benefits to be gained through compromise in this particular dispute are limited. In general, a state is much more willing to consider compromise in a territorial dispute when faced with threats elsewhere that increase the importance of improving ties with the opposing side in the dispute through territorial concessions. In short, compromise must yield some tangible benefit that exceeds the expected value of sovereignty over the land at stake and the likely costs, especially domestic ones, of compromise. If the net benefits of compromise are limited, then states should persist with a delaying strategy in a dispute.[55]

The latent rivalry between China and Japan, however, limits the degree of cooperation that each side can expect to gain by offering concessions to each other. As the two largest economies in the region, and given Japan's alliance with the United States, it is hard to see how compromising in the dispute would improve each state's own position relative to the other. It is possible that China might be more willing to offer concessions to Japan if security competition in the region with the United States intensified, but as a US ally, Japan would be unable to give China the support it might desire. The one exception might be a sustained economic or energy crisis, which would increase the importance of developing any petroleum resources that might exist in surrounding waters and require a settlement of the dispute. As natural resources are easily divisible, disputes that focus on such issues are perhaps more amenable to settlement.[56]

CONCLUSION

Despite its inherent volatility, stability has prevailed in the dispute between China and Japan over the Senkaku Islands. Looking forward, the potential for armed conflict remains low. Although China seeks to change the status quo, the costs of using force are high and, given the US security commitment to Japan, success on the battlefield is unlikely. Although the deterrent effect of US security guarantees to Japan under Article V of the treaty is key to the avoidance of armed conflict, the role played by active dispute management should not be overlooked. Indeed, both sides have managed the dispute effectively and prevented it from becoming a central issue in China-Japan relations. This successful management is noteworthy because the stability that has prevailed in the dispute is unexpected for many reasons, including the tensions in China-Japan political relations and China's past use of force in its other territorial disputes. The stability in the Senkaku dispute also illuminates some of the sources of delay in territorial disputes more broadly.

Nevertheless, the stability that has prevailed is fragile and cannot be taken for granted. The presence of the dispute allows the opportunity for armed conflict to persist, especially if management of the dispute atrophies. As territorial disputes can serve as proxies for rivalries between states, competition over the islands could increase in the future if China-Japan relations deteriorate or if the US military presence in East Asia is reduced. Thus, dispute management requires constant attention. In December 2008, for example, the presence of two Chinese government maritime survey ships within the territorial waters of the Senkakus threatened to increase tensions in the dispute, as Japan strengthened its patrolling capacity and called upon the United States to reaffirm its alliance commitments.

What can be done? First, both sides should continue to focus on functional issues, such as cooperation over energy and fishery resources. In essence, such cooperation decreases the economic importance of the islands. Second, even if the question of sovereignty cannot be resolved, the importance of resolving the question of maritime rights itself can be reduced. In this regard, the June 2008 consensus agreement between China and Japan over the development of petroleum resources in the disputed East China Sea is noteworthy.[57] Although the agreement explicitly did not address the question of sovereignty, it established a framework for joint exploration and production activities by oil companies from each side. In this way, the agreement reduced the imperative for settling the question of sovereignty by providing an alternate means to develop resources in the area and offers a creative approach that could be applied to the Senkaku dispute. Third, both sides should limit their presence in waters near the islands. China should refrain from conducting overflights of the islands that would enter into Japan's Air Defense Identification Zone and result in Japan's scrambling of fighter planes to intercept them. China should also bar its vessels, naval or civilian, from entering the territorial waters around the island, an action that will only provoke Japan and escalate the dispute. And although Japan administers the islands, it should not seek to develop them, especially for military use.

Regarding the prospects for trilateral cooperation, several points should be noted. So long as delay and the avoidance of escalation remain the preferred strategy for both sides, the presence of the dispute itself will not block or prevent cooperation in other areas. At the same time, active management of the dispute must continue so that it does not become an issue that polarizes the trilateral relationship into two camps. More generally, the presence of the dispute reveals the limits to trilateral cooperation. Given the fundamental conflict of interest over the question of sovereignty, the dispute itself cannot be settled within a trilateral framework. As a zero-sum conflict, where one side gains or maintains territory only at the expense of the other side, it is unlikely that common interests will emerge over territory in the trilateral relationship. Instead, trilateral security cooperation is most likely to materialize over security issues such as North Korea, where all three sides may share more common interests.

NOTES

1. Kalevi J. Holsti, *Peace and War: Armed Conflicts and International Order, 1648–1989* (Cambridge: Cambridge University, 1991); John A. Vasquez, *The War Puzzle* (New York: Cambridge University Press, 1993).

2. The name for these islands in Japanese is "Senkaku" while the name in Chinese is "Diaoyu."

3. Although China's conflict with Taiwan is also a bilateral one, the United States is a key player in this dispute because of its historical ties with the island and the "one China" policy in place since 1979. As America's core ally in East Asia, Japan is also a potential participant if conflict erupts between China and the United States over the Taiwan issue.

4. In the East China Sea maritime dispute, Japan could be viewed as the challenger, as its claims concern natural gas fields that China has been developing since the mid-1990s.

5. M. Taylor Fravel, *Strong Borders, Secure Nation: Cooperation and Conflict in China's Territorial Disputes* (Princeton: Princeton University, 2008).

6. On territorial disputes, see Fravel, *Strong Borders, Secure Nation*; Paul R. Hensel, "Contentious Issues and World Politics: The Management of Territorial Claims in the Americas, 1816–1992," *International Studies Quarterly* 45, no. 1 (March 2001): 81–109; Paul K. Huth, *Standing Your Ground: Territorial Disputes and International Conflict* (Ann Arbor: University of Michigan, 1996); Paul K. Huth and Todd L. Allee, *The Democratic Peace and Territorial Conflict in the Twentieth Century* (Cambridge: Cambridge University, 2002).

7. Huth, *Standing Your Ground*; Huth and Allee, *Democratic Peace*.

8. For reviews of claims in the dispute, see Greg Austin, *China's Ocean Frontier: International Law, Military Force, and National Development* (Canberra: Allen & Unwin, 1998); Unryu

Suganuma, *Sovereign Rights and Territorial Space in Sino-Japanese Relations: Irredentism and the Diaoyu/Senkaku Islands* (Honolulu: University of Hawaii, 2000).

9. Peter Kien-hong Yu, "Solving and Resolving the East China Sea Dispute: Beijing's Options," *The Korean Journal of Defense Analysis* 17, no. 3 (Winter 2005): 105–27.

10. Yukie Yoshikawa, "Okinotorishima: Just the Tip of the Iceberg," *Harvard Asian Quarterly* 9, no. 4 (2005).

11. Interestingly, China's position would have a salutary effect if extended to the Spratly Islands by limiting the importance of these islands, coral reefs, and shoals for asserting maritime rights in the South China Sea.

12. Fravel, *Strong Borders, Secure Nation.*

13. Sung-jae Choi, "The Politics of the Dokdo Issue," *Journal of East Asian Studies* 5, no. 2 (September 2005).

14. Quoted in Suganuma, *Sovereign Rights and Territorial Space,* 135.

15. Ibid.

16. Agence France Presse, "Japan Urged US to Reassure China over Defense Ties," September 20, 1996.

17. Adam Ereli, deputy spokesman, US State Department, "Daily Press Briefing (Corrected)," May 24, 2004, http://www.state.gov.

18. Reuters, "US-Japan Treaty Covers Disputed Isles," November 28, 1996.

19. Ereli, "Daily Press Briefing (Corrected)."

20. "United States Reassures Japan that Defense Pact Extends to Senkaku Islands," *Japan Times,* March 2, 2009, http://search.japantimes.co.jp/cgi-bin/nn20090302a4.html.

21. On the concept of a strategic rivalry, see Karen A. Rasler and William R. Thompson, "Contested Territory, Strategic Rivalries, and Conflict Escalation," *International Studies Quarterly* 50, no. 1 (March 2006): 145–67.

22. Richard C. Bush, "China-Japan Tensions, 1995–2006: Why They Happened, What to Do," Foreign Policy Paper Series no. 16 (Brookings Institution, June 2009). Also, see He Yinan, "History, Chinese Nationalism and the Emerging Sino-Japanese Conflict," *Journal of Contemporary China* 16, no. 50 (February 2007): 1–24.

23. Huth, *Standing Your Ground.*

24. Fravel, *Strong Borders, Secure Nation.*

25. He, "History, Chinese Nationalism."

26. In March 1978, Liberal Democratic Party members of the Diet opposed the Sino-Japanese Treaty of Peace and Friendship and publicly pressured the Japanese government to link the treaty with a Chinese recognition of Japan's claims to the Senkakus. In April, a flotilla of Chinese fishing boats, some of them armed, appeared in the surrounding waters and lingered for a week, underscoring China's commitment to its claim while Chinese officials urged Japan not to raise the issue. See Daniel Tretiak, "The Sino-Japanese Treaty of 1978: The Senkaku Incident Prelude," *Asian Survey* 18, no. 12 (December 1978): 1235–49.

27. Japan Economic Newswire, "Japan Drafts Remote Island Defense Plan Out of China Concern," January 15, 2005.

28. Christopher W. Hughes, "Japan's Remilitarisation," Adelphi Paper no. 403 (London: International Institute for Strategic Studies, 2009); Jennifer Lind, "Pacifism or Passing the Buck? Testing Theories of Japanese Security Policy," *International Security* 29, no. 1 (Summer 2004): 92–121.

29. Fravel, *Strong Borders, Secure Nation.*

30. Avery Goldstein, *Rising to the Challenge: China's Grand Strategy and International Security* (Stanford, CA: Stanford University, 2005).

31. Suganuma, *Sovereign Rights and Territorial Space.*

32. Mark Snelling, "Islands Protest Turns to Tragedy," Agence France Presse, September 26, 1996.

33. Kyodo News Service, "H.K. Activists Protest Japan's Lease of Disputed Isles," January 2, 2003; Jiji Press, "Japan Government Takes Lease on Disputed Isles," January 3, 2003.

34. Jiji Press, "In Response to Senkaku Issue, Japan Coast to Have Two Patrol Boats on Regular Watch to Strengthen Security to Stop Landings," March 31, 2004.

35. Based on a survey of Lexis-Nexis and Factiva database reports. The last apparent landing by Japanese activists was in August 2003. Kyodo News Service, "China Protests Rightwing Japanese Landing on Disputed Isles," August 25, 2003.

36. For information on the group, see http://www.cfdd.org.cn/.

37. Japan Economic Newswire, "Seven Chinese Activists Arrested by Japan on Disputed Island," March 24, 2004.

38. Ralph Jennings, "Chinese Authorities Block Senkaku Islands Boat Launch," Kyodo World Service, July 19, 2004.

39. Leu Siew Ying, "Raid on HQ Angers Diaoyus Activist," *South China Morning Post*, April 27, 2005.

40. Kyodo World Service, "PRC Authorities Detain 4 Activists Who Tried to Sail to Disputed Islets," October 31, 2007.

41. Based on a search for articles with "Diaoyu Dao" in the title of the article.

42. Based on a search for all articles that included the following words in the title: Nansha (Spratlys), Diaoyu Dao (Senkaku Islands), and Taiwan. The query to identify articles related to the Taiwan dispute included "Tai" in the title and "Taidu" (Taiwan independence) in the full text of the article.

43. Erica Strecker Downs and Phillip C. Saunders, "Legitimacy and the Limits of Nationalism: China and the Diaoyu Islands," *International Security* 23, no. 3 (Winter 1998–1999): 114–46.

44. See, for example, http://shanghaislide.stacktrace.com/2005/04/anti-japan-protest.html.

45. Du Chaoping, "*Meiguo miaozhun Diaoyudao*" [America takes aim at the Diaoyu Islands], *Dangdai Haijun* 7 (2003): 36; Gao Xinsheng, "*Daoyu yu xin shiji Zhongguo haifang jianshe*" [Islands and China's maritime defense construction in the new century], *Guofang* 11 (2006): 47.

46. Japan Economic Newswire, "Two Chinese Ships Enter Japan's Territorial Waters Near Disputed Isles," December 8, 2008.

47. "US Reassures Japan that Defense Pact Extends to Senkaku Islands," *Japan Times*, March 2, 2009, http://search.japantimes.co.jp/cgi-bin/nn20090302a4.html.

48. Fravel, *Strong Borders, Secure Nation.*

49. Ibid.

50. *Peking Review* 41 (November 3, 1978): 16.

51. James D. Fearon, "Bargaining, Enforcement, and International Cooperation," *International Organization* 52, no. 2 (Spring 1998): 269–305.

52. This, however, is questionable. In a 2000 survey, the East China Sea did not rank among the top 100 petroleum assessment areas around the world. See US Geological Survey, *World Petroleum Assessment 2000*, http://pubs.usgs.gov/dds/dds-060/.

53. On the role of domestic audiences, see James D. Fearon, "Domestic Political Audiences and the Escalation of International Disputes," *American Political Science Review* 88, no. 3 (September 1994): 577–92.

54. Peter H. Gries, "China's 'New Thinking' on Japan," *China Quarterly* 183 (2005): 831–50.

55. Fravel, *Strong Borders, Secure Nation.*

56. On this point, see Huth, *Standing Your Ground.*

57. "China and Japan Reach Principled Consensus on the East China Sea Issue," Ministry of Foreign Affairs, People's Republic of China, http://www.fmprc.gov.cn/eng/xwfw/s2510/t466632.htm.

8 | Addressing Climate Change: Why US-China Cooperation Lags behind China-Japan Cooperation

ZHANG HAIBIN

CLIMATE CHANGE IS widely recognized as a looming threat to international peace and security.[1] The UN Security Council held its first debate ever on climate and security in 2007, leading to a surge of new publications and reports aimed at understanding the security implications of large-scale climate disruption.[2] As a new security challenge in the 21st century, climate change is now firmly on the political agenda.

Addressing global challenges like climate change requires prompt and vigorous global cooperation, and no cooperation will be more important than that among the major powers.[3] In particular, China, the United States, and Japan are three key players in international climate cooperation, and their interactions—bilaterally and collectively—will be especially crucial. So far, however, there have been scarcely any comparative studies of US-China and China-Japan climate cooperation.[4] If one examines the trends in these two bilateral relationships since the late 1970s, it appears that China-Japan cooperation is much stronger than US-China cooperation. Why, then, has US-China cooperation lagged behind China-Japan cooperation? That is the core question that this chapter seeks to answer.

The chapter consists of four parts: the first summarizes the background and highlights the importance of this issue; the second compares the two bilateral relationships as they pertain to climate change policy, examining performance and progress to date; the third assesses why US-China cooperation has lagged behind China-Japan cooperation; and finally, the chapter concludes with some suggestions on how to enhance future US-China climate cooperation in particular.

Background

To start with, we must have a clear understanding of the significance of China-Japan cooperation and US-China cooperation in addressing climate change. Compared with most bilateral relationships, these two pairings are uniquely relevant for climate change policy for two reasons. First, the three countries are all extremely important to the global effort against climate change. As shown in table 1, the United States, Japan, and China are the three biggest economies in the world, with the US economy still clearly the largest. In terms of energy consumption, the United States is also the biggest consumer in the world, with China coming next and Japan ranking fourth, as represented in table 2. The huge economic output and energy consumption of these three countries mean that they have a profound impact on the global environment and climate. In fact, the latest statistics showed that in 2005 the United States had the biggest impact of any country on the global biosphere, with a total "ecological footprint" of 2.8 billion hectares.[5] China followed the United States closely with an eco-footprint of 2.78 billion hectares, and Japan ranked fourth, as shown in table 3.

Most crucially, China, the United States, and Japan are major emitters of CO_2, accounting for almost half of world emissions. According to the UN, China became the largest emitter of CO_2 in the world in 2006, the United States was the second largest, and Japan was fifth (see table 4). It is safe to say that global climate change cooperation will be doomed in the absence of participation by the United States, China, and Japan. Nonetheless, it should also be remembered that China remains far below the United States and Japan in terms of per capita GDP, ecological footprint, energy consumption, and CO_2 emissions.

Table 1. Top five economies in the world, 2007

Rank	Country	GDP (US$ millions)
1	United States	13,843,825
2	Japan	4,383,762
3	China	3,760,000
4	Germany	3,322,147
5	United Kingdom	2,772,570

SOURCE: International Monetary Fund, "World Economic Outlook Database April 2008," http://www.imf.org/external/pubs/ft/weo/2008/01/weodata/index.aspx; Chinese National Bureau of Statistics, final revision of 2007 economic data, released on January 14, 2009.

Table 2. Top five energy consumers in the world

Rank	Country	1997	2007	Percent of total global consumption, 2007
		(millions of metric tons of oil equivalent)		
1	United States	2,204.8	2,361.4	21.3
2	China	961.4	1,863.4	16.8
3	Russia	611.7	692.0	6.2
4	Japan	506.6	517.5	4.7
5	India	260.6	404.4	3.8

SOURCE: BP Global, *BP Statistical Review of World Energy June 2008* (Boston: Beacon, 2008), 40, http://www.bp.com/liveassets/bp_internet/globalbp/globalbp_uk_english/reports_and_publications/statistical_energy_review_2008/STAGING/local_assets/downloads/pdf/statistical_review_of_world_energy_full_review_2008.pdf.

Table 3. Top five ecological footprints in the world, 2005

Rank	Country	National ecological footprint (millions of hectares)	Ecological footprint per person (hectares)
1	United States	2,801	9.4
2	China	2,778	2.1
3	India	990	0.9
4	Japan	627	4.9
5	Russia	529	3.7

SOURCE: World Wildlife Fund (WWF), *Living Planet Report 2008* (Gland, Switzerland: WWF), 34–42, http://assets.panda.org/downloads/lpr_2008.pdf.

Table 4. Top five CO_2 emitters in the world, 2006

Rank	Country	Total emission of CO_2 (millions of metric tons)	Percent of total global emissions
1	China	6,103	21.5
2	United States	5,752	20.2
3	Russia	1,565	5.5
4	India	1,510	5.3
5	Japan	1,293	4.6

SOURCE: United Nations Statistics Division, "Millennium Development Goals Indicators," July 14, 2009, http://mdgs.un.org/unsd/mdg/default.aspx

Second, the bilateral relationships between China and the United States and between China and Japan are also crucial for the stability and prosperity of the Asia Pacific region and for the world as a whole. Given each of these countries' global influence, the way in which China, the United States, and Japan treat each other will to a great extent determine the nature of international peace and security. The last 30 years have seen remarkable progress in US-China relations and China-Japan relations. Despite this progress, however, underlying mutual distrust between China and the United States over each country's long-term intentions has grown and could, over time, make mutual antagonism a self-fulfilling prophecy.[6] The same can be said for China-Japan relations. The emergence of climate change as a shared and pressing global concern, however, offers a good opportunity for US-China and China-Japan relations to advance to a new stage, building on their enormous potential to have a collaborative impact on this critical field and beyond.

COMPARING CHINA-JAPAN AND US-CHINA CLIMATE CHANGE COOPERATION

US-China cooperation and China-Japan cooperation in the field of energy and climate change both started in the late 1970s. The past 30 years saw some progress in both bilateral relationships. By comparison, however, there is a noticeable gap between them in terms of performance and progress. For the purposes of this analysis, four indicators will be employed to gauge performance in this area: (1) indices of the political will to cooperate on climate change, (2) existing channels of cooperation, (3) joint projects underway on climate change, and (4) the degree to which financial assistance is being provided to foster such cooperation.

Political Will to Cooperate

One way to measure the political will to cooperate is to look at the number, official status (i.e., the level of government involved), and relevance to climate change of the existing bilateral agreements on issues associated with climate change. In terms of the first two criteria, the number and status of bilateral agreements between China and Japan and China and the United States are roughly the same.

The difference lies in the relevance of the agreements to climate change. China and Japan have signed bilateral agreements specifically on climate change while the United States and China have not. In addition, the content of the China-Japan bilateral climate agreements tend to be more concrete than those between China and the United States. Looked at in this light, generally, the political will to cooperate demonstrated by China-Japan climate cooperation agreements is stronger than that shown by US-China agreements, as demonstrated in tables 5 and 6.

Table 5. Major China-Japan agreements on climate change

Agreement	Level of signatories	Purpose
China-Japan Joint Statement on All-round Promotion of Strategic Relationship of Mutual Benefit (2008)	Heads of state	The two sides agree to actively participate in the establishment of a post-2012 international climate regime, abiding by common but differentiated responsibility principles.
Joint Statement on Climate Change between Japan and China (2008)	Cabinet	Establishes climate change partnership and specifies priority areas, methods, and funding of bilateral cooperation.
China-Japan Joint Press Communiqué on Boosting Bilateral Exchanges and Cooperation (2008)	Cabinet	Promotes general China-Japan strategic and mutually beneficial relations by launching over 70 joint programs, including more than 20 related to energy conservation and environmental protection.
China-Japan Memorandum for the Continuous Enhancement of Cooperation in the Energy Conservation and Environment Fields (2008)	Cabinet	Continues joint study of CCS (carbon capture and storage) and environmental audit of energy conservation.
Joint Statement on Further Enhancing Cooperation on Climate-Change-Related Science and Technologies (2007)	Cabinet	The two sides express their political will to further science and technology cooperation on climate change and agree to many concrete technology cooperation measures.
Joint Statement on Further Enhancing Cooperation in Environmental Protection (2007)	Cabinet	The two sides commit to addressing climate change through international cooperation and further bilateral cooperation on the Clean Development Mechanism under the Kyoto Protocol.
China-Japan Joint Statement on the Further Enhancement of Cooperation for Environmental Protection (2007)	Cabinet	Confirms that both countries attach great importance to climate change and to promoting bilateral cooperation on technology transfer.

Table 6. Major US-China agreements on climate change

Agreement	Level of signatories	Purpose
US-China Memorandum of Understanding to Enhance Cooperation on Climate Change, Energy, and the Environment (2009)	Cabinet	Establishes mechanism for regular climate change policy dialogue and cooperation and gives higher priority to climate change issues in bilateral relations
Ten Year Energy and Environment Cooperation Framework (2008)	Vice premier/ Treasury secretary	Establishes joint task forces on the five functional areas of the framework: (1) clean efficiency and secure electricity production and transmission; (2) clean water; (3) clean air; (4) clean and efficient transportation; and (5) conservation of forest and wetland ecosystems.
US-China Westinghouse nuclear reactor agreement (2007)	Cabinet	The United States approves the sale of four 1,100-megawatt Ap-1000 nuclear power plants that use a recently improved version of existing Westinghouse pressurized water reactor technology.
Joint Statement on Cooperation on Environment & Development between the United States and China (2000)	Cabinet	The two sides agree to promote North-South cooperation on climate change.
Statement of Intent on Clean Air and Clean Energy Technology Cooperation (1999)	Cabinet	Promotes environmentally sound US energy technologies in China.
US-China Environment and Development Forum (1997)	Cabinet	Establishes venue for high-level bilateral discussions on sustainable development and sets three priority areas for cooperative work: urban air quality, rural electrification, and clean energy/energy efficiency.
US-China Joint Statement (1997)	Heads of state	Targets urban air quality, rural electrification, and clean energy sources/energy efficiency.
US-China Protocol for Cooperation in the Fields of Energy Efficiency and Renewable Energy Technology Development and Utilization (1995)	Cabinet	Focuses on cooperation to (1) promote the diversification of China's energy, (2) protect the environment by using renewable energy and enhancing energy efficiency, and (3) increase US industry's competitiveness in China's energy market.
Protocol on Cooperation in the Field of Fossil Energy Research and Development (1985)	Cabinet	First major bilateral agreement on fossil energy. Now includes five annexes: power systems, clean fuels, oil and gas, energy and environment technologies, and climate science.
Atmosphere and Science and Technology Protocol (1979)	Cabinet	Establishes bilateral climate and oceans data exchange, research, and joint projects.

Channels of Bilateral Cooperation

China has established channels of cooperation at multiple levels with both the United States and Japan, including official, semiofficial, and nongovernmental cooperation. In this aspect of their bilateral relations, US-China and China-Japan cooperation are comparable. The major channels of climate cooperation are shown in table 7. US-China cooperation at the nongovernmental level, however, may be slightly stronger than China-Japan cooperation, as shown below. For a variety of historical and cultural reasons, US civil society—particularly private foundations—is more active than that of Japan, and in some ways, these US nongovernmental actors may be compensating for the lack of funding at the government level.

Table 7. Major channels of China-Japan and US-China bilateral cooperation on climate change

Level	China-Japan	US-China
Official	China-Japan High-Level Economic Dialogue	Strategic & Economic Dialogue
	Sino-Japan Friendship Center for Environmental Protection	US-China Working Group on Climate Change
	China-Japan Joint Committee on Science and Technology	US/China Energy & Environmental Technology Center at Tsinghua University
Semiofficial	China-Japan Forum on Energy Conservation and Environmental Protection	US-China Clean Energy Forum
Nongovernmental	China-Japan Nongovernmental Committee on Afforestation Cooperation	Beijing Energy Efficiency Center, EcoLinx Foundation, Energy Foundation, Environmental Defense, Ford Foundation

Joint Projects Related to Climate Change

Looking at the joint projects conducted to date, China-Japan cooperation has clearly made more progress than US-China cooperation (see table 8). First, there are more energy-conservation and environmental demonstration projects being conducted between China and Japan. Second, nearly 30 clean development mechanism (CDM) projects have been launched between China and Japan, leading to an estimated reduction of greenhouse gas (GHG) emissions equivalent to 20 million metric tons of CO_2. By contrast, there has not been a single CDM project undertaken jointly by China and the United States. Third, the scale of China-Japan personnel training programs is much bigger than that of China-US programs.

Table 8. Major joint projects on climate change between China and Japan and between China and the United States

Type of project	China-Japan	US-China
Energy-conservation and environmental protection model projects	Green Aid Plan (40 projects finished by 2008, 10 joint project agreements signed in 2008)	Some small joint projects (photovoltaic technology projects in China)
	China-Japan Environmental Technology Transfer Center established in 2007 in Wuxi	US-China model energy-saving building constructed in 2004
	China-Japan CCS project in Daqing starting in 2009 (US$200–300 million project)	Beijing Taiyanggong gas-fired thermal plant built in 2008
	Qingdao selected as a model city for a joint experiment to create a "recycling economy" in 2008	
CDM projects	28 projects (reduced GHG emissions equal to 20 million metric tons of CO_2)	None
Personnel training	Japan will provide training program for 10,000 Chinese in the field of energy conservation in 2008–2011	Much smaller (data unavailable)
	50 young Chinese scientists, including climate change experts, are invited annually by the Japanese government for short-term visits to Japan (2008–2012)	

Financial Assistance

One major difference between China-Japan and US-China climate cooperation is that Japan has been providing official development assistance (ODA) to China. In contrast, the United States has rejected the idea of providing China with direct assistance in this field, at least up until the Obama administration came into power. From 1988 to 2004, a total of

81 environmental projects in China were supported by Japanese yen loans with a total value of ¥822.8 billion. Among them, many projects focused on such areas as residential heating, desulphurization of coal-fire power plants, and afforestation, which are closely related to energy conservation and the mitigation of GHG emissions.[7] Although Japan phased out its ODA loan program for China in 2008, it has promised to continue providing funding to China for environmental projects under its "Cool Earth 50" plan. ODA is a key channel for North-South cooperation on climate change, and without it, China-US efforts in this field have been crippled.

Explaining the Gap

The four-point comparison above clearly indicates that US-China cooperation lags behind China-Japan cooperation in addressing climate change. US-China and China-Japan climate cooperation are both, in many respects, typical of North-South environmental cooperation. Clearly, the effectiveness of such North-South environmental cooperation is mainly determined by the developed countries' policies, because they possess the environmental technology and financial resources needed to make such cooperation work. Japan and the United States are both technologically sophisticated and wealthy powers, so the gap between US-China climate cooperation and China-Japan climate cooperation is primarily determined by the different environmental strategies and policies they have pursued.

More broadly, the gap has much to do with the two countries' different international environmental strategies. This difference is apparent at three levels. First, the United States and Japan differ in their objectives. The past 30 years have seen the US desire to be a global environmental leader dramatically weaken, while Japan has shown an increasingly strong desire to assume that leadership role.

Measuring the performance of US international environmental strategy by four indicators—concern over global environmental issues, participation in international environmental negotiations, implementation of international environmental agreements, and foreign environmental assistance—we find that in the 1970s the United States scored high in all four areas and was widely accepted as a global environmental leader. The 1980s, however, witnessed the United States making a "great leap backward" in the indicators, with the exception of compliance with international environmental agreements. US environmental leadership was therefore crippled. In the 1990s, the Clinton administration made some progress in increasing engagement on global environmental issues, but this turned out to be lip service rather than concrete action in most cases. As one analyst noted, the Clinton administration's "initiative to coalesce foreign policy around the environment appears designed more to raise the profile of the numerous aggressive environment initiatives than to establish a set of new activities."[8] US performance in international climate change negotiations still clearly indicated that the United States was no longer the global environmental leader.

After the Bush administration came to power in 2001, unilateralism prevailed in the US international environmental strategy. The most vivid example was its complete retreat from the Kyoto Protocol in 2001, which dealt a heavy blow to the global effort against climate change. In the early 21st century, the Bush administration not only gave up its global environmental leadership but also became a laggard in international environmental cooperation.[9]

Interestingly, Japan did precisely the opposite. Japan began to pursue global environmental leadership in the late 1980s. The Japanese government stated in 1988, "Today, our nation's economy accounts for more than one-tenth of the global economy, and Japan is the largest creditor country. Also, we play a leading role in the area of science and technology. Therefore, we are entering an era in which there will be growing expectations from different corners for us to make contributions to the world. Our nation has great potential to make contributions and our impact on the world environment is extensive, so we must take the initiative and assume a greater role in protecting the earth."[10]

Environmental ODA has been used by Japan as a major tool to achieve this goal. In 1989, Japan announced its Environmental ODA Policy at the G7 Summit, the main principles of which included (1) the expansion and reinforcement of bilateral and multilateral assistance through the disbursement of ¥300 billion over three years in the environmental field; (2) cooperation in forest preservation and research, mainly targeted at tropical forests; (3) cooperation for capacity building in developing countries to deal with environmental problems; (4) promotion of poverty reduction, based on the understanding that poverty is the root cause of the decline in tropical rainforests; (5) technical cooperation for the nurturing of expertise in the environmental field; (6) use of multilateral financial institutions for development; and (7) reinforcement of environmental considerations in general development assistance.[11] At the United Nations Conference on Environment and Development (UNCED) in 1992, Japan committed to disbursing between ¥900 billion and ¥1 trillion over five years for bilateral and multilateral assistance in the environmental field. As the world's top donor, Japan has sharply increased its environmental ODA since making this commitment.[12]

The assistance was well received by the international community. Maurice Strong, secretary-general of the 1992 UNCED, once called Japan "an environmental superpower."[13] Japan continued its assistance policy in the first decade of this century. It proposed the Environmental Conservation Initiative for Sustainable Development at the 2002 World Summit on Sustainable Development in Johannesburg, South Africa. The initiative made it clear that "Japan will positively continue to extend its environmental cooperation, mainly through its ODA, in order to support sustainable development in the world." Japan also spelled out five principles underlying its environmental cooperation: (1) capacity development, (2) the active integration of environmental considerations into its broader policy, (3) the establishment of Japan's leading role in this area, (4) the promotion of cooperation under a broad and comprehensive framework, and (5) the application of Japanese experience and scientific knowledge.[14] Under this initiative, Japan also made a number of commitments: to train 5,000 people in the environmental field over a five-year period (starting in FY2002), to provide yen loans with the most concessional terms for projects in environmental fields, to enhance Japan's grant aid for the global environment to promote international cooperation, to promote wide-ranging collaboration with international organizations, and to improve evaluation methods to make assessments of Japan's environmental ODA more effective.[15]

More recently, in 2007 the Japanese cabinet approved an important document entitled "Becoming a Leading Environmental Nation in the 21st Century: Japan's Strategy for a Sustainable Society." In it, Japan committed itself to becoming a leading environmental nation and assuming international leadership to address climate change.[16]

A second difference between Japan and the United States is the way in which they define the role of international environmental strategy within their broader international strategies. For Japan, its international environmental strategy is of special significance to its international outlook. With its amazing economic success in the 1980s, Japan gained momentum to become a political power and a "normal" state. Japan's aggressor role in World War II prevented it from assuming a bigger role in the postwar international political arena even as its wealth expanded. Japan's constitution also constrained its military role abroad. Against this background, international environmental cooperation offered Japan a unique chance to play a leading role in international affairs.[17] Little wonder then that the

Japanese government repeatedly emphasized, "Environmental protection is the most appropriate area for Japan, which proclaims itself to be a peace-loving nation, to contribute to the world . . . Under such circumstances, we must actively promote a policy of active environmental diplomacy commensurate with our nation's international position, and at the same time, we must take the global lead in creating a 'model for an environment-protecting society.'"[18]

In clear contrast, as the only superpower in the world in the post–Cold War era, the United States saw no need to elevate international environmental strategy to such a high level. International environmental strategy at best was seen in Washington as one of many tools available to serve its national interests.

Third, Japan and the United States are quite different in their approach to the international environmental technology market. The economic competition between Japan and the United States in the 1990s ended with the United States as a winner due to its advantage in information technology. In recent years, however, Japan has intensified its efforts in the race for advanced environmental technology. In fact, the Japanese government listed economic growth focused on environmental and energy technologies as a priority in its national development strategy. Japan thus decided to create a new engine for economic growth by responding to environmental issues, developing technological innovations, and improving its environmental and energy-related technology, including technologies for energy conservation, renewable energy, and nuclear energy. Japan's new strategy highlighted the significance of the international environmental protection market—an industry in which it has shown much stronger interest than has the United States. The latest data show that, in total, the United States exported more than US$40.2 billion in environmental technology goods and services in 2008.[19] The United States is a leading producer of environmental technology; however, it exports only about 11 percent of its output while Japan exports more than 20 percent.[20]

What is equally important is that China topped the list of countries with the most potential growth in environmental technology production. The Chinese market was estimated at US$13.4 billion in 2008 and is projected to reach US$34 billion by 2013, with the largest sectors being products and services aimed at addressing water pollution, air pollution, and urban solid waste.[21]

The differences in the international environmental technology strategies being pursued by Japan and the United States also indicate that Japan has had stronger aspirations to global environmental leadership and has put more emphasis on the international environmental protection market and its international environmental strategy. As a result, Japan has shown stronger political will than the United States to cooperate with China—the biggest developing country—in the climate area.

Probably the most important reason for the gap, however, lies in the different approaches the two countries have pursued in their policies toward China on the issue of climate change. Japan has sought greater consensus with China than Washington on international climate negotiations. For example, Japan shares China's support for the principle of common but differentiated responsibilities, which is a pillar of the UN Framework Convention on Climate Change. China argues that the largest share of historical and current global emissions of GHG has come from developed countries, while per capita emissions in developing countries are still relatively low and the share of global emissions originating from developing countries must grow to meet their social and development needs. For example, between 1850 and 2005, China emitted 8.3 percent of the cumulative emissions from fossil fuel use, compared with the United States, which emitted 29.3 percent, more than three times the emissions of any other country.[22] Therefore, developed countries should take the lead in reducing GHG emissions, while developing countries should place priority on achieving sustainable development.[23]

Table 9. Per capita and accumulated CO_2 emissions and number of people living without electricity

	Per capita CO_2 emissions, 2004 (tons)	Total accumulated CO_2 emissions, 1850-2005		Number of people without electricity, 2005 (millions)
		Percent of world total	Per capita (tons)	
United States	20.6	29.3	1,107	0
Japan	9.9	3.8	334.5	0
Germany	9.8	7.0	958.3	0
China	3.8	8.3	71.3	8.5
India	1.2	2.3	23.8	487.2
OECD countries	11.5	64.9	623.4	–
Developing countries	2.4	–	–	1,569.0

SOURCE: UNDP, *Human Development Report 2007*, and World Resources Institute, Climate Analysis Information Tool (CAIT), http://cait.wri.org/.

NOTE: Figures are CO_2 emissions from energy consumption.

The United States, on the other hand, has taken a completely different position. It has insisted that China and other major developing countries join developed countries in making binding GHG-control commitments. On July 25, 1997, by a 95–0 vote, the US Senate unanimously passed the Byrd-Hagel Resolution (S. Res. 98), which stated that the United States should not be a signatory to any protocol that did not include binding targets and timetables for developing nations as well as industrialized nations since this "would result in serious harm to the economy of the United States." On November 12, 1998, Vice President Al Gore symbolically signed the Kyoto Protocol, but even he and Senator Joseph Lieberman, who supported the treaty, indicated that the protocol would not be acted upon in the Senate until there was participation by developing nations.[24] More recently, immediately after the 2007 UN Climate Change Conference was held in Bali, Indonesia, the United States issued a statement emphasizing that the negotiations must proceed with the view that climate change cannot be adequately addressed through commitments for emissions cuts from developed countries alone. Major developing economies must likewise act. The statement said that negotiations must clearly differentiate among developing countries based on the size of their economies, their emissions, and their level of energy utilization and must sufficiently link the nature and degree of responsibility to such factors. It also specified that the negotiations must adequately distinguish among developing countries by recognizing that the responsibilities of the smaller or least developed countries are different from those of the larger, more advanced developing countries.[25]

The significant difference between the Chinese and US stances on these issues has undoubtedly become a major hurdle for their bilateral climate cooperation. Table 10 lists the points of agreement and disagreement on climate change among China, Japan, and the United States. This clearly shows that there are more similarities between China and Japan than between China and the United States, particularly on the key issues relevant to cooperative responses to climate change.

Another difference is that Japan's climate policy toward China is more pragmatic than that of the United States. Following the 1989 Tiananmen Square incident, hostility toward the Communist leadership precluded China from receiving ODA from the United States—aid that could have significantly hastened climate change–related projects.[26] Such aid remains the main channel for North-South cooperation on climate change, and without it, China-US efforts have been crippled. By contrast, Japan downplayed the role of ideology in climate cooperation with China and continued to provide aid to China for climate-change projects.

Table 10. Differences in Chinese, Japanese, and US positions on climate change, 2008

Issue	China	US	Japan
Accepts global warming as a reality	yes	yes	yes
Believes that global warming is mainly anthropogenic	yes	yes	yes
Believes that global warming is having a negative impact on the country	yes	yes	yes
Believes developed countries should take the lead in reducing GHG emissions	yes	no	yes
Supports the Kyoto Protocol	yes	no	yes
Supports the flexibility mechanism	yes	yes	yes
Supports the primary status of the UN Framework Convention on Climate Change	yes	yes	yes
Believes developed countries should provide technological and financial assistance to developing countries	yes	unclear	yes
Believes climate change mitigation should be achieved under the framework of sustainable development	yes	yes	yes
Believes mitigation and adaptation should be given equal attention	yes	yes	yes
Believes climate change mitigation should be based on cost-effect analysis	unclear	yes	yes
Agrees to halve global carbon emissions by 2050	unclear	yes	yes

Source: Compiled based on official statements from China, Japan, and the United States in international climate negotiations, accessed from the Earth Negotiations Bulletin, http://www.iisd.ca/enbvol/enb-background.htm.

It goes without saying that the United States and Japan both want to influence China's decision-making process on energy and environmental policy, but they took different approaches. Washington has never hidden its desire to exert as much impact as possible on China's decision making in this field.[27] Its demands have usually been presented to China in a more direct and explicit way than those of Japan, and as a result it has seemed more aggressive to Chinese policymakers. For example, at the third US-China Strategic Economic Dialogue meeting in December 2007, the United States demanded that China develop a nationwide program on sulfur dioxide emissions trading, and China made concessions.[28] Japan, on the other hand, has been very careful in how it has presented requests to China and has seemed more willing to cater to China's needs. For example, China's greatest concerns in the past have been air pollution, water pollution, and desertification. Japan deliberately focused its environmental ODA on those issues.[29] In other words, whereas the United States sought to influence China by demands, Japan sought to do so by offering help. Not surprisingly, China feels more comfortable with the Japanese approach.[30]

Last but not least, geography also helps in part to explain the gap. China is situated far from the United States, while China and Japan are neighbors. That proximity has created a stronger sense of the benefits of environmental cooperation with China among the Japanese public than the American public. In other words, the Japanese public is more concerned about China's environment and it is therefore easier for the Japanese government to mobilize public support for its initiatives in bilateral climate change cooperation.

CONCLUSION

If global efforts to fight climate change are to succeed, China-Japan and US-China climate cooperation must both be strengthened. This chapter has compared the development and performance of their cooperation in this area to date and explained why US-China efforts have lagged behind China-Japan efforts. The gap has mainly been caused by the fact that Japan and the United States have pursued different climate policies toward China.

Japan does not have significant disputes with China in international climate negotiations, while Washington has had a fundamental disagreement with China over how to understand the principle of "common but differentiated responsibilities." Japan has approached China in a more pragmatic way, while ideological factors still play an important part in US climate policy toward China. Japan has helped shape China's environmental policy by catering to China's needs, while the United States has sought to influence China's environmental policy by making direct demands. China is more comfortable with the Japanese approach and so they have cooperated more easily than have China and the United States.

This gap also has much to do with the different environmental strategies the two countries have pursued. Over the last 20 years, Japan has shown an increasingly strong desire to become a global environmental leader, while the United States has shown a declining interest in that role. Moreover, Japan has attached more importance to its international environmental strategy and to the global environmental technology market than has the United States. Therefore, Japan has had more incentive to develop climate cooperation with China.

In addition, the proximity of China to Japan has caused deeper public concern in Japan over China's environmental situation than in the United

States. Accordingly, the Japanese government has found it easier to gain public support than has the US government when pushing forward bilateral climate cooperation with China.

Looking ahead to the future, how can China-Japan and US-China climate cooperation be strengthened? First of all, China, Japan, and the United States should realize that, compared with their potential for cooperation and the necessity of effectively addressing climate change, their cooperation to date has been far from satisfactory. The three sides must redouble their efforts to deepen climate cooperation.

In terms of China-Japan climate cooperation, the critical point at this stage is for the two sides to focus on the implementation of their existing bilateral agreements. It is also imperative to reach agreement on a long-term funding mechanism for climate change. As noted earlier, Japan ended its yen loans to China in 2008, and environmental assistance is now being provided under Cool Earth 50, which was a prime ministerial initiative. Given the shifting landscape in Japanese politics, however, it is unclear whether that type of initiative is sustainable, and a firmer, longer-term commitment to cooperation is now needed.

In terms of the United States and China, there is much more to be done to improve climate cooperation. The primary problem ahead is not the lack of potential for China and the United States to work together but whether the two sides have the political will to do so—particularly in the United States. Barack Obama's presidency offers a precious chance for China and the United States to cooperate on climate and energy issues. President Obama has announced the New Energy for America plan and has said that he is determined to implement an economy-wide cap-and-trade program to cut CO_2 and other GHG emissions to 1990 levels by 2020 and then reduce GHG emissions 80 percent by 2050, making the United States a leader on climate change.[31] Meanwhile, the US Congress showed in 2009 that it is serious about moving forward on cutting GHG emissions by taking up "cap-and-trade" legislation for the first time in its history.

Also worth noting is the increased political appetite in China for international cooperation on climate change, including agreements with the United States. China's cooperative attitude at the 2007 UN Climate Change Conference in Bali won widespread praise. Also in 2007, the official report to the 17th National Congress of the Chinese Communist Party listed protection of the global environment as a goal for Chinese diplomacy. In 2008, the Communist Party Politboro held its first study meeting on climate change, where President Hu Jintao stressed that climate change is of great importance.

Currently, China's position on climate change in international cooperation can be characterized as "the hard is getting harder, the soft is getting
softer"—the former refers to the fact that China still refuses to accept a
binding reduction in GHG emissions, while the latter points to the fact
that China has become increasingly flexible and cooperative in its attitude
toward international climate cooperation. More specifically, China's view
on the Kyoto Protocol's three flexible mechanisms, and especially the
CDM, has changed from suspicion to support. In respect to financing and
technology, it is more willing to pursue a win-win technology transfer
mechanism and reciprocal technological cooperation. In addition, having concentrated on the UN Framework Convention on Climate Control
and the Kyoto Protocol in the past, China now holds a more open attitude
toward other types of international climate change cooperation. And finally,
it has shifted from a focus on domestic voluntary mitigation activities to
measurable, reportable, and verifiable mitigation commitments or actions
as are nationally appropriate.

These major changes in China's climate change politics show that there
is increasing political will for cooperation with the United States, which
hopefully will match similar aims on the part of the Obama government and provide new impetus for climate-change partnership between
the two countries. One positive sign was that, during her recent visit to
China in February 2009, US Secretary of State Hillary Clinton expressed
strong interest in promoting US-China climate cooperation, and China
responded positively.[32]

Now is the time for the two sides to take a bold step toward each other
in this area. The Obama administration could further US-China climate
cooperation by signing a summit document on climate change, helping
China with aid to invest in climate-change projects, and setting an example
by accepting binding emissions targets. This conforms with the common
but differentiated responsibility principle and equity principle guiding the
UN Framework Convention on Climate Change. The developed countries
are mainly to blame for the accumulation of GHG in the atmosphere,
which is the result of the gases emitted since the Industrial Revolution,
and current per capita emissions in developed countries are much higher
than those in developing nations. At the same time, developing countries
have a limited capacity to convert their energy systems and consumption
patterns to norms that are more sustainable as a result of low per capita
income and persistently high levels of poverty. Moreover, as the report of
the Stern Review on the Economics of Climate Change concluded, the
effects of global warming and climate change will be more pronounced

in developing countries, thus requiring even more resources to mitigate the impact.[33]

For its part, China will need to show that it can meet the ambitious energy conservation and emissions mitigation targets set in its 11th Five-Year Plan[34] and the National Climate Change Programme.[35] According to these two important documents, China is committed to making the utmost effort to achieve the following specific objectives by 2010:

- Achieve a target reduction in energy consumption per unit GDP of approximately 20 percent by 2010 (base year is 2005), and consequently reduce CO_2 emissions by about 1.6 billion metric tons, which is the most ambitious national GHG mitigation plan in the world[36]
- Optimize the energy consumption structure to raise the proportion of renewable energy (including large-scale hydropower) in the primary energy supply up to 10 percent by 2010 and the extraction of coal bed methane up to 10 billion cubic meters
- Stabilize nitrous oxide emissions from industrial processes at 2005 levels by 2010
- Increase the forest coverage rate to 20 percent and realize an increase in carbon sinks by 50 million tons above the 2005 level by 2010

China's emissions mitigation measures were well received by the international community. In 2007, Ban Ki-moon, secretary-general of the UN, spoke highly of China's efforts against climate change, noting,

> Much is made of the fact that China is poised to surpass the United States as the world's largest emitter of GHG. Less well known, however, are its more recent efforts to confront grave environmental problems. China is on track to invest US$10 billion in renewable energy this year, second only to Germany. It has become a world leader in solar and wind power. At a recent summit of East Asian leaders, Premier Wen Jiabao pledged to reduce energy consumption (per unit of GDP) by 20 percent over five years—not far removed, in spirit, from Europe's commitment to a 20 percent reduction in greenhouse gas emissions by 2020.[37]

However, there is more still to be done. China should release its medium- and long-term (2020–2050) emissions mitigation policy with some quantitative targets, as it did under the National Climate Programme in 2007, and be open to a discussion of when it will join the developed countries in accepting binding targets. In addition, China should make greater efforts to protect intellectual property rights.

Currently, what is really lacking for US-China climate cooperation is not ideas and plans but shining, win-win examples.[38] One good beginning would be to choose a small city in China as an experimental zone. The two sides could test the innovative funding mechanism, technology transfer and co-development mechanism, and intellectual property rights protection mechanism as it relates to environmental technology, using these mechanisms to promote clean coal technology, renewable energy, and energy efficiency as priority areas in the city. If it functions well, other cities can learn from this model and the two sides will have more incentive to broaden bilateral climate cooperation.

China, Japan, and the United States should also launch a cooperative trilateral initiative on climate change. This trilateral cooperation should focus on (1) coordinating their policies on international climate negotiations, (2) promoting existing regional climate change cooperation regimes like the Asia-Pacific Partnership on Clean Development and Climate or the Methane to Markets Partnership, and (3) establishing climate-change projects in China that are jointly funded and technologically developed by the three parties. Trilateral cooperation on climate change has another important role to play in terms of confidence building among the three countries. It was reported in early June 2009 that the United States, Japan, and China would hold unprecedented trilateral talks in July 2009 to find solutions to issues of common concern. The agenda would include the overall Asian situation and global issues such as climate change and energy.[39] Unfortunately, one month later the trilateral talks were postponed indefinitely due to China's concern over whether such trilateral talks might unnecessarily anger North Korea.[40] It would appear, however, that the convening of these trilateral talks is just a matter of time.

Stronger climate change cooperation between and among China, Japan, and the United States could benefit not just their own citizens but all of humanity. The world calls for wiser policies from all three countries, and especially from the United States and Japan, which must apply their full range of resources—scientific, technological, and economic—to bear on this critical challenge. Moreover, the benefits of their effective climate cooperation could spill over to other areas of their bilateral and trilateral relationships and help build mutual trust. This would, in turn, enable them to work together more effectively to address the many other challenges facing the region and the world in the 21st century. In this sense, stronger climate cooperation among these three nations would be good not only for the environment but also for global peace and partnership.

NOTES

1. See the Report of the UN Secretary-General, "In Larger Freedom: Toward Security, Development, and Human Rights for All," A/59/2005, March 21, 2005.

2. For example, see Center for Naval Analyses (CNA), *National Security and the Threat of Climate Change* (Alexandria, VA: CNA, 2007), http://securityandclimate.cna.org/; Kurt M. Campbell et al., *The Age of Consequences: The Foreign Policy and National Security Implications of Global Climate Change* (Washington DC: Center for Strategic and International Studies, 2007), http://www.csis.org/media/csis/pubs/071105_ageof-consequences.pdf; Joshua W. Busby, "Who Cares about the Weather? Climate Change and US National Security," *Security Studies* 17, no. 3 (2008): 469–504; German Advisory Council on Global Change, *Climate Change as a Security Risk* (London: Earthscan, 2008), www.wbgu.de/wbgu_jg2007_engl.pdf ; Chris Abbott, "An Uncertain Future: Law Enforcement, National Security, and Climate Change" (briefing paper, Oxford Research Group, London, 2008), http://oxfordresearchgroup.org.uk/publications/briefing_papers/uncertain_future_law_enforcement_national_security_and_climate_change.

3. At the World Economic Forum in 2009, UN Secretary-General Ban Ki-moon said, "I have taken to calling this a time of multiple crises. The economy, volatile energy markets, war and humanitarian disasters. Yet for all the troubles, we face only one truly existential threat. That is climate change." See UN News Center, "Remarks at Event Entitled 'Shaping the Climate Change Message' at the World Economic Forum," http://www.un.org/apps/news/infocus/sgspeeches/statments_full.asp?statID=417.

4. On US-China climate cooperation, see Asia Society and Pew Center on Global Climate Change, *Common Challenge, Collaborative Response: A Roadmap for US-China Cooperation on Energy and Climate Change* (Washington DC: Asia Society and Pew Center on Global Climate Change, January 2009), http://www.pewclimate.org/US-China; Kenneth G. Lieberthal and David B. Sandalow, *Overcoming Obstacles to US-China Cooperation on Climate Change, January 2009*, John L. Thornton China Center Monograph Series, no. 1 (Washington DC: Brookings Institution, January 2009); Zhang Haibin, "US-China Climate Cooperation: Challenges and Opportunities," *International Economic Review*, no. 6 (2007).

5. The ecological footprint measures humanity's demand on the biosphere in terms of the area of biologically productive land and sea required to provide the resources we use and to absorb our waste.

6. Lieberthal and Sandalow, *Overcoming Obstacles.*

7. Graduate School of Economics, Kyoto University (Hiromi Yamamoto, Kazuhiro Ueda, Yukihisa Mori, Kohei Yamamoto, and Hideaki Nagare),"Assessment and Study of the Role of Japanese Yen Environmental Loan to China—Support for China's Environmental Governance," a report prepared for the Japan Bank for International Cooperation, November 2005, http://www.jbic.go.jp/.

8. John J. Cohrssen, "US International Interests, Sustainable Development, and the Precautionary Principle," in *The Greening of US Foreign Policy*, ed. Terry L. Anderson and Henry I. Miller (Stanford: Hoover Institution, 2000), 134.

9. For further analysis of the evolution of US environmental leadership, see Zhang Haibin, *Environment and International Relations: Rational Reflections on Global Environmental Issues* (Shanghai: Shanghai People's Publishing House, 2008), 267–83.

10. Environmental Agency of Japan, *Quality of the Environment in Japan 1988* (annual white paper), Chapter 3.5, 1988, author's translation.

11. Japan International Cooperation Agency, "The Features of Japan's Environmental Cooperation: Its Track Record and Policy Agenda," http://www.jica.go.jp/english/publications/reports/study/topical/environment/pdf/environment_04.pdf.

12. Ibid.

13. Author's interview with Maurice Strong, September 6, 2007.

14. Ministry of Foreign Affairs of Japan, "Environmental Conservation Initiative for Sustainable Development (EcoISD)-Summary," http://www.mofa.go.jp/policy/environment/wssd/2002/kinitiative3.html.

15. Ibid.

16. Government of Japan, "Becoming a Leading Environmental Nation in the 21st Century: Japan's Strategy for a Sustainable Society," June 2007, http://www.env.go.jp/en/focus/attach/070606-b.pdf.

17. Yasuko Kawashima, "A Comparative Analysis of the Decision-Making Process of Developed Countries toward CO_2 Emissions Reduction Targets," *International Environmental Affairs* 9, no. 2 (Spring 1997): 95–126.

18. Environmental Agency of Japan, *Quality of the Environment in Japan 1991* (annual white paper).

19. US Department of Commerce, International Trade Administration, "Environmental Industries," http://www.environment.ita.doc.gov/.

20. Virginia Economic Development Partnership, Division of International Trade, "Fast Facts: Environmental Technology," http://www.exportvirginia.org/fast_facts.html.

21. Ibid.

22. World Resources Institute, Climate Analysis Information Tool (CAIT), http://cait.wri.org/.

23. National Development and Reform Commission, People's Republic of China, "China's National Climate Change Program," June 2007, http://www.ccchina.gov.cn/WebSite/CCChina/UpFile/File188.pdf.

24. "Clinton Hails Global Warming Pact," CNN, December 11, 1997, http://www.cnn.com/ALLPOLITICS/1997/12/11/kyoto/.

25. US White House, "Statement by the Press Secretary on the Decision of the Conference of the Parties in Bali on Climate Change," December 15, 2007, http://georgewbush-whitehouse.archives.gov/news/releases/2007/12/20071215-1.html.

26. Kelly Sims Gallagher, "US-China Energy Cooperation: A Review of Joint Activities Related to Chinese Energy Development Since 1980" (discussion paper no. 2001-21, Belfer Center for Science and International Affairs, Harvard University, November 2001).

27. Ibid.

28. Henry M. Paulson Jr., "A Strategic Economic Engagement: Strengthening US-Chinese Ties," *Foreign Affairs* 88, no. 4 (September/October 2008).

29. Graduate School of Economics, Kyoto University, "Assessment and Study of the Role of Japanese Yen Environmental Loan to China."

30. Author interviews with two senior officials from the Chinese National Development and Reform Commission and Ministry of Environment, conducted under the condition of anonymity, June 2008.

31. US White House, "Energy and Environment," http://www.whitehouse.gov/agenda/energy_and_ environment/.

32. Fintan Moran, "Clinton Urges Closer Ties between US and China," *Sunday Tribune*, February 22, 2009, http://www.tribune.ie/archive/article/2009/feb/22/clinton-urges-closer-ties-between-us-and-china/.

33. This Stern Review was a study conducted in 2006 by economist Lord Stern of Brentford for the British government on the projected impact of climate change on the world economy, which produced a widely read report. For more information, see International Energy Agency, *World Energy Outlook 2007*.

34. China has not met the targets set in its 11th Five-Year Plan in terms of energy consumption per unit of GDP and total pollution control. See the report of China's top legislator, Wu Bangguo, on the work of the Standing Committee of the 11th National People's Congress, which was presented to the Chinese parliament's second annual session on September 9, 2009, http://news.sina.com.cn/c/2009-03-09/092517367297.shtml.

35. National Development and Reform Commission, People's Republic of China, "China's National Climate Change Programme," June 2007, http://www.ccchina.gov.cn/WebSite/CCChina/UpFile/File188.pdf.

36. Remarks by Su Wei, director of the Climate Department of China's National Development and Reform Commission. See Voice of China report, July 24, 2009, http://www.ce.cn/cysc/ny/hgny/200907/24/t20090724_19490696.shtml.

37. Ban Ki-moon, "A New Green Economics: The Test for the World in Bali and Beyond," *Washington Post*, December 3, 2007, A17.

38. See Asia Society/Pew Center, *Common Challenge, Collaborative Response*; Lieberthal and Sandalow, *Overcoming Obstacles*.

39. Cui Xiaohuo, "US-Japan-China Talks to Focus on Key Issues," *China Daily*, http://www.chinadaily.com.cn/china/2009-06/08/content_8257370.htm.

40. Yonhap News Agency, "1st Trilateral Talks among US, Japan, China Postponed," July 20, 2009, http://www.breitbart.com/article.php?id=D99I2KM80&show_article=1&catnum=2.

Economic Integration and Trilateral Relations

9

Asianism Rising: Assessing China-Japan- US Dynamics in Regional Trade and Investment Realities

SAADIA M. PEKKANEN

THIS CHAPTER FOCUSES on structural changes in Asian trade and investment and their implications for managing China-Japan-US interactions. Several key questions glue the narrative together: What exactly is the nature of such changes, particularly involving China, Japan, and the United States? How, why, and in which direction are China-Japan-US dynamics headed as a result, and with what consequences for the standing of each of these individual powers and for the future of Asia as a whole? What are some concrete ways in which China-Japan-US interactions can be managed in the context of Asian economic changes? These questions force attention not just on the nature and extent of the underlying economic realities in Asia today but also on the ways, if any, in which the governments of China, Japan, and the United States have adapted to and accommodated them through various processes as we head toward a world of regions.[1] The focus of this chapter is therefore not so much on the bilateral relationship between any two of the three countries but rather on the prospects for and problems in strengthening trilateral China-Japan-US dynamics in the context of Asian regional integration.

For analytical purposes, "the management of China-Japan-US dynamics" refers in this chapter to the ways in which the governments of these countries have or have not taken concrete steps to ensure, facilitate, and smooth the continuation of regional trade and investment flows through various legal institutions. Although such mechanisms can range from the informal to the formal, the focus here is on assessing the formal mechanisms in particular, as they are a better and more tangible indicator of the seriousness with which these countries are moving to safeguard what they perceive to be their regional economic interests. For this reason, attention is given to the concrete legal agreements and treaties that they have concluded in the past, are concluding at present, or are moving to conclude in the future. In the realm of trade and investment, this specifically means the presence of free trade agreements (FTAs) and bilateral investment treaties (BITs), whether negotiated at the bilateral, trilateral, or regional level. Ideally, to show that there is a coordinated dynamic at play among these three countries, as defined above, we would expect to find evidence that the three governments have taken or are beginning to take collective, trilateral steps to construct a rules-based institutional rubric for trade and investment flows within the Asian region. Unfortunately, the evidence at the present stage suggests that that remains a very distant vision—steps toward which have been thwarted by the fact that there is still no real trilateral cooperation within the region among the three countries and also by the fact that, individually and jointly, both Japan and China have already forged ahead with legal institutions to advance Asian integration.

The remainder of this chapter is comprised of five sections. The first section sets the stage by distinguishing between the economic and institutional dimensions in current debates about changes in Asia. The second section discusses the factual realities that have brought Asia to the center of the world political economy. It provides an overview of the actual economic weight of Asia, focusing on general indicators as well as specific trade and investment patterns. The third section provides an overview of the actual economic weight of China, Japan, and the United States amid the new structural realities in Asia—that is, in terms of their export and import levels to and from the region, as well as their aggregate investment levels within the region. Additionally, it examines the interactions among the three countries. This gives us a clear sense of how much is economically at stake for each of these powers in the region relative to one another and the extent to which they are also dependent on one another. The fourth section then examines the legal institutions being constructed by these three powers in terms of FTAs, BITs, and other frameworks. This allows us to gauge the extent to which these three powers are individually or jointly forging legal institutions to safeguard regional economic operations. In light of the evidence, the fifth section ends by assessing options for managing China-Japan-US dynamics in the near future in the context of regional trade and investment realities.

Distinguishing *Asia* Rising from *Asianism* Rising

Virtually everywhere one looks in academic and policy circles, Asia as a collective and connected region commands attention.[2] For the purposes of this chapter, the region refers to both industrial and emerging Asia.[3] A wide range of sources confirm the region's importance.[4] According to the CIA, in 2007 it was home to 3 of the top 10 largest economies in the world, namely China, Japan, and India. An International Monetary Fund (IMF) estimate in 2005 suggested that Asia as a whole accounted for more than 35 percent of the world GDP and that it was fuelling close to 50 percent of world growth. The World Trade Organization (WTO) figures for 2007 show that, second only to Europe as a region, Asian countries together accounted for about 27 percent of world merchandise exports and 24 percent of world merchandise imports.[5] Again, according also to the CIA, the top 2 holders of foreign exchange reserves in the world in 2007 were both Asian countries, namely China and Japan; and of the top 10 holders, only 3 were non-Asian.[6] Not to be forgotten, the region also has about 60 percent of the world's population and three of the world's four largest standing armies.

Even those who are reluctant to attribute a pivotal role to Asia alone in the "rise of the rest"—as opposed merely to the "decline of the West"—still focus on the changes in Asia as being the most visible of all shifts occurring in "the rest" at this stage.[7] The aspects of Asia that have drawn so much attention around the world are first and foremost economic in content— meaning the connectedness and integration of trade, investment, and financial flows among East Asian countries. The dramatic changes in these economic fundamentals have, to some extent, even detracted attention from the importance of carefully defining Asia as a region along material-ist, ideational, and behavioral dimensions.[8] In fact, for better or for worse, in many assessments this appears not to matter, as the symbolic aspects of the region have begun to outweigh the material aspects—at least from the outside looking in at the frenzied activities of a core set of countries in the region, such as China and Japan.

Although no one can say exactly what it is, the worldwide perception is that something very Asian is in the global air. The economic rise of Asia in the global economy is well understood, as discussed above. This chapter, however, will focus on the rise of "Asianism," by which is meant that we need to take account of both *structural* shifts (i.e., economic shifts) brought about by economic flows in the region and, especially, *process* transformations (i.e., the establishment of formal legal institutions) brought about by the principal governments with stakes in those economic changes. This idea parallels an earlier concept that, in looking at ties across East Asia, distinguished between the forces of regionalization, which develops from the bottom up through societally driven actors, and regionalism, which focuses on the processes of creating institutions.[9] For most analysts, this author included, there is little question that it is the process part of the East Asian integration story that is now playing catch-up with the structural economic shifts that have occurred in the region over the past few decades, largely through cross-border economic flows.[10]

The present global financial turmoil has not completely deflated or devastated the economic prospects for Asia in the way the Asian financial crisis did back in 1997.[11] No major Western or Asian power will escape the current economic downturn unscathed. But it is likely, as indicators are beginning to suggest already, that Asian countries will continue to be major players in the world economy in the near future.[12] They will thus also continue to have an interest in the legal institutions that govern the economic flows in which they already have and are rapidly expanding their material stakes. From the perspective of shaping the institutional landscape this, then, is the important point: in contrast to the past, the current economic shifts have pushed public and private actors toward rules-based institution building within the region as never before. As discussed below, this is why the ASEAN+3–based processes—those emerging from even the sometimes competitive activities involving ASEAN members as well as China, Japan, and South Korea—are becoming integral to any future schemes for regional economic integration.[13]

Altogether these trends suggest that at this stage in world history we can speak more credibly than ever before of "Asianism rising"—that is, not just economic shifts but also an expansive institution-building agenda largely for and by regional Asian actors, at least at this stage. These trends are taken up in succession below as a background to understanding the relative actions and standing of China, Japan, and the United States. Why these countries in particular? For starters, they represent the three largest single-country economies in the world. As such, their actions and interactions carry not just great significance for the global economy but also the prospects for regional integration in Asia as a whole. It is also especially important to understand their uneven patterns of interdependence and vulnerabilities with respect to one another and within the region because there is little question that they are the main players jockeying for influence in this great new Asianism game. The analytical steps below allow us to better discuss the management of China-Japan-US interactions in the context of Asian regional economic integration.

ASIA'S WEIGHT IN THE WORLD

This section explores some general indicators, as well as specific trade and investment patterns, to highlight Asia's relative standing in the world economy. Asian countries are certainly not newcomers to the global economic stage. As is well known, their ups and downs have commanded considerable attention throughout the postwar period: the highs reflected in the shining developmentalism of Japan and the newly industrialized countries beginning in the 1960s, the lows in the form of the depressing doldrums that afflicted both Japan and ASEAN in the 1990s, and presently the resurgence as seen in the spectacular ascent of China that is pulling along its regional neighbors in the 2000s. To be clear, this latest resurgence should not be confused with Asia going it alone economically. The reality is that despite talk of their decoupling from the global economy, Asian countries are still economically interdependent with the rest of the world and are likely to remain so for the foreseeable future.[14] As the negative impact on regional economic growth from the current financial crisis shows, Asia is highly dependent on exports, particularly in terms of final demand in Western industrial markets.[15] The fall in net exports is not the only culprit. Weak domestic demand in almost all the countries in the region is also problematic, although some of these countries are reportedly undergoing a transition to domestic-led growth, no matter how slow or painful this may be.[16] With this in mind, what exactly are some of the facts on the ground that have fuelled talk of Asian resurgence?

General Indicators

To place things in a comparative context, it is helpful to begin with a general consideration of the region's share of world production, competitiveness rankings, productivity gains, demographic trends, and educational workforce quality. On all of these dimensions, Asia has begun to stand out.

The global share of real GDP of East Asia (including Taiwan and Hong Kong SAR) went from 21.5 percent in 1980 to 27.6 percent in 2005, surpassing that of the EU and appearing to be on track to catch up with that of the North American Free Trade Agreement (NAFTA).[17] In the global competitiveness index, 5 of the top 15 spots are held by Asian players: Singapore is ranked at number 7, Japan at 8, Korea at 11, Hong Kong SAR at 12, and Taiwan at 14. (China itself is ranked at 34.)[18] Additionally, although the United States still leads productivity rankings, China and other parts of East Asia now show the highest productivity growth in the world.[19] Even keeping in mind that they are coming from far behind, their relative productivity gains are remarkable. In 2006, productivity rose 3.3 percent at the global level, 2.1 percent in the industrial world, and 8.5 percent in East Asia.

The demographic weight of Asia should also be kept in mind. Together, East and Southeast Asia have about 32 percent of the global population, and with India, that figure rises to 57 percent.[20] The high quality of the science-and-technology education that is being nurtured in these countries has also been the subject of attention. In an international evaluation of educational trends conducted in 2003, Singapore, Taiwan, South Korea, Hong Kong SAR, and Japan held the top five spots in studies of mathematics at the eighth-grade level and the top four spots (along with Japan at number six) in studies of science at the eighth-grade level.[21] In the same evaluation, the United States was ranked 15th for mathematics and 9th for science. In terms of sheer numbers, one estimate also suggested that in 2004 China graduated 600,000 engineers, India 350,000, and the United States a mere 70,000.[22] Although both the quantity and quality of Chinese and Indian engineers has been called into question in such estimates, the US National Academy of Science used such trends in 2005 to warn that the United States could soon lose its world leadership position in science.

Trade and Investment Patterns

The more specific regional trade and investment realities in the Asian region have also been widely noted. As trade volumes have increased in the region, there has also been a corresponding growth in economic inter-connectedness among Asian countries as indicated by the trade intensity index, intraregional trade flows relative to interregional trade flows, share of intermediate goods in trade flows, and cross-regional investment flows. In turn, as will be discussed below, these changing economic realities have also called into question Asia's reliance on non-Asian markets.

Between 2000 and 2005, the degree of trade intensity between East Asian countries increased, meaning simply that their trade relationships have become closer than in the past.[23] The ratio of intraregional trade to East Asia's total trade (including Taiwan and Hong Kong SAR) rose sharply from about 35.7 percent in 1980 to 55.8 percent in 2005.[24] To put things in perspective, this figure was substantially higher than that for NAFTA, which was at 43 percent in 2005, and it appeared poised to catch up to and possibly surpass the EU's ratio, which was at around 62 percent. The proportion of intermediate goods in intraregional trade has risen from 42 percent in 1980 to 60 percent in 2005, indicating that Asian economies are engaged in a cross-border division of the manufacturing process. These figures indicate overall that Asian economies are not only trading more with each other, but they are also increasingly specializing in line with their strengths. To put this in a global perspective, another estimate suggests that the share of intermediate goods in trade flows within Asia in 2005 stood at about 65 percent, as compared with about 40 percent among developed nations and around 30 percent between emerging Asia and the developed economies.[25]

Without detracting from Asian countries' dependence on world markets, other estimates from a variety of sources have also begun to make the same point that changing trade patterns are increasing regional interdependence. In 2007, the WTO figures show that interregional trade flows as a share of total regional merchandise exports stood at about 50 percent between Asian countries, compared with about 51 percent between North American countries and about 68 percent between the EU members.[26] The IMF data also show a similar pattern, namely that while the interregional trade ties between emerging Asia and other countries rose fivefold from 1990 to 2006, the intraregional trade within emerging Asia increased by a factor of 8.5.[27] And it is not just the emerging economies that show this trend. The share of imports by countries in industrial Asia (which includes Japan) from countries in emerging Asia changed from 27 percent in 1990 to 43 percent in 2006. Conversely, the share of exports by countries in industrial Asia to those in emerging Asia has increased from 30 percent in 1990 to 47 percent in 2006. Like the WTO data, the IMF figures also suggest that intraregional trade now accounts for about 50 percent of total trade in Asia, putting it closer to both NAFTA and the EU in terms of regional orientation.

Not surprisingly, the figures above can be interpreted as mirroring the decline of exports from the industrial Asian economies to countries in NAFTA and the EU. For Japan, in particular, some experts have suggested that in direct contrast to the rising economic importance of East Asian countries, the importance of countries such as the United States and Australia has been declining through the 1990s.[28] For the remainder of Asia, including China, Hong Kong SAR, Korea, and the ASEAN countries, there is a markedly greater reliance on each other for export markets in contrast to a decreasing collective reliance on the US market.[29] At one point, before the true toll of the 2008–2009 global financial crisis became clear, these falling extraregional trade trends fuelled academic and policy speculation about Asia's "decoupling" from the global business cycle.[30] As noted earlier, however, contractions in GDP levels, industrial production, as well as export and import levels have challenged the basis for that speculation. It is more likely that, even as intraregional trade trends increase and solidify, Asian economies will continue to be reliant in the medium term on markets in developed countries as the main destination for final good exports, especially because their exposure to interregional exports has also increased since the 1990s.[31]

Finally, foreign direct investment (FDI) inflows to Asia and Oceania have continued to grow steadily, climbing to US$260 billion in 2006, which accounted for about two-thirds of inflows to all developing countries that year.[32] Outward FDI from this region also increased by 50 percent over the previous year, reaching about US$117 billion. Many of these investment flows are also becoming intraregional, involving those from Japan and the newly industrialized economies (Hong Kong SAR, Korea, Singapore, and Taipei China) to ASEAN and mainland China, as well as those from ASEAN countries to other ASEAN countries and mainland China.[33] The UN Conference on Trade and Development estimates these changes by examining data on cross-border merger and acquisition (M&A) deals undertaken by transnational corporations based in the region, which show a notable concentration in two clusters, the intra–Greater China area and the intra-ASEAN area. In 2004, 40 percent of M&A deals by transnational corporations in these areas were intraregional in character and this increased to about 55 percent in 2005 and 2006. The Asian Development Bank's online estimates suggest that Asia's intraregional FDI share went from about 51 percent in 2004 to a peak of almost 80 percent in 2005.[34] There is an additional dimension that stands to affect Asian investment patterns both globally and regionally in the near future. This refers to the fact that Asian countries collectively held an estimated US$3.9 trillion in foreign exchange reserves near the end of 2007—a figure that is expected to soar beyond US$5 trillion by the end of 2009.[35] Since Asian investments (particularly those from Japan and China) have often been rebuffed in a high-profile manner in Western markets due to alleged national security concerns, the region's sovereign wealth funds may well begin to think about using these reserves to invest more strategically throughout both emerging and industrial Asia—a process that could also spur intraregional investment flows.[36]

In short, while Asian countries are interdependent with other parts of the world, the region's growing relative importance and its deepening integration should not be disregarded. Numerous general indicators—such as the share of world production, competitiveness, productivity, demographic levels, and science and technology education—show the increasing importance of Asian countries in the world economy. Intraregional trade and investment flows are not only rising but are also increasingly oriented toward both industrial and emerging Asia—all of which has added a new perspective on the continued reliance of Asia on world markets outside the region. Of course, based on any number of factors, such levels and trends can reverse, stagnate, or disappear. But at this stage, what is of greatest relevance to this analysis is that these trends have already had a substantial impact on the prospects for legalizing and institutionalizing Asian economic affairs in an unprecedented way.

Economic Realities Involving China, Japan, and the United States

In order to gain a clearer picture of the economic involvement of China, Japan, and the United States in the Asian region, it is useful to examine trade and investment flows among the three countries as well as between them and the region. These realities are summarized in tables 1, 2, and 3. Although these present snapshots in time rather than shifting longitudinal trends, they provide a departure point for analysis and allow us to see how these players are, relative to each other, involved in the trend toward the greater legal institutionalization of Asian economic affairs. Additionally, they provide us with a clearer basis for assessing the prospects for China-Japan-US dynamics in shaping the direction of Asian regionalism.

As table 1 reveals, roughly half of the trade for both Japan and China involves Asian countries, a trend that is on the increase. It is helpful to remember, of course, that country trends tend to fluctuate from year to year, but this comparative information is instructive in indicating which countries have greater stakes in the region as we near the end of the first decade of the 21st century. This is especially true for export and import levels involving China and Japan with both industrial and emerging Asia. In this regard, the United States, while still a sizable actor, is less dependent on the region relative to the other two players. A similar story comes to the surface with respect to investment levels. While much of the Chinese and Japanese FDI is concentrated in the Asian region, at this stage the United States is still behind these two countries in terms of its overall investment in the region despite ongoing increases.

Table 1. Trade and investment engagement in Asia[37]

	China[38]	Japan[39]	United States[40]
Trade with Asian countries, as % of total trade	Exports: 24%–33% Imports: 45%–66% (2007)	Exports: 54% Imports: 46% (2007)	Exports: 27% Imports: 31% (2007)
Investment in Asian region, as % of total FDI	36% (2005)	26% (2007)	13% (2007)
Overall assessment	While all three countries have significant trade involvement in the Asian region, at this stage Chinese and Japanese trade structures are relatively more oriented toward Asian economies than that of the United States.		

SOURCES: Data on trade are from International Monetary Fund (IMF), Direction of Trade Statistics 2008 (DOTS–CD ROM) 2008 and DOTS Yearbook 2005 (Washington DC: IMF, 2005). Data on investment are estimated from Leonard K. Cheng and Zihui Ma, "China's Outward FDI: Past and Future" (unpublished manuscript, Hong Kong University of Science and Technology and Renmin University China, July 2007), esp. table 4, www.nber.org (accessed May 13, 2009); Japanese Ministry of Finance, Historical Data on Outward/Inward Direct Investment, www.mof. go.jp (accessed May 13, 2009); US Department of Commerce, Bureau of Economic Analysis, US Direct Investment Abroad: Balance of Payments and Direct Investment Position Data—Position on a Historical-Cost Basis (2007), www.bea.gov (accessed May 13, 2009).

Table 2. Trade among China, Japan, and the United States

	China	Japan	United States
Percentage of total trade with each country (2007)	With Japan Exports: 8% Imports: 13% —— With US Exports: 18% Imports: 7%	With China Exports: 26% Imports: 24% —— With US Exports: 20% Imports: 12%	With China Exports: 9% Imports: 19% —— With Japan Exports: 5% Imports: 7%
Overall assessment	Japan's dominant trade partner is China and its overall trade structure is increasingly reliant on the Chinese market. The United States is not a dominant exporter to the Chinese or Japanese markets but is still a significant market for both China and Japan. China has strong trade interests related to Japan and the United States.		

SOURCES: Data on trade are from IMF, Direction of Trade Statistics 2008 (DOTS–CD ROM) 2008 and DOTS Yearbook 2005 (Washington DC: IMF, 2005). See also notes in table 1.

Table 2 provides an assessment of China-Japan-US trade realities, which deserve some explanation as there has been much interest in total trade flows between these three players. As is well known, China has become one of the top trade partners for both Japan and the United States.[41]

Table 3. Investment among China, Japan, and the United States

	United States[42]	Japan[43]	China[44]
Percentage of total investment	In China: 3% In Japan: 4% —— From China: 0.4% From Japan: 11% (2007)	In China: 12% In US: 21% —— From China: 1% From US: 60% (2007)	Outward investment in 2005 reached new high of US$13 billion. —— From Japan: 4% From US: 3% (as % of realized FDI value, 2008)
Cumulative stock in other countries	In China: US$15 billion In Japan: US$80 billion (2004)	In China: US$32 billion In US: US$142 billion (2004)	As of 2006, China's cumulative FDI abroad was estimated to be US$73 billion.
Overall Assessment	Both the United States and Japan have considerable cumulative stock and continuing FDI flows in each other's economies that far outweigh their engagement with China. While China is of interest as an investment destination to both the United States and Japan, China itself is a negligible player thus far in these two countries' investment portfolios.		

SOURCES: US FDI estimations are based on data from the US Department of Commerce, Bureau of Economic Analysis, "US Direct Investment Abroad: Balance of Payments and Direct Investment Position Data—Position on a Historical-Cost Basis (2007)," www.bea.gov (accessed May 13, 2009). All cumulative stock estimations for the United States are from the US Government Accountability Office (USGAO), "China Trade: US Exports, Investment, Affiliate Sales Rising, but Export Share Falling," *Report to Congressional Committees GAO-06-162* (Washington DC: USGAO, December 2005), pp. 32–34.

Estimation of Japan FDI is based on data from the Japanese Ministry of Finance, Historical Data on Outward/Inward Direct Investment, www.mof.go.jp (accessed May 13, 2009). All cumulative stock estimations for Japan are from the Japan External Trade Organization (JETRO), "Japanese Trade and Investment Statistics (FDI Stock [based on International Investment Position, net])," www.jetro.go.jp (accessed May 13, 2009).

Estimation of China FDI is based on data from Chinese Ministry of Commerce/Investment Promotion Agency of MOFCOM, Invest in China, "Table of Investment Utilization of FDI from Jan to December 2008," January 22, 2009, fdi.gov.cn (accessed May 13, 2009). For an assessment of China's cumulative stock, see the US-China Business Council, "Foreign Investment in China," February 2007, available online at www.uschina.org (accessed 13 May 2009); "China's Overseas Investment in 2005 Hits New High," September 5, 2006; and "Outbound FDI up 123% in 2005," September 5, 2006, both available online at www.mofcom.gov.cn (accessed May 13, 2009).

Although much has been made of the fact that China has become Japan's largest trade partner, it has also passed Japan to become the second most important trade partner for the United States. In 2007, two-way trade volume between the United States and China was US$386 billion, while it was about US$208 billion between the United States and Japan. At the same time, two-way trade volume between Japan and China was estimated to be about US$236 billion. As table 2 reveals, the aggregate volumes of trade mask some asymmetries. Both China and Japan continue to be highly dependent on the United States as an export market. For China, the US market is of sizable importance; for Japan, although the United States has diminished in overall trade importance and there is greater reliance on the Chinese market, the United States nevertheless remains a vital market. The United States itself is far less dependent on either Japan or China for exports or even imports. In fact, both Japan and China continue to be relatively small players in the overall US trade portfolio.

Table 3 provides an overview of China-Japan-US investment realities. Compared with the trade flows, the investment picture is different, with the United States emerging as a pivotal player. It also shows that it is Japan and the United States that have been the most active in terms of investing in each other, with China not appearing to be much of an investor in either country. Both Japan and the United States have acquired sizable cumulative investment stocks in China, with Japan's estimated to be twice as large as that of the United States. Additionally, both the United States and Japan retain substantial cumulative investment values in each other's economies, with Japan's estimated to be again roughly twice as large as that of the United States.

This brief survey of China-Japan-US economic realities tells us two things. First, despite the fact that trends are slow, uneven, and subject to setbacks, changes, and reversals, there is an Asia-centric economic reality out there. Specifically, this refers to the Sinicization of Asian economic relations, meaning that China is becoming the most significant (but by no means the only) locomotive of regional economic growth.[45] Second, while China, Japan, and the United States have considerable trade and investment stakes in the region, it is Japan and China that are becoming more pivotal than the United States in terms of the region's trade in particular but also in terms of investment flows. These realities provide a foundation on which to begin an analysis of how to manage China-Japan-US dynamics in the near future, a task that is taken up below.

Legal Institutions Involving China, Japan, and the United States

In light of the discussion above, it is safe to say that Asia is emerging as a cohesive regional economic entity in a way that is quite different from the past.[46] Of course, as stated above, patterns and trends are reversible: exogenous shocks, internal implosions, natural calamities, and even political and security barriers can affect economic scenarios in the Asian region. But three factors make the current situation different from the past. First, the economic transformation in Asia today has social foundations and consequences as well. The rise of an "emergent middle class" across the region—one with different national situations but nevertheless with similar lifestyles and ambitions—has fuelled personal consumption to unprecedented levels.[47] In 2002 alone, personal consumption in East Asia was worth an estimated US$5 trillion, a figure comparable to that of the EU and not far behind the United States. Embedded in the new economic structures, the rising professional class across Asia not only helps to solidify the expanding regional consumer market but also stands to enhance a regionwide consciousness over the long term.

Second, Asian economic integration is driven by specific and very concrete economic interests. From a self-interested commercial perspective, it is of course not difficult to accept that Asian countries such as China and Japan, which have considerable economic stakes in the region, have a strong incentive to reinforce those interests. But who exactly benefits? Historically, many economic factors have brought Asia to this stage: the opening of China and its integration into the world economic order; the maturation and spread of Japan's trade interests, especially in Asia; the forging by the United States of one of the world's largest trade blocs in its home region; and the collective experiences of Asian countries in the aftermath of the Asian financial crisis.

But behind these major, large-scale changes, the most critical elements in forging Asian links have actually been private as well as public economic interests. In other words, it is not government-led institutions that have been central to the organization or functioning of the region's economy. Rather these economic links have been driven primarily by concrete economic interests, especially private interests that have gained or stand to gain substantial production and operational stakes in the region.[48] It is such interests that have been directly engaged in shaping the economic patterns described in this chapter and that obviously have a stake in sustaining them. This holds true also for public interests that have come to the fore especially with Chinese economic operations thus far, but may become even more prominent with the movements of foreign exchange reserves by both China and Japan in the near future. Having had to operate under various opportunities and constraints—such as economic competition, the pressures of globalization, and technological progress—the important point here is that both private and public interests have been driven more by a concern with profits than with any grand designs for the future standing of Asia in the world. Nonetheless, the sum total of their narrow moves has, over time, changed the actual landscape of and future prospects for Asian economic integration.

Third, it is the protection of concrete economic interests across both emerging and industrial Asia that has turned out to be the primary factor in bringing regional governments more solidly into the Asianism game. This is reflected in the search for legal institutions to provide exactly such protections, irrespective of whether the underlying economic interest is private or public. Although this chapter is concerned primarily with China, Japan, and the United States in the Asianism game, it is helpful to understand the more general premises. Once private or public entities acquire stakes in cross-border operations, they need to stabilize market access, ensure favorable investment environments, shelter direct and indirect assets and personnel, reduce discriminatory treatment, and generally protect against the arbitrary whims of foreign governments, actors, and jurisdictions.[49] Their respective home governments are then drawn into the game of providing protection through various formal instruments, such as FTAs or BITs.

The motivation for home governments to do so cannot just be relegated to platitudes about their diplomatic, strategic, or reputational interests. Rather, their motivation stems from the specific ways in which such instruments become concrete means for shaping economic outcomes across international, regional, and foreign realms. Any such instruments constrain the actions and conduct of public and private interests in different jurisdictions, help support business operations across borders, facilitate the direction and speed of regional economic integration, provide a binding rules-based framework for dealing with trade partners, and, other things being equal, potentially boost national welfare over the long term. The governments surely also calculate that securing and locking in their economic interests for the world to see may also allow them to project their influence more forcefully in global and especially regional settings at either an individual or collective level down the line.

Formal instruments therefore matter greatly and allow us to begin gauging the prospects for managing the dynamics of key players, such as China, Japan, and the United States in, for example, the Asian region. But what are the indications that governments are taking steps to secure their respective economic interests through formal legal institutions? There is, most visibly, an FTA frenzy in Asia today in which the dominant players, China and Japan, appear to be engaged in head-to-head competition for leadership within the region. But while such stories certainly make for headline news around the world, they do not speak to the actual legal-institutional strategies being pursued to lock in and secure economic interests across the region. Competitiveness, in this context, is surely a spur to further integration, whether at the corporate, governmental, or regional level. The governments of all the major Asian players today—mainly, but not limited to, China, Japan, and ASEAN—have fuelled talk of Asian integration, precisely by concluding formal legal instruments such as FTAs and BITs in bilateral, trilateral, and multilateral settings, which is something not previously done.

There is, in short, a rules-based transformation taking place in Asia today. Putting this in the context of China-Japan-US interactions, the question is, what should the three countries be doing to strengthen trilateral management in light of the legal institutions accompanying the structural economic shifts? To answer this question requires some understanding of where the three governments actually stand in terms of formal legal institutions individually, bilaterally, trilaterally, and even multilaterally. As stated above, such institutions are a clear means to affect not just national economic interests but also the shape of Asian economic integration. All three governments are of course part of the Asia Pacific Economic Cooperation (APEC)—Japan and the United States since 1989 and China since 1991. This affiliation gives them a regional, multilateral entry point into regional affairs and makes them part of one of the more dynamic economic regions of the world. However, in terms of legal-institutional centrality, APEC is not where the action is. Rather, it is to be found in bilateral FTAs and BITs, as well as in trilateral issue-specific ventures (such as those related to investment) in an East Asia FTA, in ASEAN+3, and so on. Thus, more consequentially for the relative standing of China, Japan, and the United States in Asia, we need to know how and in what ways the Chinese, Japanese, and American governments have actually focused on the Asian region and Asian actors in their legal-institutional diplomacy. Table 4 provides information on this front.

In keeping with the structural shifts that have integrated their economies ever more in the Asian region, China and Japan have concentrated their legal institution–building agenda in Asia. For Japan, despite the continued emphasis on cross-regional agreements, such as those with Mexico or Switzerland, the bulk of its initiatives are focused on the Asian

Table 4. Involvement in Asian legal-institutional frameworks

Frameworks	China[50]	Japan[51]	United States[52]
Proportion of actual and proposed FTAs that involve Asia—FTAs with Asian countries/total known FTAs	13 /23 (2009)	13 /20 (2009)	2 /20 (2009)
Proportion of actual and proposed BITs that involve Asia—BITs with Asian countries/total known BITs	24 /121 (2008)	9 /12 (2008)	4 /47 (2008)
Proportion of Trade and Investment Framework Agreements (TIFAs) that involve Asia—TIFAs with Asian countries/total known TIFAs	—	—	12/42 (2009)
Involvement with major regional-multilateral initiatives in Asia	All e.g., APEC, ASEAN+1, ASEAN+3, East Asia FTA, Trilateral CJK [China-Japan-Korea] FTA, CJK investment treaty	All e.g., APEC, ASEAN+1, ASEAN+3, East Asia FTA, Trilateral CJK FTA, CJK investment treaty	Few e.g., APEC, Enterprise for ASEAN Initiative
Overall assessment	The three governments have considerable engagement with Asia-centric frameworks but, relative to the United States, both China and Japan are more focused on the Asian architecture. Japan is the most Asia-centric of the three in its legal-institutional diplomacy.		

SOURCES: Data on Chinese and Japanese FTA agreements are from Asian Development Bank, Asian Regional Integration Center, Free Trade Agreement Database for Asia, http://aric.adb.org (accessed May 13, 2009). US data on FTAs and TIFAs data are from the United States Trade Representative (Trade Agreements), available online at www.ustr.gov (accessed May 13, 2009). Data on BITs for all three countries are from UNCTAD, country-specific list of BITs, available online at www.unctad.org (accessed May 13, 2009).

region. For China, a similar pattern emerges, as much of its highest-profile economic diplomacy is concentrated in the region. Both Japan and China have also been engaged in the protection of their investments and are now engaged in hammering out the contours of a trilateral investment treaty involving South Korea—a region-centered move that leaves out the United States entirely.[53] Meanwhile, as can also be readily seen from table 4, the United States still lags behind in its legal-institutional diplomacy in Asia altogether. Like the Asian governments, the United States, too, has shown a particular interest in the advancing legalization in the investment arena, and it has been most notably involved in BIT negotiations with China since June 2008.[54]

From an evolutionary perspective, Asia proper is thus being engineered into existence through the use of formal, competitive, rules-based, legal-institutional building blocks that will take it forward over the remainder of the century. The activities of both China and Japan have been critical to this venture; the United States to date has not been a key player but may well parlay its burgeoning trade and investment framework agreements (TIFAs) and investment stakes to make more of a mark in the region. What does all this suggest about the future of the China-Japan-US relationship?

MANAGING CHINA-JAPAN-US DYNAMICS AMID ASIANISM

As described in this chapter, Asian economic integration is an emerging reality and looks set to be so for the foreseeable future. Asia is also moving toward the formation of distinct, new, and unprecedented legal institutions to govern its economic changes. From the bottom up, these are helping to construct a genuine regional architecture to govern the Asia-centric economic reality. The reason these frameworks are important is because they serve the concrete economic interests of some of the most pivotal players and give them avenues to shape outcomes across the region. Within this Asian economic reality, thus far, both China and Japan are increasing their weight relative to the United States. Both China and Japan, individually and together, also thus far have more legal institutions to safeguard their shifting economic interests in the Asian region, some of which pointedly exclude the United States. It is the Americans, in short, who are trying to catch up with the Chinese and Japanese moves already in play within the region.

What, then, are some specific options for managing China-Japan-US dynamics in the context of Asian regional integration in order to ensure that they remain positive and advantageous for all three countries? This final section sets out four options for the governments of China, Japan, and the United States, ending with a discussion of those that are most likely at present to secure the shared economic interests of all three countries in ensuring the continuation of regional trade and investment flows.

Return to a Focus on the Existing WTO-Centered System

Even with their burgeoning regional interests, the Chinese, Japanese, and American governments can opt to return to the WTO as the focal point for rules-based integration. This would not just advance the region's interests but would also ensure that it remains open and linked to other dynamic areas of the global economy. Simply by virtue of including all major economies in the world, the gains from trade would be the highest of any other forum that the three countries could possibly conclude. However, while this would genuinely be the best option for the United States, which has historically been dominant within the General Agreement on Tariffs and Trade (GATT)/WTO framework, China and Japan may not be equally enthusiastic about a forum where they have long been the rule takers and not the rule makers. While all three countries are likely to remain active users of the WTO for dispute settlement under the existing rules, the prospects for using this global multilateral forum for trade liberalization purposes remain dim. There is a widely held view that the WTO is cumbersome, is currently stalled in any event, and cannot possibly keep pace with the rapidly changing realities in Asia. Also, a number of top trade officials in Japan have written off the mega-multilateral trade liberalization option as archaic.[55] Unless there is a dramatic turnaround and show of leadership by China, Japan, and the United States in the context of the ongoing Doha Round, this option is not very likely to be exercised in the near future.

Return to a Focus on Existing Regional Institutions

China, Japan, and the United States also have the option of using the common experiences and rules from their various bilateral agreements in the context of existing institutions like APEC. The virtue of this option is that it could lead to some of the biggest economic gains for the three countries across substantial parts of the world economy and draw them into a cross-regional arrangement that could help solidify their interests more broadly. However, there are several constraints. For one, APEC has been used as a regional vehicle for liberalization before and it has been found lacking, particularly in the aftermath of the debacle associated with the attempt to promote EVSL [Early Voluntary Sectoral Liberalization]. Although this does not mean that the forum cannot be used as a vehicle to further liberalization and integration, the weight of its tarnished past combined with the relative speed and flexibility of bilateral forums may make it less appealing to the three governments. For another, from the perspective of

China, the presence of Taiwan as an equal in the forum makes it considerably less attractive. Altogether, this option requires extensive coordination among members with divergent interests and probably has a lower chance of being exercised in the near future.

Continue to Focus on FTAs and BITs

The Chinese, Japanese, and American governments can continue to move forward with their individual agreements with other countries or sets of countries. If things stay the course, this approach is most likely to predominate in the immediate future as it merely reinforces the present trend. These agreements themselves are competitive and overlapping, and might actually have a minimal impact on boosting national economic welfare as opposed to sectoral interests. They do, however, help provide a common rules-based vocabulary that can serve as a building block for more genuine trilateral ventures.

In fact, there is little doubt that China, Japan, and the United States will continue their various bilateral efforts. However, in order to secure greater economic gains, the centrality of ASEAN to regional initiatives should be kept in mind as it has already concluded agreements of varying complexity with the key regional players. The United States, too, has an initiative focused on trade and investment with ASEAN. Region-wide FTAs are therefore most likely to progress on the basis of either the ASEAN+3 (including China, Japan, Korea) or ASEAN+6 (including China, India, Japan, Korea, New Zealand, and Australia) formats, possibly with the added involvement of the United States. Although this option need not be exercised formally as it is already in motion at both the bilateral and regional levels, it does require that the governments in China, Japan, and the United States be vigilant in ensuring it be inclusive with respect to one another.

Continue to Focus on Block-Based Agreements and Treaties

Instead of focusing on bilateral, regional, or multilateral forums per se, the prospects for China-Japan-US interaction would be greatly enhanced if the three governments focused on narrow and specific *blocks* of economic activity in the region, such as services, intellectual property, investment, and so on.[56] On investment in particular, China and Japan have already taken concrete steps with South Korea in this precise direction by starting to negotiate a treaty to protect the concrete cross-border operations of private actors in the region. Known in negotiating circles as the "CJK trilateral investment treaty," it had already entered the sixth round of negotiations as of April 2009.[57] The important thing about this treaty, which can be a model for further integration prospects in the region, is that it is focused on a block of economic activity—in this case, investment—and utilizes some general principles from the WTO framework to facilitate investment flows. There is a distinct Asian flavor to many such block-based approaches, and this is most aggressively reflected in the negotiations over the CJK treaty. However, this option does not have to be exclusionary. This is not an issue of whether the United States is an Asian power, about which debate will continue.[58] Although the United States needs to stand aloof from Asian economic integration processes much in the same way that it did when European integration took its formative and then more concerted steps in the early postwar period, it should still safeguard its economic interests in conjunction with the other dominant powers in the Asian region. The United States can, for instance, request to join the CJK investment treaty negotiations by building upon its own investment negotiations with China, with a view to protecting and promoting its own investments broadly in the region, and with a longer-term view of incorporating such rules into a global multilateral or perhaps even APEC-centered minilateral investment treaty.

∗ ∗ ∗ ∗ ∗

There is little doubt that the connectedness and integration of trade and investment flows is on the rise, especially among East Asian countries. Despite setbacks, ongoing changes, and perhaps even the shadows of history, these flows look set to fuse the economic map of the region. Nor is there any remaining doubt that governments, whether inside or outside of the region, are playing catch-up in terms of establishing formal legal institutions for the ongoing economic integration brought about by these flows. In turn, their very presence suggests that the most remarkable thing about Asia today is that this is no longer a region where things simply happen at the mercy of outside influences. Rather, it is one in which regional players such as China and Japan, as well as other South and Southeast Asian nations, are determined to play a forceful role in shaping its legal institutions at present and into the foreseeable future.

Asianism, in short, is a reality in terms of structural economic shifts as well as in terms of the unprecedented legal institutions that are deepening and expanding them. Both these dimensions need to be kept in mind when one assesses prospects for the management of China-Japan-US dynamics in the region. Asian countries would not be attracting so much attention were it not for the scope of these economic shifts and the promise that is associated with them. Nor would other countries be so focused on the region without the burgeoning legal institutions that can clearly keep them in or out, or can put them at an advantage or disadvantage, in this great new Asianism game.

NOTES

1. See Peter J. Katzenstein, *A World of Regions: Asia and Europe in the American Imperium* (Ithaca: Cornell University Press, 2005), esp. 208–48.

2. See, for example, T. J. Pempel, "Introduction: Emerging Webs of Regional Connectedness," in *Remapping East Asia: The Construction of a Region*, ed. T. J. Pempel (Ithaca: Cornell University, 2005), 1–28; Kishore Mahbubani, *The New Asian Hemisphere: The Irresistible Shift of Global Power to the East* (New York: PublicAffairs, 2008); Naoko Munakata, *Transforming East Asia: The Evolution of Regional Economic Integration* (Washington DC and Tokyo: Brookings/RIETI, 2006); David Shambaugh, "Introduction: The Rise of China and Asia's New Dynamics," in *Power Shift: China and Asia's New Dynamics*, ed. David Shambaugh (Berkeley: University of California, 2005), 1–20; Amitav Acharya, *Asia Rising: Who is Leading?* (Singapore: World Scientific, 2008); Jason T. Shaplen and James Laney, "Washington's Eastern Sunset: The Decline of U.S. Power in Northeast Asia," *Foreign Affairs* 86, no. 6 (November/December 2007): 82–97; and Victor D. Cha, "Winning Asia: Washington's Untold Success Story," *Foreign Affairs* 86, no. 6 (November/December 2007): 98–113.

3. In terms of defining Asia, the International Monetary Fund (IMF) makes a distinction between "Emerging Asia" (China, India, Hong Kong SAR, Korea, Singapore, Taiwan, Indonesia, Malaysia, Philippines, Thailand, and Vietnam) and "Industrial Asia" (Japan, Australia, and New Zealand) as identified in IMF, *Regional Economic Outlook: Asia and the Pacific* (Washington DC: IMF, 2007), vi. Although this is a useful distinction, this paper focuses mostly on the countries in emerging Asia, as well as Japan.

4. For the general facts and figures noted here, see Central Intelligence Agency (CIA), *The 2008 World Factbook*, "Rank Order—GDP (purchasing power parity)" and "Rank Order—Reserves of Foreign Exchange and Gold," at www.cia.gov/library/publications/the-world-factbook/rankorder/2001rank.html and www.cia.gov/library/publications/the-world-factbook/rankorder/2188rank.html respectively (both accessed June 6, 2008); IMF, "Asia's Role in the World Economy," *Finance & Development* 43, no. 2 (June 2006), www.imf.org/external/pubs/ft/fandd/2006/06/picture.htm; World Trade Organization (WTO), *International Trade Statistics 2008* (Switzerland: WTO, 2008), 10–11; United Nations (UN), Department of Economic and Social Affairs, Population Division, World Population Prospects: The 2008 Revision—Population Database, esa.un.org/unpp (estimated via tables for world and Asia populations) (accessed May 10, 2009); and Jason T. Shaplen and James Laney, "Washington's Eastern Sunset: The Decline of U.S. Power in Northeast Asia," *Foreign Affairs* 86, no. 6, (November 2007): 82.

5. WTO, *International Trade Statistics 2008*, 10–11. Figures exclude Australia and New Zealand.

6. The top-10 rank order was China, Japan, Russia, Taiwan, South Korea, India, Brazil, Singapore, Hong Kong SAR, and Germany.

7. See Fareed Zakaria, *The Post-American World* (New York: Norton, 2008), 2, 86, 87–166. Zakaria's more extensive analysis of the "rest" focuses largely on the two most import rising powers in the world today, China and India.

8. Peter J. Katzenstein, *A World of Regions*, 2, 6–13; T. J. Pempel, "Introduction," 24–28; Munakata, *Transforming East Asia*, 178.

9. T. J. Pempel, "Introduction," 19–24.

10. Following on this distinction, see especially Naoko Munakata, "Has Politics Caught Up with Markets? In Search of East Asian Economic Regionalism," in *Beyond Japan: The Dynamics of East Asian Regionalism*, ed. Peter J. Katzenstein and Takashi Shiraishi (Ithaca: Cornell University, 2006), 130–57.

11. David Pilling and Geoff Dyer, "Asia Looks to IMF Relations 10 Years After its Own Crisis," *Financial Times*, November 10, 2008; and Patrick Barta, "Sharp Slowdown in Asia Nears," *Wall Street Journal*, October 27, 2008.

12. Jeffrey Garten, "Amid the Economic Rubble, Shangkong Will Rise," *Financial Times*, May 11, 2009; James Lamont, Kathrin Hille, and Kevin Brown, "Asia Markets Buoyed by Growth Data," *Financial Times*, May 5, 2009; and Kishore Mahbubani, *The New Asian Hemisphere*, 52. Mahbubani relies on the predictions made in a Goldman Sachs BRICs study, which asserted that, in order, China, the United States, India, and Japan would be the major players.

13. See Richard Stubbs, "ASEAN Plus Three: Emerging East Asian Regionalism?" *Asian Survey* 42, no. 3 (2002): 440–55.

14. See Anne O. Krueger, "Mutual Interdependence: Asia and the World Economy" (speech, Institute for Global Economics, Seoul, Korea, June 30, 2005, www.imf.org/external/np/speeches/2005/063005.htm). For specific facts and figures, see IMF, *Regional Economic Outlook*, 41–53; and Munakata, "Has Politics Caught Up with Markets?" 136–7.

15. "Asia's Suffering," *Economist*, January 29, 2009; and "Asia's Export-Dependent Economies Feeling the Pain of Slowdown," *China Post*, March 2, 2009.

16. David Pilling, "Mixed Signals from Asia's Animal Spirits," *Financial Times*, May 14, 2009; and James Kynge, "Chinese Tap an Inner Dynamic to Drive Growth," *Financial Times*, May 11, 2009. There are now indications that at least China is beginning to rely on inner dynamism to fuel its economic growth rates, a trend that could go on to have positive repercussions for future Asian economic fusion.

17. Ministry of Economy, Trade and Industry (METI), *White Paper on International Economy and Trade 2007* (Tokyo: METI, 2007), esp. 157–8.

18. See World Economic Forum, Global Competitiveness Index 2007–2008, *The Global Competitiveness Report 2007–2008*, www.gcr.weforum.org.

19. "US Leads Productivity Ranking; China Gains," *New York Times*, September 4, 2007.

20. See United Nations, *Demographic Yearbook 2004* (New York: UN, 2007), esp. table 2, www.unstats.un.org.

21. See Ina V. S. Mullis et. al. (IEA), *TIMSS 2003 International Mathematics Report* (Chestnut Hill MA: TIMSS & PRLS International Study Center, Boston College, 2004), 34; and Michael O. Martin et. al., *TIMSS 2003 International Science Report* (Chestnut Hill MA: TIMSS & PRLS International Study Center, Boston College, 2004), 36.

22. Zakaria, *The Post-American World*, esp. 187–8.

23. The following draws on METI, *White Paper on International Economy and Trade 2007*, 162, 165–166. In its white paper, METI has defined East Asia as Japan, China, Korea,

ASEAN, India, New Zealand, and Australia. Separately, the Asian Development Bank (ADB) also provides indicators that the intraregional trade intensity index has increased. See ADB/Asia Regional Integration Center (ARIC)—Integration Indicators Database: Trade Integration Indicators, www.aric.adb.org (accessed May 9, 2009).

24. See also Masahiro Kawai, "Evolving Economic Architecture in Asia," ADB Institute Discussion Paper no. 84, December 2007, 2–4 (esp. table 1).

25. Paul Gruenwald and Masahiro Hori, "Intra-Regional Trade Key to Asia's Export Boom," *IMF Survey Magazine: Countries & Region*, February 6, 2008, esp. chart 1, www.imf.org (accessed June 6, 2008).

26. WTO, *International Trade Statistics 2008*, 9, 207.

27. IMF, *Regional Economic Outlook*, esp. 41–43.

28. Tadahiro Yoshida, "East Asian Regionalism and Japan," IDE APEC Study Center Working Paper Series 03/04, no. 9 (March 2004), esp. 13–15.

29. See ADB, *Asian Development Outlook 2007*, esp. table 1.5.3, www.adb.org.

30. See Barry Eichengreen and Yung Chul Park, "Asia and the Decoupling Myth" (policy paper, University of California Berkeley and Korea University, May 2008, www.econ. berkeley.edu/~eichengr/policy.html), esp. 11–14.

31. Gruenwald and Hori, "Intra-Regional Trade Key to Asia's Export Boom," esp. chart 2.

32. UNCTAD, *World Investment Report 2007* (New York and Geneva: UN, 2007), 40–45.

33. Masahiro Kawai, "Evolving Economic Architecture in Asia," 2–4 (esp. table 2).

34. See ADB/ARIC—Integration Indicators Database: FDI Integration Indicators, www.aric. adb.org/indicator.php (accessed August 2, 2009).

35. IMF, *Regional Economic Outlook*, 7, 10–11; John Berthelsen, "Asia Ponders Its Astounding Foreign Exchange Reserves," *Asia Sentinel*, January 14, 2008, www.asiasentinel.com (accessed June 4, 2008). See also the data provided by the Sovereign Wealth Fund Institute in the Foreign Exchange Reserves by Country or Geopolitical Entity section of its website, swfinstitute.org/research/fxr.php (accessed June 4, 2008).

36. See, for example, Stephanie Kirchgaessner, "China Hits Out at US 'Protectionism,'" *Financial Times*, June 11, 2008.

37. Table 1 uses trade data from the IMF's Direction of Trade Statistics (DOTS) yearbook and data series. These classify the following countries under Asia: Afghanistan, Bangladesh, Brunei Darussalam, Cambodia, China, Hong Kong SAR, Macao SAR, Fiji, Guam, India, Indonesia, Korea, Lao PDR, Malaysia, Maldives, Mongolia, Myanmar, Nauru, Nepal, Pakistan, Palau, Papua New Guinea, the Philippines, Samoa, Singapore, Solomon Islands, Sri Lanka, Thailand, Vanuatu, Vietnam, and Taiwan Province of China (only world tables). The IMF DOTS CD-ROM data excludes Taiwan at the request of Mainland Chinese authorities and use is therefore made of the *IMF Yearbook 2005*. The *Yearbook* also does not contain separate country pages for Taiwan, but Taiwan's export and import levels are based on those appearing under the general world tables in the Asia column using 2004 data. All world totals refer to the DOTS World Total category for each country. China world totals sum up those for Mainland China, Hong Kong SAR, and Macao SAR.

38. Trade estimations for China are given as a range depending on whether export and import figures on greater China (i.e., including Mainland China, Hong Kong SAR, Macao SAR, and Taiwan) are excluded (lower figure) or included (higher figure) in the calculations. As for investments, in 2005, for the first time, China's FDI flows to Latin America (53 percent) exceeded those to Asia. Until then, Asia had received a little over half of China's FDI in 2003 and 2004.

39. Estimations of Japanese exports and imports to Asia include Taiwan.

40. Estimations of US export and imports to Asia include Taiwan and Japan.

41. See Paul Blustein, "China Passes US in Trade with Japan," *Washington Post*, January 27, 2005, www.washingtonpost.com/wp-dyn/articles/A40192-2005Jan26.html (accessed June 10, 2008); "China-Japan Economic, Trade Ties Have Great Potential to Tap," *China View*, May 4, 2008, news.xinhuanet.com/English/2008-05/04/content_8104901.htm (accessed June 10, 2008); and data from the US Census Bureau, Foreign Trade Statistics.

42. Data on US investments to and from China include Mainland China, Hong Kong SAR, and Taiwan. Also, as a benchmark, it is helpful to know that in 2004 the cumulative stock of US investment was US$952 billion in the EU, US$217 billion in Canada.

43. Mainland China, Hong Kong SAR, and Taiwan are included in data on Japanese investments to and from China and all cumulative stock estimations for Japan in China.

44. Information on China's inward and outward FDI is scant, though a picture of its FDI patterns can be established by also examining both data from the United States and Japan, as is done here. A significant portion of China's incoming FDI is from Hong Kong SAR (44.4 percent), followed by the Virgin Island (17.3 percent).

45. Zhang Yunling and Tang Shiping, "China's Regional Strategy," in *Power Shift*, 51–53; Peter J. Katzenstein, "East Asia—Beyond Japan," in *Beyond Japan*, 10–14; and Macabe Keliher, "Replacing US in Asian Export Market," *Asia Times*, February 11, 2004.

46. See Gerald Curtis, "Rethinking US East Asia Policy" (English translation of a *Tokyo Shimbun* article that originally appeared on January 11, 2004), on the RIETI website's Newspapers & Magazines section, www.rieti.go.jp/en/papers/contribution/curtis/03.html.

47. Takashi Shiraishi, "The Third-Wave: Southeast Asia and Middle-Class Formation in the Making of a Region," in *Beyond Japan*, 237, 267–71; and also Peter J. Katzenstein, "East Asia—Beyond Japan," in *Beyond Japan*, 27–28.

48. See T. J. Pempel, "Introduction," in *Remapping East Asia*, 20–22; Saadia Pekkanen, *Japan's Aggressive Legalism: Law and Foreign Trade Politics Beyond the WTO* (Stanford: Stanford University, 2008), esp. 231, 233; and Munakata, *Transforming East Asia*, 37–61.

49. Saadia Pekkanen, *Japan's Aggressive Legalism*, 3–4.

50. The estimate of Chinese FTAs includes FTA/agreements under implementation, proposed, under consultation, under study, or signed. Hong Kong SAR (two FTAs, of which one is Asian) and Taiwan (seven FTAs, of which one is Asian) are not included in the count. Likewise, Chinese BITs estimates include those that are signed and may or may not be in force. Hong Kong SAR (15 BITs, of which 3 are Asian) and Taiwan (21 BITs, of which 6 are Asian), are not included in the count. For the purposes of both the FTAs and BITs Australia and New Zealand are not counted as Asian.

51. The estimate of Japan's FTAs includes FTA/agreements under implementation, proposed, under consultation, under study, or signed. Japanese BIT estimates include those that are signed and may or may not be in force. For the purposes of both the FTAs and BITs, Australia and New Zealand are not counted as Asian.

52. The total count of US FTAs includes both those signed and those in force. For TIFAs, Asia includes South Asia, Central Asia, Southeast Asia, and the Pacific. Additionally, different types of TIFAs with one country still only count as one by country. Meanwhile, BIT estimates include only those that are signed and may or may not be in force, and therefore the US-China BIT negotiations are excluded from the count. For the purposes of both the FTAs and BITs, Australia and New Zealand are not counted as Asian.

53. Interview with METI officials, Tokyo, October 18, 2007.

54. Cai Congyan, "China-US BIT Negotiations and the Future of Investment Treaty Regime: A Grand Bilateral Bargain with Multilateral Implications," *Journal of International Economic Law* 12, no. 2 (2009): 457-506.

55. Interview with METI official, Tokyo, October 16, 2007.

56. For more on this approach, see Michael Green and Matthew Goodman, "Why Saying 'Sayonara' is the Hardest Thing to Do," *Financial Times*, June 26, 2006, who focus on such "building-blocks" in the context of a "Super-FTA" between the United States and Japan. See also Saadia Pekkanen, "Assessing the Prospects for a US-Japan FTA," in APEC, *The New International Architecture in Trade and Investment: Current Status and Implications* (Singapore: APEC Secretariat, March 2007), 94–98, who advocates a "BITs and Blocks" approach in the context of fostering concrete integration between the United States and Japan—a strategy that can be generalized also to China, Japan, and the United States, as proposed here.

57. Interview with METI official via e-mail, April 1, 2008.

58. See M. Taylor Fravel and Richard J. Samuels, "The United States as an Asian Power: Realism or Conceit?" Audit of the Conventional Wisdom (MIT Center for International Studies) 05-2 (April 2005), web.mit.edu/cis/pdf/Audit_5_05_Samuels_Fravel.pdf.

10 Cooperation and Competition in the Chinese Automobile Industry: The Emerging Architecture of China-Japan-US Economic Relations

KATSUHIRO SASUGA

INTERNATIONAL ECONOMIC RELATIONS are regarded as immensely important by China, Japan, and the United States, and thus there is a tendency in analyses of their relations to concentrate on formal procedures and institutionalized decision making. However, this does not give us the whole picture of how trilateral economic relations have evolved. Even though there are few clear formal institutional frameworks among the three governments, economic interdependence among China, Japan, and the United States has still deepened dramatically. Closer examination of economic relations at the ground level reveals that, in addition to central governments, firms, local governments, and other nonstate actors have played key roles in driving this process of economic integration and have been influential in shaping the dynamics of China-Japan-US trilateral relations.

To better understand how the interplay among these various actors affects trilateral economic relations, it is useful to look empirically at ground-level interactions among the three countries. In this context, the automobile industry provides a particularly illustrative case study. The automobile industry is the largest industry in many developed and emerging economies, and in China it is the only industry in which each core project takes the form of a joint venture with a foreign company. The production processes and the delivery of products to consumers increasingly cross state borders. In fact, China's rapid economic development cannot be understood independently of the changing dynamics of global sourcing and the transformation of production networks, and the growth of China's automobile industry—the production of both whole vehicles and automobile parts—can be seen as one of the most significant developments in the process of China's modernization.

This chapter seeks to examine and analyze the development of the Chinese automobile industry and the emergence of production networks linking China, Japan, and the United States in order to shed light on the deepening economic linkages among the three countries. It also focuses on China's institutional arrangements at the national and subnational levels and, in particular, on how networks among local governments and Chinese and foreign companies are shaping and influencing the formation of a cross-border architecture linking China, Japan, and the United States. In attempting to understand how China's economic linkages to Japan and the United States are evolving, focusing on the developmental state is necessary but not sufficient. It is also important to understand the nature and dynamics of operational networks comprising both individuals and collectives, as well as the roles of public and private actors pursuing common goals. Their regularized practices are often what drive cooperation, the institutionalization of patterns of interaction, and governmental action.

The Globalizing Automobile Industry

The global automobile industry has been under extreme pressure since the outbreak of the financial crisis in 2008. It is facing one of its most challenging periods in history, and uncertainty is spreading worldwide. In 2008, global automobile production fell 3.7 percent from the previous year to approximately 70.5 million units, down from 73.3 million units in 2007.[1]

One of the most dramatic changes occurring in the globalizing automobile industry is the sharp rise in production in newly industrializing countries such as China, Brazil, and India over the last 10 years, as reflected in table 1. This is a logical shift given that while the mature markets of Europe, North America, and Japan consist largely of replacement sales, these types of emerging regions can generate more new sales. For General Motors (GM), for example, 38 percent of all its vehicle sales took place in emerging markets in 2007.

It is notable that China has suddenly emerged as the fastest-growing automobile producer, surpassing Germany in 2006 and even the United States in 2008. As a result, Japan, China, and the United States are now the three leading nations in terms of automobile production: in 2008, Japan produced 16.4 percent (11.6 million units) of total world production, China produced 13.3 percent (9.3 million units), and the United States produced 12.3 percent (8.7 million units). Together, these three countries dominate world automobile production, accounting for roughly 42 percent of the global total.

At the same time, China is also the fastest-growing market for vehicles in the world. Sales of automobiles have grown sharply in recent years, surpassing those in Japan in 2006 and those in the United States in 2009, making China the world's largest auto market. In 2007, total vehicle sales jumped 21.8 percent to 8.8 million units—twice the number sold in 2003.[2] Despite the outbreak of the financial crisis, China's vehicle sales continued to grow in 2008, reaching 9.4 million units. By contrast, due to the huge impact of the financial crisis in 2008, vehicle sales in the United States dropped sharply, falling 18 percent from the previous year to 13.2 million units, while in Japan vehicle sales in 2008 were down 5 percent to 5.1 million units.[3]

Table 1. World automobile production, 2008

Country	Four-wheeled vehicles	
	Vehicles produced (thousands)	Share of world total (%)
Japan	11,564	16.4
China	9,345	13.3
United States	8,705	12.3
Germany	6,041	8.6
South Korea	3,807	5.4
Brazil	3,220	4.6
France	2,569	3.6
Spain	2,542	3.6
India	2,315	3.3
Mexico	2,191	3.1
Others	18,228	25.8
World Total	70,527	100.0

SOURCE: OICA (International Organization of Motor Vehicle Manufacturers), 2009.

NOTE: Includes passenger cars and commercial vehicles.

The automobile industry has emerged as the world's largest manufacturing industry. The automotive sector in Japan, for instance, is estimated to account for 22.1 percent of the country's exports (2007) and 7.9 percent of its employed workforce (2006).[4] It plays a similarly vital role in many countries in terms of investment, business volume, trade, and employment, and affects various social structures such as roads and travel. The wealth-creation effect of the industry has been extremely important for the industrial development of many countries. Historically, the automobile industry has survived for more than 100 years, transforming itself from craft production to mass production and now to lean production and networking.[5] The United States dominated car production technology from the earliest stages up to the middle of the 20th century, when European competitors became strong and started to compete with the US manufacturers. During the 1980s, the Japanese car industry emerged as a strong competitor as well. This triadic nature of the industry, however, is now changing as automakers operate production facilities on a global basis.

In recent years, there has been growing interest in the importance of network-based multinational corporations (MNCs) in the global economy. The process of globalization—the deepening integration of globalized capitalist economic activity encouraged by the rapid development of information technology and transportation—has been a defining feature of the contemporary international political economy. As in the past, a firm's competitiveness is the key determinant for its success in the market. A competitive strategy relates to researching and establishing a profitable and sustainable position in an industry.[6] But in a globalizing world, firms have more strategic options, and firms in many sectors have decided to source globally to enhance their competitiveness. This globalized sourcing strategy entails more complex factors that need to be taken into account, such as longer and more costly transportation, legal and regulatory import restrictions, and exchange rate and currency fluctuations. Firms that have decided on global sourcing must choose which country, which suppliers, and how to structure these relationships.

The manufacture of automobiles is now a very complex process with a number of unique features in its production system. An automobile is in general estimated to be composed of 20,000 to 30,000 separate parts, and not even the largest manufacturer can produce all of them. Thus, the automobile industry has been seen for a long time as essentially an assembly industry. Automakers have been seen as "assemblers" who fashion parts and components from many suppliers into completed cars. The leading automakers, however, do not just assemble parts but are also capable of designing and producing engines and platforms using high technology. Obtaining economies of scale to reduce costs is an important strategy for these automakers. Assembly plants require just-in-time deliveries from parts suppliers, and thus a spatial concentration is likely to emerge when economies of scale exist in the industry and transportation costs are low.[7] In such a situation, major parts and components suppliers have been faced with the decision to locate their plants near the core company. In addition, they have had to develop their capacity to produce major components, such as braking systems and front panels, as the diversification of automobile production has seen the assemblers pass on more responsibility to their suppliers.

Table 2. Automobile companies ranked by annual revenues, 2008

Rank in auto industry (in all industries)	Company	Country of headquarters	Revenues (US$ millions)
1 (10)	Toyota	Japan	204,352
2 (14)	Volkswagen	Germany	166,579
3 (18)	General Motors	United States	148,979
4 (19)	Ford	United States	146,277
5 (23)	Daimler	Germany	140,328
6 (51)	Honda	Japan	99,652
7 (64)	Fiat	Italy	86,914
8 (67)	Nissan	Japan	83,982
9 (75)	Peugeot	France	79,560
10 (78)	BMW	Germany	77,864
11 (87)	Hyundai	Korea	72,542

SOURCE: http://money.cnn.com/magazines/fortune/global500/2009/full_list.

Table 2 indicates the scale of globally competitive automobile producers. Although a number of independent small players do exist, the automobile industry is clearly dominated by a limited number of MNCs. In the automobile industry, economies of scale have always been a crucial factor, and as a result of global competition, automakers have attempted to create economies of scale by maximizing their capability, opting for mergers and acquisitions, or becoming subsidiaries of other firms. As a result, there are now a number of complex alliances and relationships among these firms.

This trend has also inevitably led to the consolidation of the parts and components suppliers. Although it is perhaps an oversimplification, the supply networks in the automobile industry can essentially be characterized as falling into three hierarchical tiers. The first-tier suppliers provide complex components to lead automakers, the second-tier suppliers produce parts for the assemblers or the first-tier suppliers, and the third-tier suppliers make more basic parts. Among such hierarchical tiers, the first-tier suppliers are involved in shared management with the lead automakers and play a key role in terms of innovation and best practices.[8] The first-tier suppliers have themselves become assemblers with research and development (R&D) and design expertise.

Some first-tier suppliers such as Bosch (Germany), Delphi (United States), and Denso (Japan) have emerged as large firms that are comparable in scale to the automakers themselves. For the automakers, technological developments have been made possible by the use of shared platforms between different car models, resulting in reduced production costs, including R&D. Another significant change is the development of module systems composed of multiple parts, which leads to a decrease in the overall number of parts to be assembled. Such technologies were originally developed in the electronics industry, but the automobile industry has also become increasingly dependent on such modular system–based architecture.

Due to global competition, assemblers require parts and components suppliers to deliver quickly (just in time), to deliver at a lower cost on a continuous basis, and to raise the quality of their components. Suppliers face pressure to relocate their component module manufacturing operations closer to the assembler in order to deliver on time. Thus, industrial agglomeration, which is the spatial clustering of similar or related industrial activities in a particular place and the collocation of firms engaged in a given industry, has become important in global business.[9]

Economic activity has made the subnational region the most significant site of competition. The firm's competitiveness in the age of globalization is now greatly affected by institutional settings, as the firm inevitably engages in politics, cultural practices, and social interactions in specific social settings. Political regimes at national and subnational levels directly or indirectly influence the firm's outcomes through regulations as well, although such regulatory institutional environments are constructed through practices and negotiations among participating actors. As national and subnational governments also pursue their respective economic goals, globalizing transnational operations increasingly promote interconnectedness and interdependence across different territorial regions. On the other hand, such networks attempt to take advantage of geographical differences in the distribution of factors of production and in state policies and increasingly influence the economies of specific regions and countries. Thus, an understanding of the complex network of relations among economies of scale, supplier networks, and territoriality in the automobile industry helps us to grasp the nature and dynamics of globalizing networks as well as their relationship to economic development in specific regions.

CHINA'S AUTOMOBILE INDUSTRY AND FOREIGN
DIRECT INVESTMENT

The history of the Chinese automobile industry began when the first auto factory was founded in the 1950s in the city of Changchun in northeastern China with the technological support of a Chinese ally, the Soviet Union. In 1975, a second auto factory, which focused on truck manufacturing, was established in Hubei Province. During the era of the "centrally planned economy" in China, the production of automobiles was under the control of the central government. Strategic concerns meant that factories were located in remote regions that Chinese leaders—especially Chairman Mao—thought would be safe from foreign attack. In the pre-reform period, efficiency of production was not a primary objective and economies of scale were not taken into account. Between 1953 and 1978, a total of 53 small-scale automakers and 166 auto parts producers were set up under the centrally planned economy, and that can be seen as the origin of structural problems such as the fragmentation of production sites and the small scale of production.

China's technological level was therefore very low until the introduction of economic reforms in the late 1970s. Chinese leaders recognized that the main problems with Chinese industry were outdated technology, dispersed production, and low quality. In 1981, the Chinese auto industry produced only 176,000 four-wheeled vehicles, in contrast to the Japanese auto industry, which produced 11 million vehicles.[10] China's seventh Five-Year Plan (1986–1990) identified the automobile industry as a "pillar industry" and adopted an import-substituting strategy based on the introduction of technology from foreign partners in joint ventures and the start of complete knockdown (CKD) assembly. The plan clearly focused on the development of the passenger car as a core of the auto industry, and the objective was to consolidate production and upgrade technological capabilities through the creation of linkages with foreign auto companies.

In developing its industries, nothing was more important than China's capacity to utilize foreign direct investment (FDI). During the 1990s, China received more FDI than any other developing country. In 2007, foreign investment in China totaled almost US$74.76 billion (utilized FDI), and 54.7 percent of that was invested in the manufacturing industry.[11] FDI has played a critical role in China's economic performance, but it is important to recognize the various motives of those investing in China. Much of the manufacturing FDI is aimed at cutting the investor's production costs by escaping rising costs at home. China is a destination offering low-cost labor and less strict regulations, and most of its finished products are exported. In fact, foreign firms account for almost 60 percent of China's exports. Since economic reform began in the late 1970s, the Chinese government has also used a unique initiative to attract this type of cost-cutting FDI, namely the processing trade arrangement (PTA), a mechanism that alleviates customs or duties on materials and components imported into China for assemblage and export as finished products. Roughly half of China's foreign trade now involves PTAs.[12]

In addition to cost cutting, another objective of automobile-related FDI in China is to gain market access to 1.3 billion potential consumers.[13] In the 1980s, the Chinese market was highly restricted through the regulation of managerial control, and access to the domestic market was therefore difficult for foreign firms. In the early 1990s, the investment environment improved and foreign investors were granted greater access to the domestic market, although the Chinese government has carefully managed to control FDI. MNCs from Europe, the United States, Japan, and South Korea began to play a significant role in the Chinese economy. Giant foreign automakers then expanded the scale of their businesses in China, and a huge amount of FDI poured into the Chinese automobile industry, greatly contributing to its economic success. The growth in this sector has created desirable and stable jobs for Chinese workers and benefited the wider economy, in particular through spillover into the parts and components sector.

At the same time that FDI has spurred production, China's domestic demand for cars has continued to grow thanks to the support of government policies, the increasing purchasing power of individuals, and the depreciation of car prices under intensifying competition as a result of China's entry into the World Trade Organization (WTO). In fact, since WTO accession in 2001, the Chinese automobile industry has grown at an average annual rate of 20 percent. Table 3 shows the top 10 passenger-car companies in terms of sales in China in 2007 and 2008. Total sales of passenger cars reached 6.8 million units in 2008, up 7.3 percent from the previous year, while sales of commercial vehicles reached 2.6 million in 2008—also up 5 percent.[14]

China was not able to avoid the global economic downturn of 2008, so the rapid pace of growth has slowed. However, China has already become a critical market for foreign automakers. For example, sales by Volkswagen (VW) of almost 1 million units in China in 2008 made it the top-selling passenger-car maker in China and ensured that the Chinese market surpassed VW's home market of Germany.

Table 3. Top passenger-car companies in China by units sold

Rank	Company	Units sold 2008	Units sold 2007	Change in rank from 2007
1	First Auto Works (FAW)–Volkswagen	498,953	459,359	↑
2	Shanghai Volkswagen	490,087	436,343	↑
3	Shanghai General Motors	432,001	500,308	↓
4	FAW Toyota	366,045	281,952	↑
5	Chery	356,093	381,000	↓
6	Dongfeng Motor Co. (Nissan)	350,520	272,915	↑
7	Guangzhou Honda	305,998	295,000	↓
8	Beijing Hyundai	294,504	231,137	→
9	Geely	221,823	219,512	→
10	ChangAn Ford	204,674	217,000	→

SOURCE: Compiled from the Auto Channel and *Nihon Keizai Shimbun*, "Chugokushijo gensokude meian," January 27, 2009.

Figure 1. Auto production and sales in China (millions of units)

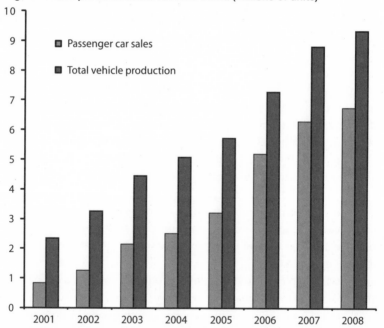

SOURCE: Compiled from Honda Motor website (http://www.honda.co.jp/investors/annualreport/); *CJH (Chugoku joho handobukku)*, 2007 ed. (Tokyo: Sososha, 2007); and Fourin, *Sekai jidosha tokei nenkan* [World automobile statistics yearbook 2009] (Nagoya: Fourin, 2009).

As shown in figure 1, both auto sales and production in China have been growing rapidly. However, one fact that stands out among the 2008 sales figures for China is that only 2 of the top 10 companies are local Chinese manufacturers (Chery and Geely), while the rest are joint venture enterprises allied with European, American, Japanese, and Korean MNCs. While only 510,000 passenger cars and commercial vehicles were produced in China in 1990, production has since soared, reaching 2.07 million in 2000 and 9.34 million in 2008. This is clearly linked to the continued expansion by the foreign automobile industry of its production capability in China. By 2008, VW was operating 11 production sites, GM had 9, and Toyota had 6 sites producing completed cars and another 10 for manufacturing parts.

The Chinese Central Government, Local Governments, and Foreign Automobile Companies

It was VW that first brought radical technological changes to the Chinese automobile industry. VW started to negotiate with the Shanghai municipal government in 1978, when China initially announced economic reform. In October 1984, VW established a joint venture with the Shanghai Automotive Industry Corporation (SAIC), called Shanghai VW, and started to produce a passenger car named the Santana. The SAIC was part of the Shanghai local government bureaucracy; it was 75 percent owned by the Shanghai municipal government and the rest was owned by the Shanghai International Trust and Investment Company. The Shanghai municipal government also focused on the auto sector as having the potential to spur industrial upgrading and local development. The increase of local content rate in the production of the Santana was the primary interest of the SAIC. On the other hand, VW's initial concern was not rapid localization but rather to build a safe and high-quality product that was consistent with foreign standards.

VW, however, received full support (in the form of what is known as "pioneer status") from both the central and municipal governments. The central government offered tax advantages and preferential treatment in terms of foreign currency and the supply of materials. For its part, the Shanghai municipal government offered many supportive institutional measures. In 1986, for example, the Shanghai municipal government formed the Santana Localization Small Group under the leadership of the Shanghai

Economic Commission, and then established the Automobile Industry Leading Small Group in 1987, which was directly under the control of the mayor's office. Along with such reforms of its bureaucratic apparatus, the municipal government gave specific advice concerning equipment and technology to local parts suppliers and even provided necessary financial backing. The SAIC assisted the development of supply firms through investments, and Shanghai VW worked to strengthen interfirm relationships with local parts makers as well. VW also provided technical assistance and guidance for local partners.

Although initial localization efforts were not successful, efforts to upgrade local supply companies resulted in a steady rise in local content rates; the Santana's domestic content increased from 2.7 percent in 1987 to 92.9 percent in 1997. Moreover, by 1997 almost 90 percent by value of that local content was produced within the municipality of Shanghai.[15] With the strong support of then Mayor Zhu Rongji (who later became the country's premier), Santanas were purchased by the government, state-owned enterprises, and state-owned taxi companies. As a result, Shanghai VW's share of the auto market in China exceeded 50 percent by 1996. Thus, Shanghai VW's success derives from various factors, including favorable treatment through the tax system, foreign currency supplies, the central government's supply chain facilitation, and clear communication between the firm and various levels of government.

Different policy targets often bring about different management decisions at the local level. Central governments have to consider the entire national economy, whereas local governments only focus on their own jurisdiction. From the view of the central government, VW's project required approval at the highest political level. In the 1970s, the central government started to devolve economic autonomy, including automobile production, to local governments. Decentralization has been the main feature of China's economic reform, and fiscal decentralization was one of the fundamental factors that have affected central-local economic relations. The localities increased incentives to promote local economic development in order to try to maximize local revenue. Firms were central factors in the development of local industry, and so under the decentralization process, local governments were required to help them.

However, there was no single dominant approach to development at the local level, which instead formed a "mosaic" of local patterns within a national framework.[16] When considering the abilities of Chinese local governments, it is important to look at intergovernmental relations in the field of economic policy. Relations between the central and local governments depend largely on ad hoc measures and on bargaining power, which are often tied to individuals and party politics. In the case of Shanghai VW, the former municipal mayor, Zhu Rongji, who actively supported the project from its start, rose to the national level in 1991, when he became vice premier. This gave Shanghai VW a powerful voice at a high central political level, thereby facilitating the creation by Shanghai VW of cooperative alliances with the Bank of China and the China National Automotive Industrial Corporation.[17] Zhu's support was also seen as key to increasing Shanghai VW's steel quota to meet the company's needs.

As part of its economic reforms, the Chinese government adopted a protective strategy for the domestic auto industry by controlling foreign automakers, regulating finished car imports, and restricting the portion of ownership of foreign capital automakers to 50 percent or less. The central government proposed the "Big Three, Little Three" scheme in 1988. First Auto Works (FAW)-VW, Dongfeng Peugeot Citroën Automobile, and Shanghai VW were selected as the "big three," which meant that they fell under the auspices of the central government. Beijing Jeep (now part of Beijing Benz-DaimlerChrysler Automotive), Guangzhou Peugeot, and the Tianjin Automotive Industrial Corp.–Daihatsu were designated as the "little three" and were therefore under the control of local governments. This reflected the policies of the central government, which restricted entry into the passenger car market by using regulatory control over FDI and allocated car production to selected manufacturers. The 1994 automobile industry policy aimed to achieve economies of scale and promote production efficiency, as well as to protect the automobile market with high trade tariffs and tight entry controls. Indeed, during the 1990s, China's automobile import tariffs were between 100 and 220 percent, which effectively prevented competition from foreign automobile makers.[18]

However, in the 10th Five-Year Plan (2001–2005), which responded to China's accession to the WTO, the central government announced the reduction of tariffs, the relaxation of import restrictions, and the deregulation of types and models of car products that could be produced in China. In 2004, the government then announced its New Automobile Industrial Development Policy, which opened up distribution and retail and made it possible for foreign automakers to build a vertically integrated distribution system. Furthermore, in 2005, the central government announced the need for approval by the producer when dealers sell vehicles. These policies are oriented toward the construction of a distribution system led by the producers from developed countries.

Then, in 2006, the central government ratified the 11th Five-Year Plan (2006–2010), which set targets for the scale of vehicle sales and production in China at under 10 million units and aimed to improve the fuel efficiency of vehicles. Growing attention to global warming and excessive consumption of energy forced the government to adopt policies geared toward controlling the sharp expansion of the automobile industry. In January 2009, for example, the central government reduced the purchase tax for small cars, which immediately affected the sales performance of automakers in China.

China's industrial policy has clearly vacillated, despite the central government's efforts to consistently promote the expansion of the automobile industry. As Eric Thun has pointed out, the central government has usually defined "strategic" according to political rather than economic priorities, resulting in the direction of financial resources to the least competitive companies out of consideration for political consequences.[19] One of the features of the Chinese automotive industry is that there are a large number of firms with small-scale production, resulting in low productivity.[20] Indeed, the number of companies producing automobiles in China actually increased from 127 in 1999 to 144 in 2004. During the same period, the number of foreign-affiliated firms increased from 21 to 48.[21] It seems that every municipality wants to have an auto manufacturing industry within its own jurisdiction. This is partly attributable to decentralization, but it also relates to the pre-reform strategic structure that resulted in hundreds of auto manufacturing sites. With strong local government support—such as the procurement of completed vehicles by the local government—a number of small carmakers can continue to survive despite lacking the capability to produce engines on their own.

Under such conditions, the Chinese automobile industry developed a uniquely diversified structure composed of vertically integrated state-owned large firms and vertically disintegrated small- and medium-sized local companies.[22] China's unique vertical disintegration has further encouraged the development of modular types of assembly, such as engines trading, which has led to the growth of Chinese automakers such as Chery that are not joint ventures and that are not capable of producing engines on their own. However, Chery has been actively involved in procuring auto parts from foreign suppliers such as Delphi, Federal-Mogul, GKN, and TRW Automotive. Moving in the other direction, the Japanese brand Mitsubishi established an engine plant in China in 1997. Since it was not allowed to produce a finished product, Mitsubishi has played a key role in supplying engines for local Chinese automakers. All the same, despite its rapid development, the Chinese automobile industry has not yet resolved certain structural problems, such as the large number of small or even tiny companies, fragmentation of production sites, low levels of technology (and hence dependence on foreign technology), and small scales of production. Thus, the production networks in the Chinese automobile industry have not yet been well established.

GM and Ford are the world's longest established transnational automobile producers and were already involved in China in the early 20th century. After the Communist revolution, however, both ceased car exports to China and refrained from investing there. The US automakers were not involved in Chinese joint ventures until the mid-1990s. Ford, the third largest automobile company in the world, gained a local foothold in 1995 when it purchased a stake in the Jiangling Motors Corporation. Two years later, GM, the world's largest automaker at that time, entered China by forming a joint venture with the SAIC, which had already formed its first joint venture with VW.

Thanks to the experience of the Shanghai VW joint venture, the SAIC already had a reputation as the most profitable Chinese automobile company. GM actively started to invest in China, forming three other joint ventures across the country during the 1990s. The Chinese government required that GM establish a technical center with the SAIC. GM was the first foreign company to do so, creating what is called the Pan Asia Technical Automotive Center (PATAC). The primary activity of PATAC has been the redesign of GM models for the Chinese market, which plays a central role in strengthening local design skills. Shanghai GM was the flagship of GM's operations in China, starting production of the Buick with 47 percent of its parts made by local Chinese suppliers.[23]

GM has made an effort to modify and upgrade its vehicles to produce better cars with higher performance. It has also brought in more modern technology than other US investors. Its aggressive commitment stemmed from the lessons of previous foreign entrants in the Chinese automobile industry. For example, VW kept producing the same older models for a long time and therefore began to lose market share. By 2000, GM had increased its localization rate to 60 percent for the Buick sedan, and by 2006 it was selling more Buicks in China than it was in the United States. In 2007, GM's total vehicle sales in China, including commercial vehicles, reached 1 million units, which made it the top-selling firm in the Chinese market, ahead of VW and its Japanese rivals. It had achieved a surprising tenfold increase in Chinese vehicle sales from 2002 to 2007.

GM has also maintained cooperative relations with the Chinese authorities. In 2008, GM announced the construction of its Asia Pacific headquarters and an R&D center in Shanghai to respond to the government's desire to promote environmentally friendly vehicles. GM also jointly established a research institute with Shanghai Jiao Tong University that focuses on R&D and technical training. In 2008, GM announced the establishment of the China Automotive Energy Research Center, to be run jointly with Tsinghua University in Beijing. GM offered US$5 million for the center to carry out R&D with the university and the Chinese government to promote energy efficiency within the automobile industry.

THE JAPANESE AUTOMOBILE INDUSTRY IN CHINA

Compared with European automakers, who entered the Chinese market as early as the 1980s, Japanese automakers are latecomers to car production in China, but in recent years their presence has grown rapidly. In the 1980s, the major Japanese auto companies preferred to earn profits from assembled vehicle sales to China. In addition, increasing trade frictions with the United States during that decade were seen as a more pressing issue by Japan. As a result, the Japanese automobile industry chose not to enter China at that time, with the exception of a few mid-sized automakers.

That changed, however, in the late 1990s. With China's imminent accession to the WTO, along with the arrival of foreign automakers, the level of competition in China increased dramatically. Competition among local governments became intense as well, as they were under great pressure to maximize their capabilities. It was at this time that Guangzhou appeared as a new competitor for Shanghai. Guangzhou is the capital of Guangdong Province in the southern part of China, an economically backward area where agricultural production predominated until the beginning of economic reform. The Guangzhou automobile industry was stagnant until the late 1990s, when Honda began local operations in 1999, followed by Nissan in 2003 and Toyota in 2006. With the expansion of production capacity, Guangzhou alone produced 555,200 units in 2006. It is now emerging as a major automobile production base with the development of an industrial cluster of associated parts and components manufacturers.

Why did Guangzhou's automobile industry grow so rapidly through industrial agglomeration? Traditionally, automobile industry agglomeration in China has been focused in the cities of Shanghai and Tianjing, as well as in Hubei Province, but none existed in the southern part of China. Guangzhou is a city with a population of nearly 11 million. Located 1,887 kilometers to the south of Beijing, Guangzhou's location has always been ideal for international links and has also enabled the city to enjoy some freedom from Beijing's scrutiny. The central government granted Guangzhou the freedom to pursue experimental reform policies without interference, but in exchange, the city could not seek resources from the central government.

In 1986, at almost the same time as the start of the Shanghai VW operation, the Guangzhou Peugeot Automobile Corporation was established in the form of a joint venture. The French automaker's share was 22 percent, which meant that it did not have overall control. Although Guangzhou Peugeot's production initially increased, it produced old models and its sales performance steadily declined. Furthermore, the Tiananmen Square Incident in 1989 soured relations between China and France. Another impediment was that, in contrast to Shanghai VW, the municipal government did not channel investment capital into supply companies. Peugeot finally decided to withdraw completely in 1997. In the case of Guangzhou Peugeot, technological cooperation with parts suppliers did not materialize and technological assistance was not provided to the local Guangzhou enterprise. Furthermore, the Guangzhou municipal government did not play a large role in the support of local content rates.[24] In 1997, the Guangdong provincial government finally made the decision that the automotive industry was no longer a target industry for government support.[25] Some assert that, in comparison with the automotive industry in other parts of China, Guangzhou did not know how to build an organizational structure that was conducive to developing the manufacturing capability of a supply network.[26] The capability (or lack thereof) of the local government thus produced a very different result as compared with that of Shanghai.

After Peugeot's withdrawal, Honda arrived as a new pioneer of the automobile industry in Guangzhou. While the Guangdong and Guangzhou governments had given up on the development of an automobile industry, they regained the opportunity to develop the industry after Guangzhou Honda, a joint venture between Guangzhou Automobile Group and Honda, started production in 1998. For foreign companies, a joint venture partner has to be found among a limited number of existing local enterprises. Honda, however, had some advantages because of its Chinese motorcycle business, which it had established in 1981. Honda was able to utilize this experience and extend it to the production of parts for cars. The Guangzhou municipal government persuaded Honda to invest in China and repeatedly announced its strong support for Honda in order not to repeat its past mistakes. Guangzhou Honda was thus established to produce a complete car and Dongfeng Honda was established to supply engines.

Limitations on production capacity at Chinese locations often occur due to a shortage of roads, railways, electrical power, and other infrastructure issues, as well as problems connected to the tax system and to a lack of Japanese interpreters. The Guangzhou municipal government has made a great effort to work with Honda to solve these types of problems. As one example, it constructed a railway system that enables Honda to ship its finished vehicles by rail. This support made it possible for Honda to begin car production in China earlier than its Japanese rivals.

In addition, although Honda realized that the factories that had been established by Guangzhou Peugeot did not fit their requirements exactly, they were still able to utilize those factories, equipment, and workers, thereby reducing their initial investment costs. When Guangzhou Honda started production, it required its Japanese parts suppliers to move to Guangzhou too, in order to maintain quality and raise the local content rate. Automakers may undertake a full model change every four to five years but will make minor cosmetic changes more frequently in order to maintain the interest of the market. As such, automakers, parts companies, designers, and machine manufacturers need to develop and maintain a relationship of trust through enhanced communication and collaborative learning. In particular, Japanese automakers adopt a single-sourcing system in which they offer a special deal to parts manufacturers involved in the development of a new model, and they give similar priority to suppliers that build plants near the company's overseas factories.[27]

The localization policy of the Chinese government is crucial in affecting the decisions of foreign investors. Even after accession to the WTO, the Chinese government imposed high tariffs on the import of finished cars and raised nontariff barriers, hence encouraging more parts suppliers to build plants in China. At the municipal level as well, the Guangzhou government aimed to develop the automobile industry as a pillar of that city's industrialization policy.[28] In order to encourage auto industry agglomeration, local government support is essential, particularly in terms of policies on infrastructure, labor, customs, the legal system, financial services, and medical services. Some of the notable features of Guangzhou's industrial policy for automobile agglomeration included the following: (1) the establishment and management of six industrial zones in Guangzhou and surrounding cities; (2) support for the Guangzhou Automobile Industry Group (established in 2000 through a merger of the Guangzhou Automobile Group and the

Guangzhou Motors Group), which now operates 14 joint ventures including Guangzhou Honda, Guangzhou Toyota, and Guangzhou Automobile Group Component; and (3) the active promotion of joint ventures between state-owned firms and foreign firms by giving foreign investors preferential tax treatment and efficient, one-stop service at government offices.[29]

As in the case of Shanghai, the role of individual local government leaders has also proved to be important. The position of mayor in China is often seen as a steppingstone to provincial leadership or a high position in the central government, and the mayor of Guangzhou, Zhang Guangning, who is known as the "automobile mayor," has made a great effort to attract foreign investment. With its industrial policies and strong leadership, the Guangzhou government has actively promoted the development of infrastructure, as seen in the opening of a new Guangzhou international airport in 2004.

These are the types of local policies that facilitated the creation of Guangzhou Honda, whose first factory was established in the Guangzhou Economic and Technological Development Zone in 1998, and whose second factory was constructed in the Zengcheng Industrial Zone in 2005. As a result, from 2001 to 2005, most of Honda's first-, second-, and third-tier suppliers moved into Guangzhou.[30] Meanwhile, all the key components companies established in Guangzhou to support Toyota were wholly Japanese owned.[31] As a result, 156 Japanese automobile components companies had already been established in Guangdong by 2005, and of those, 84 were established in Guangzhou. Thus, the Guangzhou municipal government has been a key player in encouraging local political and economic institutions to implement an industrial agglomeration policy, and as a result, the Japanese automobile industry has been allowed to transplant its production system from Japan.

The efforts made by the local government can also be seen in the case of Dongfeng Motor Company (Nissan), a joint venture between Dongfeng Motor Corporation and Nissan in the Huadu District of Guangzhou. In 2004, Dongfeng Motor Company (Nissan) started to operate factories producing vehicles and engines as well as an R&D center. The Huadu District government planned to create an automotive cluster known as Huadu Auto City next to the new international airport. It has been very supportive in offering a stable electrical supply and building infrastructure such as roads, railways, and a port. The staff of Huadu Auto City have actively worked to attract FDI and have negotiated to gain approval from the local government. They have also visited Japanese companies to explain the local business environment and available support systems.[32] Although the fact that parent companies require their parts suppliers to build overseas plants is obviously a powerful factor, the parent company is not necessarily responsible for the success of the parts supplier's business activities once they decide to invest in a foreign site. The role of the local government in providing support and undertaking other measures is therefore crucial. Guangdong's geographical proximity to Hong Kong, the increasing presence of the Japanese automobile industry (led by Guangzhou Honda's operations), the range of support from local governments, and the reorganization of production were all undoubtedly elements that attracted Nissan, and this has led its related parts and components manufacturers to follow in turn.

AUTOMOBILE PRODUCTION NETWORKS ACROSS REGIONS

China has recently entered the automobile export market. Compared with its figures for sales and production, China's auto exports and imports are relatively small, but the rate of exports of vehicles from China has grown sharply, as reflected in figure 2. The majority of exported vehicles are light trucks and commercial vehicles, almost all of which are shipped to Russia or to developing countries in Asia, the Middle East, and Africa. The Chinese automobile industry has targeted low-cost vehicles at emerging economies where the automobile industry has not yet matured. China has also rapidly increased its vehicle exports, reaching 658,670 units in 2008.[33]

Figure 2. China's vehicle imports and exports (thousands of units)

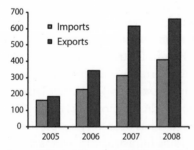

SOURCE: Fourin China Auto Weekly (2008) and Fourin (2009).

Table 4. China's top trade partners for completed vehicles by units sold, 2007

Rank	Import source	Export destination
1	Japan	Russia
2	Germany	Syria
3	South Korea	Ukraine
4	US	South Africa
5	UK	Vietnam
6	Slovakia	Algeria
7	Sweden	Iran
8	Mexico	Venezuela
9	Austria	UK
10	France	Kazakhstan

SOURCE: Fourin China Auto Weekly (2008).

The sharp growth is due mostly to local Chinese brands such as Chery, Geely, and ChangAn. On the other hand, China imported 408,781 units in 2008—mostly high-quality passenger cars from developed countries, with Japan being the most common source. The average price of China's vehicle imports was three times the average price per unit of its export vehicles.

Foreign automakers are not only seeking markets in China but are also pursuing opportunities to manufacture automobiles in China for export. This strategy often coincides with the interests of the local governments. The 2005–2010 Guangdong Province Automobile Industrial Development Plan envisions an enlargement of the scale of car production to strengthen the competitiveness of the automobile industry, with a central focus on Guangzhou Honda and Dongfeng Motor Group Company. In particular, it encourages Honda's worldwide export of small cars and aims to develop a national-level export base.[34] Until recently, light trucks were the main automobile export from China. In 2003, however, Honda established a new factory in a joint venture with Guangzhou Motor and Dongfeng Motor Group Company. This was the first exclusively export-focused factory approved by the Chinese government, and Honda was allowed to hold an exceptional 65 percent ownership position. In 2005, Honda started to produce a small car to export to Europe (the model is sold under the brand name Jazz in Europe and as Fit in Japan, China, and the Americas). It is estimated that almost 70 to 80 percent of Jazz units sold in Europe are made in China.[35]

Of the business strategies needed to operate overseas production in the automobile industry, management know-how for local procurement is especially important. Japanese automakers in China have gradually increased local procurement rates in order to reduce the costs of taxation and transportation. Guangzhou Honda's local procurement rate in June 2004 was 74 percent for the Accord and 87 percent for the Fit. Almost 80 percent of local procurement was supplied by Japanese companies with operations in China, 10 percent from local Chinese companies, and the rest from Thai and Malaysian companies in China.[36] In early 2008, the new Accord achieved approximately 85 percent local procurement.[37] In 2005, Dongfeng Motor (Nissan) purchased 67 percent of its parts from companies located in southern China, including Guangzhou.[38] Since Japanese parts suppliers moved into the Guangzhou area, the local content rate has steadily risen.

However, some high-performance components such as transmissions and antilock brake systems still have to be imported from Japan. As a result, nearly 90 percent of Guangdong's automotive components imports are from Japan. Japan's automobile parts and components trade has continued to increase from 3.1 percent of its total foreign trade in 1998 to 14 percent in 2006.[39] China's auto industry as a whole relies heavily on auto parts imports, resulting in a huge deficit with Japan, Germany, the United States, and South Korea. In fact, in 2007, 80 percent of China's auto parts imports came from these four countries, with Japan as the largest source, representing 34 percent of the national total in 2007. On the other hand, technological development has now made it possible for Toyota to supply engines produced in Guangzhou to its factories in Japan.

The concentration of the Japanese automobile industry has even started to affect the trade and industrial structure of Guangdong. In 2000, the automobile industry accounted for only 1.8 percent of Guangdong's total industrial output, but by 2007, it had grown to 4.1 percent and was the province's fastest growing major industry. Passenger car production in Guangdong even overtook that of Shanghai in the second half of 2008, making it the highest producing province in the country.[40]

Table 5. US auto parts exports and imports

Export destinations (percent of US exports)

	2000	2001	2002	2003	2004	2005	2006	2007	2008
NAFTA	78.5	77.1	78.4	78.0	78.3	77.5	75.9	75.2	72.9
Japan	4.1	4.0	4.6	4.2	2.9	2.6	3.0	2.8	2.7
China	0.4	0.5	0.7	1.1	1.2	1.1	1.4	1.8	1.6
Germany	1.8	2.2	1.9	2.1	2.4	2.5	2.7	2.6	3.0
South Korea	0.8	0.7	0.7	0.6	0.9	1.0	1.0	1.0	0.7

Import sources (percent of US imports)

	2000	2001	2002	2003	2004	2005	2006	2007	2008
NAFTA	54.2	54.2	54.0	53.2	51.9	50.4	49.2	48.8	46.1
Japan	21.7	21.0	19.5	18.5	18.6	17.8	16.2	14.4	14.9
China	2.4	2.8	3.2	3.7	4.7	5.9	7.3	8.6	10.0
Germany	5.8	6.0	6.3	7.3	7.4	7.3	7.5	8.3	8.2
South Korea	1.6	1.8	2.0	2.1	2.2	2.9	3.9	4.0	4.3

SOURCE: Compiled from the US Department of Commerce, US Automotive Trade Data, 1998–2009.

China's auto producers still play a relatively minor role in the completed auto trade data; however, they have already started to play a significant role in the auto parts trade. Table 5 shows the trend of auto parts imports in the United States. According to the figures, the proportion of imports from NAFTA countries, which were major auto parts supplier to the United States, continued to decline from 54.2 percent to 46.1 percent. Much of the rest came from Japan, Germany, and, notably, China. NAFTA countries are also the major destinations for US auto parts exports, accounting for more than 75 percent of total exports. During this period, however, table 5 clearly shows that China has steadily increased its share among major auto parts exporters to the United States. The volume of China's auto parts exports to the United States jumped more than fivefold between 2000 and 2008, climbing from us$1.6 billion to us$9.0 billion.[41] As a result, China is now the fourth largest auto parts exporter to the United States, surpassing Germany. Behind this trend is the fact that a number of US auto parts suppliers have begun to produce in China, and the major US assemblers are now procuring auto parts from their factories in China. For example, GM announced that it expected to increase its original equipment parts purchases from China from us$200 million in 2003 to us$10 billion in 2009.[42]

This increased outsourcing of projects to China is likely to lead to a decline of auto parts production in the United States as well as subsequent job cuts. Indeed, the downward cost pressures seem to be directly affecting the wages of workers in US auto parts firms. According to research undertaken by McKinsey & Company, auto parts produced in China cost approximately 20–30 percent less than similar parts produced in the United States.[43] On the other hand, China's sheer distance from the United States may lead to higher transportation costs—especially given rising oil prices—and limit China's role as a supplier, in particular due to pressures associated with the just-in-time system of production. The situation was further complicated when the WTO Dispute Settlement Body decided in February 2008 that China needed to lift its restrictions on auto parts imports. This was seen as a way to encourage auto parts exports to China. All the same, the rapid growth of Chinese auto parts manufacturers is likely to have an important impact on the US auto parts industry.

Globalizing production networks in the automobile industry have further encouraged complicated outsourcing arrangements that involve all three countries—China, Japan, and the United States. In March 2008 a Japanese company, Mitsubishi Motors, announced a plan to export cars from its production base in the United States for sale in China. The decline of Japan's share of auto exports to the United States, as represented in table 5, does not translate into a decline of the total Japanese auto and parts industry worldwide. Rather, the Japanese automobile industry has already played a significant role in China-US relations, not only through the auto parts trade but also through its role in the completed car trade using either China or the United States as a production base for sales to the other side.

More significantly, the Chinese automobile industry has already advanced in overseas automobile sales and production. By 2008, Chery had already begun knockdown assembly at two overseas sites in Uruguay and Russia and, furthermore, had licensed technology to overseas partners in Iran, Russia, Egypt, Ukraine, and Indonesia.[44] Despite the remaining uncertainty over the global automobile industry, the recent expansion of China's auto parts exports demonstrates the strong demand for the Chinese automobile industry, and it seems we will see the continued expansion of auto trade between China, Japan, and the United States.

Conclusion

This chapter has sought to explore and explain the key components and characteristics of the rise of the Chinese automobile industry with particular reference to the role of cross-border production. China's emergence as a global automobile manufacturer has corresponded to the shift of global production networks, and these help shape the relations among China, Japan, and the United States. Thus, it is worth asking what the case of automobile manufacturing can tell us more broadly about the economic dynamics shaping trilateral relations.

First, there is a consensus among observers, both in academia and in the automobile industry, that China is becoming a global automobile player and a critical market for global automakers. This is bound to have important implications for trilateral economic relations. For the time being, Chinese exporters have focused on producing low-cost vehicles for emerging markets, but moves to become more competitive in the export of higher-quality vehicles can add to trade tensions among the three countries. Also, the impact of outsourcing to China in the auto parts industry has already contributed to job losses in the United States. These dynamics bear watching, although the integration of China-Japan-US relations and the fact that American and Japanese firms are likely to profit from Chinese exports means that we need to be careful to avoid characterizing trade competition among the three countries as a zero-sum game.

Second, the way in which networks have developed in the Chinese automobile industry illustrates the degree and nature of the growing interdependence among China, Japan, and the United States. This has been driven from the bottom up by firms and by the dynamics of global sourcing rather than by governments. The transformation of production networks is progressively deepening the links among the Chinese, Japanese, and US economies, even though there are few clear formal institutional frameworks among the three countries. Notably, these closer linkages have not necessarily benefited one country to the detriment of another. For example, despite its late entry into China, GM has succeeded in penetrating the Chinese automobile market. The Japanese automobile industry, an even later entrant, is emerging as a strong competitor by benefiting from a favorable business environment created with the support of local governments.

China's impact on the auto parts trade as a result of globalizing production networks is already evident. Yet China's technological dependence on the major American, Japanese, and European manufacturers; its small scale of production; and the large number of very small companies active domestically have continued to show that China has not yet achieved its political goal of building a consolidated automobile industry and producing a national champion. The cross-border production networks led by auto-related FDI have greatly contributed to the development of production networks in the Chinese automobile industry and are therefore likely to underpin the future development of the industry. In reality, the further development of the Chinese automobile industry depends on cooperative and competitive production-network relations across regions within China, as well as with Japan and the United States and globally.

Third, one intuitive but often overlooked point is that it is not just state actors that are important in trilateral relations but also local governments and the private sector. Therefore, it is important to consider not just state-to-state dynamics in analyzing China-Japan-US relations but also the dynamics of local-national-global relations. As a result of global competition, the strategies of economic actors are more diverse and different levels of government have reacted in different ways according to their particular capabilities and priorities.

In the case of the Chinese automobile industry, the dynamics of local-national-global relations involve looser processes of influencing and negotiating with a range of public- and private-sector actors to achieve desired goals. Economic decentralization has been a primary characteristic of China's economic reform; however, despite some weakening of central power, the state continues to be a key determinant in selecting major players, regulating investment, and carefully controlling interactions with the world economy.

On the other hand, the role of state actors has been changing in response to global competition, and local governments have used their increased autonomy and power to encourage foreign investment as a driving force for regional economic development. It is clear that local governments are increasingly becoming key agents of networking and are thereby affecting local industrial transformation. There are huge regional variations in China, and as seen in the case of Shanghai and Guangzhou, it is important to note that there are institutional differences between local governments, as well as different policies and different capacities to put in place the types of institutional arrangements needed to support foreign firms and attract foreign investment. Related to this is the fact that the leadership of local governments is closely linked to the national political structure, which gives leaders important incentives to improve local institutional characteristics in response to the global economic environment.

The cases of the US and Japanese automobile industries in Shanghai and Guangzhou demonstrate the increasingly critical role of place- and industry-specific institutional settings and show that there is no single approach to development. The strategic industrial policies implemented by the central and local governments have created an opportunity for both the US and Japanese automobile industries to set up production sites and to exploit China's emerging market. With the strong support of the Guangzhou municipal government, Japanese firms have been allowed to transplant their production systems with less interference from the central government. Guangzhou has exploited its comparative advantage vis-à-vis Shanghai and provided the ideal base for the Japanese automobile industry. The concentration of Japan-related parts suppliers has built a huge production capacity in Guangzhou, making it a competitive automobile manufacturing city.

Finally, the dynamics that are seen in the development of the automobile industry—such as increasingly intertwined cross-border production networks and the growing influence of subnational and private-sector actors—will also affect how China, Japan, and the United States deal with some of the broader policy challenges they face. One example is the issue of energy and the environment. The improvement of energy efficiency is the most urgent and critical issue for sustainable development of the automobile industry, and there are great opportunities for China, Japan, and the United States to promote technological cooperation and take trilateral action on regulations and other institutional factors related to the environment. The transfer of technologies to improve the energy efficiency of manufacturers and to make automobiles more fuel efficient, especially in a rapidly growing consumer market such as China, should be a major component of trilateral cooperation on climate change. However, the case of the automobile industry demonstrates how complex the challenges of making progress really are, even on issues where the three clearly share interests. Any meaningful actions to improve energy efficiency in the automobile sector will require not just the full participation of the three national governments but also local governments, and any policies need to be crafted in such a way as to enlist the private sectors in the three countries.

Overall, empirical analysis reveals that the trilateral China-Japan-US economic dynamics are more complex and involve a more diverse set of actors than many observers initially assume. Production networks in the three countries have become increasingly integrated and the economies are much more interconnected than even a decade ago. This means that policymakers focusing on China-Japan, Japan-US, or US-China relations need to consider not only trilateral state-to-state relations but also the dynamics among the various overlapping networks of national government, local government, and private-sector actors in the three countries if they are to forge effective policy responses.

Notes

1. OICA (International Organization of Motor Vehicle Manufacturers), "World Motor Vehicle Production by Country and Type, 2007–2008" (Paris: OICA, 2009), http://oica.net/category/production-statistics/.

2. Government of China, http://english.gov.cn/2008-01/13/content_856987.htm.

3. Fourin, *Sekai Jidosha Tokei Nenkan 2009* [World automobile statistics yearbook 2009], (Nagoya: Fourin, 2009).

4. *Nikkei Sangyo Shimbun*, "Shin Enerunessansu" [New energy renaissance], February 12, 2009.

5. Andrew J. Staples, *Responses to Regionalism in East Asia: Japanese Production Networks in the Automotive Sector* (Basingstoke, UK: Palgrave Macmillan, 2008), 137.

6. Michael Porter, *Competitive Strategy: Techniques for Analyzing Industries and Competitors* (New York: Free Press, 1980).

7. Paul Krugman, *Geography and Trade* (Cambridge MA: MIT, 1991).

8. David A. Dyker, "Contrasting Patterns in the Internationalisation of Supply Networks in the Motor Industries of Emerging Economies," *Post Communist Economies* 18, no. 2 (2006): 190.

9. Peter Maskell, Heikki Eskeline, Ingjaldur Hanninbalsson, Anders Malmberg, and Eirik Vatne, *Competitiveness, Localised Learning and Regional Development: Specialisation and Prosperity in Small Open Economies* (London: Routledge, 1998), 9.

10. Eric Thun, *Changing Lanes in China: Foreign Direct Investment, Local Governments, and Auto Sector Development* (New York: Cambridge University, 2006), 55.

11. *Chugoku Joho Handobukku* [China data handbook], 2008 ed. (CJH) (Tokyo: Sososha, 2008), 520.

12. CJH, 2007 ed. (Tokyo: Sososha, 2007), 366.

13. Thun, *Changing Lanes in China*, 65.
14. Fourin, *Sekai Jidosha Tokei Nenkan 2009*.
15. Thun, *Changing Lanes in China*, 105.
16. Ibid., 9.
17. Eric Harwit, *China's Automobile Industry: Policies, Problems and Prospects* (New York: M. E. Sharpe, 1995), 108.
18. Lihui Tian, "Does Government Intervention Help the Chinese Automobile Industry? A Comparison with the Chinese Computer Industry," *Economic System* 31, no. 4 (2007): 366.
19. Thun, *Changing Lanes in China*, 56.
20. Deqiang Liu and Yanyun Zhao, "Ownership, Foreign Investment and Productivity—A Case Study of the Automotive Industry in China," JCER Discussion Paper no. 104 (Tokyo: Japan Center For Economic Research, August 2006).
21. Ibid.
22. Tomoo Marukawa, *Gendai Chugoku no sangyo—Bokkou suru Chugoku no tsuyosa to morosa* [Contemporary Chinese industry] (Tokyo: Chuo Koron, 2007).
23. Kelly Sims Gallagher, "Foreign Direct Investment as a Vehicle for Deploying Cleaner Technologies: Technology Transfer and The Big Three Automakers in China" (doctoral thesis, Fletcher School of Law and Diplomacy, Tufts University, 2003), 71.
24. Shigeki Higashi, "Jidosha buhin sangyo no seicho—jiba sapuraiyaa no koudoka" [Development of auto parts industry from the view of technological upgrading of local suppliers], *Chugoku sangyo koudoka no choryu—sangyo to kigyo no henkaku* [China's industry picking up speed—changes in industry and business], ed. Kenichi Imai and Ding Ke (Tokyo: Institute of Developing Economies, 2007), 123.
25. Mizuho Research Institute, "Kantonsho no jidosha sangyo" [The auto industry in Guangdong Province], Mizuho Report (2006), 3, http://www.mizuho-ri.co.jp/research/economics/pdf/report/report06-0706.pdf.
26. Thun, *Changing Lanes in China*.
27. Tomoo Marukawa, "The Supplier Network in China's Automobile Industry From a Geographic Perspective," 2006, 12, http//www.iss.u-tokyo.ac.jp/~marukawa/supplier network.pdf/.
28. Mizuho Research Institute, "Kantonsho no jidosha sangyo," 7.
29. Akifumi Kuchiki, "The Flowchart Model of Cluster Policy: The Automobile Industry Cluster in China," Discussion Paper no. 100 (Tokyo: Institute of Developing Economies, 2007), 23–7.
30. Ibid., 15.
31. Thun, *Changing Lanes in China*, 241.
32. Ichiro Furukawa, "Katoku no maaketingu senryaku" [The marketing strategy of Huadu District], in *Chugoku jidosha taun no keisei—Kantonsho koshushi Katoku no hatten senryaku*, ed. Mitsuhiro Seki (Tokyo: Shinhyouron, 2006), 238.
33. Fourin, *Sekai Jidosha Tokei Nenkan 2009*.
34. Mizuho Research Institute,"Kantonsho no jidosha sangyo," 40–42.
35. "Honda no yushutu senyo kojo furuseisan—Oshu mitometa Chugokusha" [Honda's export factory at full production], *Nikkei Sangyo Shimbun*, June 4, 2007.
36. Higashi, "Jidosha buhin no seicho," 125.
37. Interview with the president of Guangzhou Honda, JETRO News, http://www5.jetro.go.jp/news/.
38. Kuchiki, "The Flowchart Model," 18.

39. Fourin China Auto Weekly, October 2007.

40. Guangdong Province Statistics Bureau, "Main Indicators of Industry," *Guangdong Statistical Yearbook 2008*, www.gdstats.gov.cn/tjnj/ml_e.htm.

41. Based on data from the US Department of Commerce website, "US Automotive Trade Data, 1998–2009," http://trade.gov/mas/manufacturing/OAAI/auto_stat_index.asp/.

42. Stephen Cooney, "China's Impact on the US Automotive Industry," CRS Report for Congress, no. RL33317 2006 (September 17, 2006), 17.

43. As cited in Takanari Sasaki, "Beichu boeki ga Beikoku no jidosha buhin sangyo ni ataeru eikyo" [The impact of US-China trade on the US auto parts industry], *Kokusai boeki to toshi* [International trade and investment] no. 70 (Winter 2007): 40.

44. Fourin China Auto Weekly, "Chugoku jidosha sangyo" [Chinese automobile industry], March 2008.

MUTUAL PERCEPTIONS IN CHINA-JAPAN-US RELATIONS

11 Changing Japanese Perceptions and China-Japan Relations

RUMI AOYAMA

SOUND CHINA-JAPAN relations are essential to the stability of trilateral China-US-Japan relations. Japan is the second-largest economy in the world, and China, a permanent member of the UN Security Council, now has the third-largest economy. The trajectory of their bilateral relationship will inevitably affect not only the Asia Pacific region but global politics as well.

Among the three bilateral legs of the China-US-Japan triangle, China-Japan relations have been relatively less stable in the post–Cold War era than US-China and US-Japan relations. This is in part because both Japan and China have made US policy their first priority and have made tremendous efforts to maintain good relations with the United States, the single most powerful actor in the international regime. Over the past two decades, US-Japan relations have generally been stable, and the majority of Japanese people hold a positive view of both the United States and US-Japan relations. Meanwhile, the US-China relationship has experienced some turbulence, but the two countries are now coordinating their foreign policies and co-operating on many fronts. Even though there is still substantial divergence on substantive issues between these two giants, US-China relations are commonly understood to be stable. On the other hand, the China-Japan relationship has seen significant instability during this period. This suggests that a better understanding of the bilateral China-Japan dynamic is thus important in identifying how to manage the overall dynamics of the trilateral relationship.

China-Japan relations are often compared with US-China relations. The current US-China relationship is perceived as "stable," whereas China-Japan relations appear to be substantially more fragile. Since 2008 marked the 30th anniversary of both the announcement of China's reform and opening-up policy and its normalization of bilateral ties with the United States, a general reassessment of the last 30 years of US-China relations was undertaken in China. Most Chinese scholars agree that ties between the two countries were greatly strengthened under the second term of the Bush administration. They point to the approximately 40 channels of extensive high-level contacts that have now been established in various fields and to the fact that the US media has begun covering a broader range of issues in a more positive manner in recent years. While it is true that the foundation of bilateral China-Japan ties has largely been destabilized by an array of tensions (history issues, shrine visits, the cancellation of leaders' meetings, territorial disputes, expressions of mutual distrust, and so on), it is also true that US-China relations have not been immune to such tensions over the past two decades either. And yet they seem to be on more solid footing. This leads to a simple question: how well are the conflicts between Japan and China being managed, and why are China-Japan relations less stable than US-China relations?

The bilateral relationship between Japan and China has drawn tremendous academic attention due to its importance for trilateral relations and for the stability and prosperity of the Asia Pacific region. However, in part because of the longstanding habit that scholars have of focusing exclusively on actual conflicts, the practice of conflict management between the two countries is rarely mentioned.[1] Conflict management refers to "the design and implementation of strategies to minimize the dysfunctions of conflict and to maximize its constructive functions for a more peaceful world."[2] Even though all conflicts may not be eliminated or permanently resolved, potentially violent conflicts can be transformed into peaceful processes through conflict-management diplomacy.[3] In this sense, research focused on how conflicts are managed is essential to assess the state of China-Japan relations.

By focusing on conflict management, this chapter examines the changing bilateral relationship between Japan and China in the post–Cold War era in terms of the evolution of perceptions, the broader foreign policy context of the bilateral relationship, and the way in which the management of conflicts has been conducted in China-Japan relations. The relationship between these two countries has undergone notable changes since the end of the Cold War, and these changes have coincided with shifts in each country's foreign policy priorities during this period. If we trace the trajectory of these shifts, post–Cold War China-Japan relations can be divided into three phases: the departure from the Cold War framework (1989–1995), adjustment to a rising China (1995–2006), and movement toward a new equilibrium (2006–).

Departure from the Cold War Framework (1989–1995)

The overall image of China in Japan after the Cold War was negative. In the 1980s, most Japanese admired China and had nostalgic or romanticized impressions of the country.[4] But these sentiments gradually faded away in the post–Cold War era. As figure 1 demonstrates, the crackdown on the pro-democracy protests in Tiananmen Square in June 1989 had a fundamental impact on Japanese perceptions, and those holding positive opinions of China dropped sharply from 68.5 percent to 51.6 percent in a single year.

Figure 1. Japanese sentiments toward China (percent)

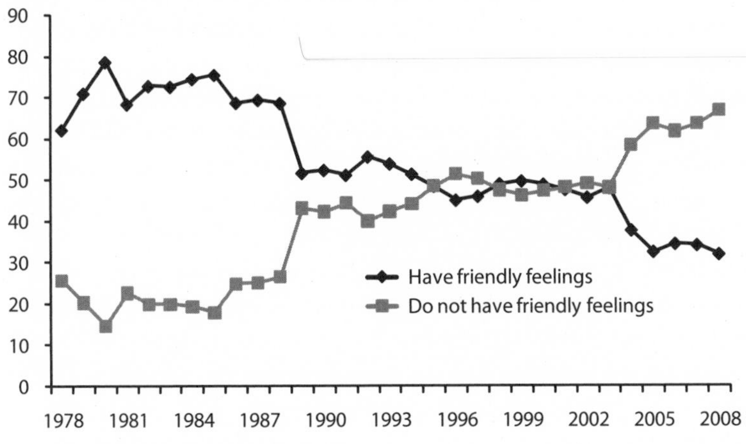

SOURCE: Cabinet Office of Japan (2008)

Despite this deterioration in public opinion, however, the two governments managed to develop and maintain a cooperative, amicable relationship. This relationship was conspicuously reflected in public opinion in Japan. As shown in figure 2, the majority of Japanese people in the early 1990s perceived that Japan and China had good relations.

Figure 2. Japanese views on China-Japan relations (percent)

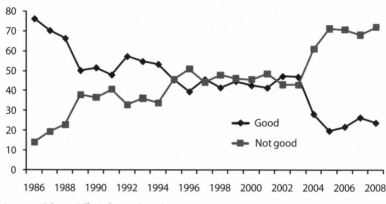

SOURCE: Cabinet Office of Japan (2008)

This cooperative relationship was considered to be in the best interests of both countries. Japan's post–Cold War strategy was based on a dual strategy that addressed the importance both of relations with the United States and of relations with other Asian countries, especially with China. This strategic framework was clearly outlined in a speech given by Prime Minister Kiichi Miyazawa at the National Press Club in Washington DC in July 1992.[5] First, Miyazawa stressed the need to develop a comprehensive security framework in the Asia Pacific region. To promote "political dialogue" in the Asia Pacific, he called for a framework that would involve a wide range of countries, including the four major powers (Japan, the United States, China, and Russia) and the ASEAN countries. Second, he called for the United States to maintain its military presence in Asia. Third, he called for the promotion of "US-Japan global partnership," stating that it is indispensable for Japan to play a larger political role in the international community. And fourth, Miyazawa called for Japanese support of China's open door policy, believing that the ongoing economic reforms in China would subsequently lead to future political reform.

Thus, while Japan sought to strengthen relations with the United States, at the same time it reasoned that friendly relations with other Asian countries were crucial in order to minimize concerns among Japan's neighbors over stronger US-Japan ties.[6] Under this strategy, the general Japanese approach to China was engagement.

Strengthening ties with Japan was one of the top diplomatic priorities for China as well. In the aftermath of the Tiananmen Square incident, China faced a harsh international climate. To break through the isolation,

China launched a new diplomatic policy that placed relations with the United States at the top of its agenda, with China-Japan relations as the second priority.[7]

Against a backdrop of lingering US-Japan trade tensions and strained US-China relations following the Tiananmen Square incident, China and Japan were eager to maintain friendly relations at the start of the 1990s. Tiananmen Square had prompted Western countries to impose strict sanctions on China in the form of bans on political and military contact with China and the cutting off of economic aid and cooperation. Yet Japan promoted its own foreign policy line, adopting a strategy to prevent China from becoming isolated. At the 1989 G7 Summit in France, Japan clearly stated that China should not be cut off, and it was successful in getting this goal included in a final "Declaration on China." In November 1990, Japan was first among the industrialized nations to resume official development assistance (ODA) disbursements to China. In January 1991, Finance Minister Ryutaro Hashimoto traveled to China, and in August of that year, Prime Minister Toshiki Kaifu became the first head of state from a major industrialized nation to visit China since the Tiananmen Square incident. In 1992, the emperor of Japan made a visit to China, further helping to restore China-Japan relations to normalcy.

The fact that Japan broke ranks with the West was a significant positive gesture from China's point of view and, as a consequence, China then expected Japan to mediate in restoring its relations with the West.[8] Thus, a confluence emerged between the two countries' strategic goals, allowing what has been called the "friendship framework" to function effectively.[9] This began to spill over to the private sector as well. After the Japanese emperor's visit, for example, Japanese direct investment in China increased rapidly.

Behind these friendly bilateral relations, however, there were also tangible signs of conflict. China signaled the advent of a new confrontation by expressing its concern about the war history issue and watched with alarm as Japan and the United States moved to redefine their alliance and agreed to cooperate on missile defense system research. Nevertheless, up until the signing of the US-Japan Joint Declaration on Security: Alliance for the 21st Century—a treaty signed in April 1996 by President Bill Clinton and Prime Minister Hashimoto in an effort to strengthen the US-Japan security alliance—most scholars in China were cautiously optimistic, thinking that the US-Japan alliance might serve to keep a lid on the resurgence of militarism in Japan.

In the meantime, China's double-digit military spending and rapid economic growth created an uneasy atmosphere in Japan. In 1995, many journals and newspapers had special editions devoted to reports on the "China threat." Amid mounting anxiety, most foreign policy opinion leaders remained relatively calm. Tadao Ishikawa, former president of Keio University and a leading area studies specialist, argued, "The nationalism that bolsters the military buildup requires more attention than the military buildup per se. In order to lead China in a reasonable direction, the best choice is to engage China."[10]

Although the Japanese government did express its concerns to China, it did not change its general approach. In the process of framing the National Defense Program Outline in 1995, Japan's politicians were divided on using the expression "the China threat," a term that was included in the initial draft prepared by the Defense Agency. In the end, the Murayama administration decided to delete the expression in an effort to accommodate China's sensitivity.[11]

A number of additional issues affected public perceptions of China during this period as well. The arrival of "boat people" from China—economic refugees who came to Japan pretending to be Vietnamese—drew public attention to domestic security in Japan and led to a deteriorating image of China. Starting in 1989, when the first boatload of Chinese arrived, the number of mock refugees to Japan continued to increase throughout the early 1990s.

The environment, which is of particular concern to Japanese people, also came to the forefront in the early 1990s. A study conducted at that time by an expert from the Maizuru Marine Observatory stated that the acid rain in Japan was caused by the air pollution in Huabei, China. Commenting on this report, Japan's Environmental Agency dismissed the "China environmental threat," saying that there are many factors that may cause acid rain and that the extent to which China's air pollution affects the environment in Japan was still not clear.[12] In fact, the Japanese government perceived cross-border pollution as a North-South problem and viewed it as one of the most appropriate areas in which Japan could contribute internationally. The government resolved to play a leading role in tackling this issue by providing both advanced technology and financial support to developing countries, including China.

This official stance was supported by the public. For example, local governments and many nonprofit organizations enthusiastically involved themselves in planting trees in desert areas in China under the slogan of "bringing green to China" (*Chugoku ni midori o*), and the Sino-Japan Friendship Center for Environmental Protection was established with Japanese ODA in 1995.

Many of the major areas of conflict that exist today between Japan and China can be traced back to the 1990s. Nevertheless, both Japan and China managed these conflicts under the friendship framework. In the beginning of the 1990s, the Japanese government recognized the global importance of its relations with China, and a statement made by former Prime Minister Miyazawa in 1995 clearly illustrates the Japanese response to a rising China at that time.[13] Regarding the military buildup and rapid economic growth in China, Miyazawa said, "China will ultimately become a major economic power, and probably a major military power as well. The Chinese leaders may be preoccupied with hegemony. Even so, it is impossible to contain China and we should not contain China. Hence, it is important for us to engage China."[14]

Behind the friendship framework, however, mutual suspicions were on the rise. Japanese concerns about China were being raised on a wide range of issues—from security to the environment—while China had a different perspective, focusing on the historical legacy and Japan's military intentions. All of these tensions rose to the surface in the latter half of the 1990s.

ADJUSTMENT TO A RISING CHINA (1995-2006)

The Changing Perception of China in Japan

The public perception of China in Japan, which had worsened after the Tiananmen Square incident, deteriorated further in the mid-1990s as a result of incidents that occurred in 1995. China executed an underground nuclear test in May 1995, in response to which Japan voiced its strong opposition, calling it a violation of the ban on nuclear tests stipulated in the Comprehensive Test Ban Treaty and demanding that China refrain from further testing. Nevertheless, a second test was conducted in August of that year. In contrast to its response following the Tiananmen Square incident, this time Japan promptly notified China on August 30 of its intention to cut off development aid. Freezing aid in this case was fundamentally different from the 1989 freeze because it was not a product of pressure from the Western camp but was instead a move made by Japan of its own accord, suggesting a change in its China policy.[15]

In the midst of these tense Japan-China relations, the "China threat" argument began to emerge from both Japan's ruling party and the opposition. This peaked in 2005, when Seiji Maehara, president of the Democratic Party of Japan (DPJ), and Foreign Minister Taro Aso openly stated that

China was a threat to Japan. All along, however, the official position of the government of Japan was that it did not regard China as a threat. Prime Minister Koizumi denied that China was an immediate threat, and Defense Agency Director General Fukushiro Nukaga also dismissed the China threat argument, describing China as a "competitive partner."

The Japanese government did, however, express concerns over China's increased military spending. The description of China's military status in Japanese defense white papers changed incrementally. In the post–Cold War period, Japan has gradually begun to look at the Taiwan question as a security issue.[16] Since 1996, Japan's white papers on defense have expressed concerns about China's military buildup, and particularly about the uncertainties caused by the tense relations between China and Taiwan. The 1999 white paper included information for the first time on the fact that "China maintains around 100 intermediate-range ballistic missiles that could reach the entire continent of Asia." The 2000 white paper gave the first concrete statistics on Chinese naval vessels and oceanographic research ships that had been spotted by Japan's Self-Defense Forces conducting operations (and suspected of gathering intelligence) in the waters surrounding Japan. The 2004 white paper expressed concern over China's activities in the airspace surrounding Japan, while the 2005 edition raised the issue of its military use of outer space.

There were changes at the Ministry of Foreign Affairs (MOFA) as well. Based on the conviction that it was important to reinforce US-Japan security relations, Japan embarked on a democratic values–laden foreign policy that adhered to the principle that more affluent and stable democratic societies will be beneficial to the stability of the international community. A foreign policy line based on promoting democracy as a universal value started to become evident. In 1999, the difference in political systems between Japan and China was referred to for the first time in MOFA's diplomatic bluebook.

In December 2005, Foreign Minister Aso portrayed Japan as a "thought leader" for Asia and as a promoter of democratic values. Although democratic values have long been one of the important principles of Japan's foreign policy, the introduction in 2006 of the geopolitical term "arc of freedom and prosperity" triggered strong criticism from China.[17]

By 2006, opinion leaders in Japan were divided on the China threat issue. Shigeo Hiramatsu, an expert on Chinese military issues, warned of China's military expansion, citing the country's military buildup and the recent increase in naval activity in the East China Sea.[18] Mineo Nakajima, an expert on China, also considered China to be a threat, labeling the country as an irredentist that intends to recover its lost kingdom.[19] On the other hand, Akio Takahara, another leading expert on China, rebutted, "The threat is not about China per se. Rather, it stems from the political and economic uncertainties and the social unrest in China."[20] Thus, two contrasting images of China coexisted in Japan: one of a rising and threatening China, the other of China as a fragile power. Although different in essence, both posed a "threat" to Japan, and each one required a different approach from Japan.

In contrast, few people in Japan have viewed China as an economic threat. Strictly speaking, the argument that China was an economic threat emerged in 2001 and evaporated in 2002. Trade disputes in the towel industry and over such agricultural products as rushes (used in tatami mats), scallions, and mushrooms started in early 2001. In the midst of rising concerns over the possibility that the increasing moves by major Japanese companies to shift their production bases to China might cause the hollowing out of the Japanese industry, Prime Minister Koizumi denied that China was an economic threat. In a keynote speech at the first annual conference of the Boao Forum for Asia in April 2002, Koizumi underlined the importance of strengthening bilateral, "mutually complementary" economic ties, saying that "the advancement of Japan-China economic relations [is] an opportunity to nurture new industries in Japan and to develop their activities in the Chinese market."[21] Similar views also came from scholars in the economic field. Hideo Ohashi of Senshu University argued that Japanese firms unexpectedly benefited from a "Chinese special procurement boom" (*Chugoku tokuju*) after China's accession to the World Trade Organization, which accelerated the pace of Japan's economic recovery from a decade-long stagnation.[22]

Since 2000, the public in Japan has viewed China as the most important country for Japan economically, displacing the United States, which is still of greater political importance to Japan, as illustrated in figures 3 and 4. Along with the strengthened bilateral economic ties, a relatively neutral term, "China risks"—as opposed to "economic threat"—gained widespread use in the economic arena.[23]

Whereas the debates on the China threat were intense among politicians and elites, the general public has by and large perceived North Korea as the biggest military threat to Japan. Only 10 percent of the Japanese public felt that China was the country that posed the greatest military threat to Japan according to a survey in 2007.[24] Moreover, for the general public, the issue of greatest interest was safety and security within Japan. Data from the Japanese National Police Agency shows that crimes by foreigners in

Japan increased rapidly from the beginning of the 1990s on. By 2006, about 84 percent of Japanese surveyed thought that public safety in Japan had gotten worse, and 55 percent of respondents cited rising crime by foreigners as a primary cause of the worsening public order.[25] That perception was due in part to the 2003 "Fukuoka incident," which occurred amid a national campaign against crimes by foreigners. Three Chinese students murdered a family of four during a robbery, and this heinous crime no doubt exacerbated the negative image among the Japanese public of Chinese people and of China itself.

Figure 3. Public perceptions of politically important countries for Japan (percent)

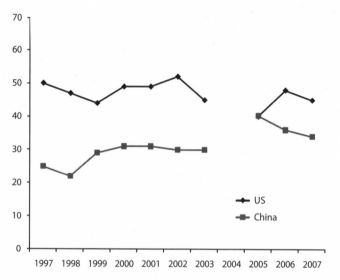

SOURCE: Annual polls conducted by Yomiuri Shimbun–Gallup.

Another domestic security issue related to China was food safety. In 2002, one Japanese person died and 11 others developed liver disorders after taking Chinese diet aids. In the same year, a wide range of products containing contaminated vegetables from China were recalled after high levels of residual agricultural chemicals were detected in imported spinach.

China also drew increased attention over the issue of pollution. As the "don't blame China" consensus that prevailed in the early 1990s faded away, Japan's image of China worsened.[26] Since the 1990s, sandstorms in Japan have been increasing in frequency and intensity, and western

Figure 4. Public perceptions of economically important countries for Japan (percent)

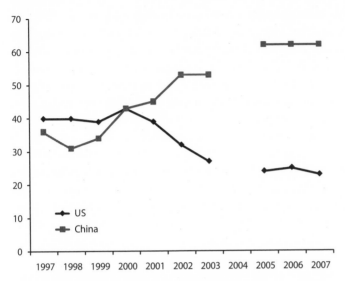

Source: Annual polls conducted by Yomiuri Shimbun–Gallup.

Japan—especially Kyushu, Chugoku, and Kansai—have been particularly hard hit. Concerns about the effect of sandstorms on human health are on the rise. Although, as the Chinese government has argued, the sandstorms come mostly from Central Asia and not just from China, many in Japan still view China as the main cause of the problem.[27] The level of photochemical smog has also increased since 2000, and China is accused of causing this problem too.[28] The fact that Japan has yet to finalize regulations on the emission of nitrogen oxides and volatile organic compounds, which can create photochemical oxidants, is barely mentioned in Japan. Similarly, in the case of acid rain, most of the ionic sulfate is believed to have come from inland areas of China via the Yellow Sea and the Korean Peninsula. Even though sulfur dioxide emissions in both China and South Korea have been pointed to as the likely sources of the pollution, only Chinese emissions are seen as the cause by most Japanese people.[29]

Thus, the image of China in Japan during this period varied greatly. Although the Japanese government never officially labeled China a threat, there were strong concerns about China's military buildup among politicians and opinion leaders, and there was a prevailing wariness about crimes by foreigners and China's environmental pollution.

China's Japan Policy and China-Japan Relations

Japan's engagement approach to China in the beginning of the 1990s was based on an assumption that Japan as an industrialized country was supporting a weak China. The strong proclivity for accommodating China's sensitivities steadily lost ground during this period as the Japanese economic bubble collapsed and China's economy grew rapidly. With the general uneasiness over China's rapid economic development on the rise, Japan no longer saw China as an appropriate target for a mere "engagement" policy, and it became more assertive on areas of conflict.

As Japan's foreign policy gradually moved away from its Asian platform and toward a greater emphasis on the US-Japan alliance, China began developing its multifaceted diplomacy.[30] Since 1996, the three major pillars of China's foreign policy have been relations with the major industrialized powers, China's neighboring countries, and the developing countries. Japan, which is both China's neighbor and a major industrialized country, was thus of substantial importance to China's foreign relations.

China's foreign policy had to overcome two challenges during this period: resurgent nationalism within China and strong criticism coming from Japan. In 1996, *The China That Can Say No* (Zhongguo keyi shuo bu), a nationalistic, anti-Western critique of American influence on China, became a best-selling book. At the same time, the voices calling for a tougher foreign policy grew louder and criticisms of the government stance were growing stronger. And when President Jiang Zemin visited Japan in 1998, the perception gap between Japan and China on history issues was thrust into the spotlight. But following these bitter experiences, China began to soften its tone in 2000 in an effort to boost ties with Japan.

In the midst of this policy shift, debate was rampant in China over the "new thinking" (*xinsiwei*) school of thought. In 2002, Ma Licheng, who was an editor at *People's Daily* (Renmin ribao) at the time, published an article titled, "New Thinking Toward Japan" (Dui Ri guanxi xinsiwei), and Shi Yinhong, a professor at the International Relations Department of Renmin University, published a paper titled, "Sino-Japanese Rapprochement and Diplomatic Revolution" (Zhongri jiejin yu waijiao gemin).[31] They both suggested shelving the history issue, acknowledging Japan as a major power, and strengthening political and economic ties with Japan. Though these suggestions met with fierce criticism, it is important to note that even the critics recognized the importance of Japan to China, since their arguments were based on the assumption that tense political relations would not damage the active bilateral economic relations. It is not clear whether the

Chinese government was behind the emergence of this new thinking, but it did quietly start to make serious efforts toward improving the image of Japan in China from 2004 onward.[32]

Despite China's adjustments to its Japan policy, Japan during this timeframe was adopting a more assertive stance on such issues as the gas fields in the East China Sea. The anti-Japanese demonstrations in 2003 and 2005 negatively affected the image of China in Japan, and the 2004 incident in which a Chinese submarine briefly entered Japanese territorial waters further bolstered the "China threat" argument in Japan. All of these incidents triggered a debate over the continuation of development aid to China. Although there were some voices pointing out the important role that ODA played in pushing China—which was still a developing country despite its formidable political power—to become further integrated into the international community, the prevailing view was that Japan should not give the Chinese military a boost by providing it with ODA.[33] A decision was consequently made to end payments in 2008, to which China quietly conceded.

Management of Conflicts

Overall, China-Japan relations from 1996 to 2006 can be labeled as "hot economics, cold politics," but even in the midst of the political chill, there was significant interchange not just in the economic field but in a broad range of fields, and that dialogue and cooperation in fact supported the relationship from below.

During President Jiang's visit to Japan in 1998, Chinese-Japanese disputes over historical matters received a great deal of attention, but the importance of the Japan-China Joint Declaration on Building a Partnership of Friendship and Cooperation for Peace and Development that was issued by the two leaders, and their agreement on 33 initiatives—including the creation of an intergovernmental hotline, security talks, and energy cooperation—were hardly mentioned. These 33 initiatives actually set the framework for future cooperation between the two countries.

Subsequently, a number of agreements were reached that sought to reduce tensions and strengthen ties between the two countries. To tackle the problems of crimes committed by Chinese nationals in Japan, the two governments agreed to open dialogues between their public security authorities in 1999. The next year, during Premier Zhu Rongji's visit to Japan in October, both sides further agreed to open regular talks between customs authorities. To prevent incidental territorial disputes, both sides agreed in August 2000 to create a framework for mutual prior notification of ocean survey operations. To strengthen economic ties, Prime Minister Koizumi and Premier Zhu agreed in principle at the first Boao Forum for Asia in April 2002 to set up the Japan-China Economic Partnership Consultation, and Foreign Minister Yoriko Kawaguchi later confirmed that those talks would commence by the end of the year. Also that year, an incident involving the Japanese Consulate General in Shenyang in May triggered a bilateral dialogue on creating a framework for consular cooperation.[34]

At the summit between Prime Minister Koizumi and President Hu in St. Petersburg in May 2003, the two sides agreed to establish the New Japan-China Friendship Committee for the 21st Century, a government advisory committee comprised of public intellectuals. In autumn of 2004, the Chinese side relayed its desire to construct a framework for strategic dialogues, leading to the launch of the Japan-China Comprehensive Policy Dialogue in May 2005. One year later, a summit between the Japanese and Chinese foreign ministers was held in Qatar, where agreement was reached on four points: increasing strategic dialogues; boosting economic and trade relations, including cooperation on energy-efficient and environmentally friendly technology; promoting interaction between civilians, particularly the youth of both countries; and conducting talks at the vice foreign minister level on international security, as well as continuing friendly exchanges between military forces.

To tackle environmental problems, new cross-border cooperation was begun and existing programs were strengthened. Starting in the early 1990s, Japanese ODA had focused on controlling emissions in China. As noted above, during President Jiang's 1998 visit to Japan, an agreement was reached on 33 initiatives, among which environmental cooperation was at the top of the agenda. Even since 2000, when ODA to China began to be scaled back, funding for environmental projects continued. Moreover, cross-border cooperation was expanding from the bilateral level to the multilateral level as well. In 2003, the governments of Japan, China, South Korea, and Mongolia launched a project to collect data on the increasingly frequent yellow sandstorms and to come up with countermeasures.[35]

With deepening economic interdependence, exchanges of people between Japan and China have become an important factor supporting bilateral relations. In 1972, roughly 9,000 people traveled between Japan and China; by 1987, the number had risen to 490,000, and in 2007, no fewer than 5.1 million people traveled between the two countries. In 1989, there were 109 sister-city relationships. Two decades later, this number had increased to 314. Approximately 50 Japanese private-sector organizations are now planting trees in China every year, covering almost 25 provinces.[36] In this way, Japan-China relations started to broaden beyond the central-government context as regional governments, the private sector, and individuals became increasingly engaged in bilateral ties.

Even in the decade of "cold politics," various actors were working to facilitate greater interaction between the two countries and, as a result, Japan and China began cooperating more closely on a wide range of issues, including domestic security, economic cooperation, and the environment.

Movement Toward a New Equilibrium (2006–)

Since 2006, both Japan and China have shown enthusiasm for establishing a more stable footing for the bilateral relationship. After Prime Minister Shinzo Abe took office in September 2006, Japan gradually moved back to its dual approach of strengthening relations with both the United States and Asia. Repairing political relations with China was high on the agenda of the Abe administration.

The change in Japan's China policy coincided with a similar shift in China that also aimed to bolster bilateral relations. In April 2005, amid anti-Japanese demonstrations, the Chinese government issued a document on China-Japan policy that laid out its policy on bilateral relations and its stance on Japan's bid for permanent membership on the UN Security Council. In early 2006, a Japan policy coordination group was established, directly under the lead of State Councilor Tang Jiaxuan.

In this context, the relationship between Japan and China improved substantially. During the 2006 Beijing summit, Prime Minister Abe and President Hu reached consensus on building a "mutually beneficial strategic relationship" to promote cooperation—especially in the economic and environmental fields. After Prime Minister Abe's "ice-breaking trip" and Premier Wen Jiabao's "ice-thawing visit" to Japan in April 2007, bilateral relations entered a "warm spring" when President Hu visited Japan in May 2008. Prime Minister Yasuo Fukuda and President Hu agreed to deepen cooperation on the environment and signed a joint statement on climate change.

Above all, the most remarkable sign of the improvement in relations between Japan and China is the fact that the two countries have finally come to agree on what the disputed problems are. Since the latter part of the

Figure 5. Japanese public perceptions of the top issues troubling Japan-China relations, 2002 and 2006 (percent)

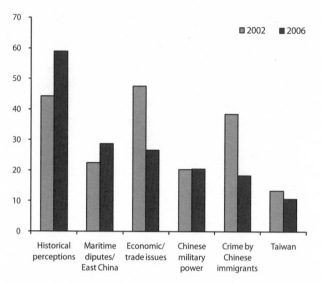

SOURCE: "Nitchu kankei ni kansuru yoron chosa" [Opinion poll on Japan-China relations], Ministry of Foreign Affairs of Japan.

1990s, Japan and China have had various confrontations, but the primary concerns and priorities of the two countries have differed. For China, the main problems it had with Japan in the late 1990s and early 2000s were the history issue, the territorial dispute over the Senkaku (Diaoyu) Islands, the Taiwan issue, and the US-Japan alliance. Issues such as the East China Sea dispute, China's increasing military capabilities, and crimes committed by Chinese nationals living in Japan received a great deal of attention in Japan but were not mentioned by the Chinese. In fact, China viewed many of Japan's concerns as being overblown. For example, in late 1997, a book titled, *Behind the Scenes of Demonizing China* (Yaomohua Zhongguo de beihou) became very popular in China. The main message of the book was that the major Western media outlets were demonizing China—an idea that was shared by both the Chinese government and the public. The majority of Chinese dismissed Japanese anxieties over food security and pollution as biased and exaggerated.

After decades of disputes, however, Japan and China have finally come to agree to disagree. There is a growing public perception that, for the most part, the big issues that bother the other side are indeed valid issues and should be resolved, even if the publics in both countries may disagree on the most desirable solution. Largely because domestic safety has become a major concern in China as well, the majority of the Chinese public is now showing an increased understanding of Japan's concern about food safety and environmental pollution in China.[37] At the same time, as indicated in figure 5, the majority of the Japanese public has come to recognize that the history issue needs to be overcome.[38]

Moreover, both governments have shown restraint on issues where conflicts exist. No sitting prime minister has visited the controversial Yasukuni Shrine since Prime Minister Koizumi's visit in August 2006, and recent leaders have also confirmed that Japan will "firmly maintain" its position on a one-China policy as expressed in the 1972 Joint Communiqué. For its part, Chinese leaders have refrained from mentioning the history and Taiwan issues. After taking office, Japan's Prime Minister Aso also refrained from reviving his controversial call for the creation of an "arc of freedom and prosperity." China, in return, has refrained from mentioning the "resurgence of Japanese militarism." In the meantime, China has repeatedly and openly expressed appreciation for the ODA that it received from Japan and has shown understanding about Japan's wish to play a larger role in the international community. During his trip to Japan, President Hu remarked positively on Japan's postwar years as a peaceful nation and its contributions to world peace and stability, and he acknowledged Japan for the first time as a major power in the global arena. Although some issues such as the gas fields and the Senkaku Islands dispute have not yet been resolved, they are at the very least being managed.

In contrast to the warming of bilateral relations at the government-to-government level, however, Japanese public sentiment toward China has continued to fluctuate. In 2008, amid a series of recalls of Chinese products in the United States, "poisoned dumplings" imported from China were discovered in Japan. Great attention was drawn once again to the safety of Chinese food, and around 93 percent of the Japanese said that they felt very anxious about the safety of imports from China.[39]

The massive earthquake that struck Sichuan Province in 2008, however, brought a softening in Japanese sentiments toward China. Immediately after the earthquake, the Japanese government announced that it would provide emergency grant aid of us$1.7 million for humanitarian assistance. It also dispatched a disaster relief rescue ream and a medical team to search for and rescue victims. The Chinese public welcomed the help from Japan and expressed their appreciation. The image of Japan in China improved dramatically (though not enough to overcome wartime memories or to allow the use of Japanese Self-Defense Force aircraft in the relief operations in

China). Conversely, the improvement in the image of Japan in China has also to some extent bolstered the image of China in Japan.

Table 1. Main dialogue channels between Japan and China

Title	Inauguration
Japan-China Committee on Science and Technological Cooperation	Jun. 1981
Japan-China Security Dialogue	Dec. 1993
Japan-China Joint Committee on Environmental Protection and Cooperation	Dec. 1994
Japan-China Consultation on Disarmament and Non-proliferation	Feb. 1999
Japan-China Public Security Authorities Consultations	Dec. 1999
Japan-China Meeting of Cooperative Fisheries Delegates	Jun. 2000
Japan-China Economic Partnership Consultation	Oct. 2002
New Japan-China Friendship Committee for the 21st Century	Dec. 2003
Japan-China Climate Change Dialogue	Mar. 2004
Japan-China Consultations Concerning the East China Sea	Oct. 2004
Regular Exchange between the House of Representatives and China's National People's Congress (NPC)	Apr. 2005
Japan-China Comprehensive Policy Dialogue (Japan-China Strategic Dialogue)	May 2005
Consultations between Japan and China Concerning UN Reform	Dec. 2005
Japan-China Ruling Party Dialogue [Chinese Communist Party (CCP)–Liberal Democratic Party dialogue]	Feb. 2006
Japan-China Press Secretary Consultations	Aug. 2006
CCP-DPJ Dialogue	Jan. 2007
Regular Exchange between House of Councillors and NPC	Mar. 2007
Japan-China Energy Ministerial Policy Dialogue	Apr. 2007
Consultations between Japan and China concerning Africa	Sep. 2007
Japan-China High-Level Economic Dialogue	Dec. 2007
Japan-China Policy Dialogue on the Mekong Region	Apr. 2008

As shown in table 1, since the end of the Cold War, a considerable number of bilateral talks have been established between Japan and China, and a variety of other issues are under negotiation as well. These efforts by the two governments, however, have had little direct impact on public opinion. This is in part because the resolution of areas of conflict, such as environmental issues, takes time. The outcome of intergovernmental efforts such as these tends to be incremental and efforts rarely produce immediate, tangible results. Nonetheless, they appear to be having a longer-term impact in terms of conflict management.

CONCLUSION

Japan and China have never before been powerful at the same time in history, and from the mid-1990s on, the two countries have been working to adjust to each other's new and evolving status, carefully weighing the extent to which the other should be treated as a threat or a partner.

Japan's image in China might be volatile and emotional, but this largely stems from Japan's perceived military intentions and its historical actions. The image of China in Japan has been somewhat mixed. In the beginning of the 1990s, Japan viewed China's domestic instability and its possible collapse as a threat. With China's rapid economic growth, there are now two contrasting images: a rising China that requires caution and a fragile China that needs engagement.

Both Japan's affinity for China and China's affinity for Japan have been put to the test since the end of the Cold War. The deteriorating public images have not always resulted in a worsening Japan-China relationship, however. Shortly after the end of the Cold War, the friendship framework functioned effectively, sustained by the assumption that "a strong Japan embraces a weak China." With China's increasing presence in the world community, both Japan and China experienced difficulties in adjusting their relationship to suit the new situation, which led to a period of "cold politics" between the two countries. Since 2006, however, political relations appear to be thawing as Japan and China have finally recognized each other as major powers, acknowledging the other's standing in the international community and the legitimacy of the other's concerns regarding their bilateral relations.

Although Japan and China have experienced bumpy relations in the post–Cold War era, there have been efforts at various levels of government to keep official relations from spiraling out of control, as evidenced by the establishment of more than a dozen channels of high-level dialogues. Even though talks between the top leaders have been suspended at times, the bilateral relationship has been supported by the central governments as well as by regional governments, the private sector, and individuals. It may be a while yet before permanent solutions to all the issues troubling Japan and China are found, but there is no doubt about the positive effect that intergovernmental and civil society dialogue is having on preventing existing problems from becoming worse.

After a decade of adjustment and learning, Japan and China have come to recognize each other as major global powers, have agreed that each other's concerns should be treated as valid, and are holding talks to resolve their disputes. This is only the first step, but it is a very significant step toward creating a new equilibrium.

In order to further stabilize this new equilibrium and to make conflict-management diplomacy more effective, a cooperative architecture based on traditional and nontraditional security agreements is indispensable. First, there is a need to sustain existing governmental dialogue to ensure that negative perceptions do not translate into heightened conflicts. Second, there is a need to expand joint China-Japan initiatives to the regional and global levels. The two governments have already worked together on issues such as the environment, food safety, and crime. A wider range of cooperation beyond the bilateral level may help identify shared challenges and enhance political trust. Third, there is a need to build up the underpinnings of China-Japan relations to improve mutual perceptions over the long term. Due to the fact that both China and Japan are undergoing dramatic social changes, the improvement of mutual perceptions may require a good deal of time, and the role of scholars and journalists will be crucial in helping the publics of both countries understand and accept those shifts.

Finally, it is important to point out that China-Japan relations are heavily influenced by US policy toward these two countries since both China and Japan address US policy as their first priority. In this sense, the stability of China-Japan relations depends not only on the degree of success that China and Japan have in building future cooperation but also on how much progress can be made in constructing a new architecture for the trilateral China-Japan-US relationship.

Notes

1. Samuel S. Kim, "China's Conflict-Management Approach to the Nuclear Standoff on the Korean Peninsula," *Asian Perspective* 30, no. 1 (2006): 7, http://www.asianperspective.org/articles/v30n1-a.pdf.

2. Samuel S. Kim and Abraham Kim, "Conflict Management," in *Encyclopedia of Government and Politics*, 2nd ed., ed. Mary Hawkesworth and Maurice Kogan (London: Routledge, 2003), 980.

3. For a more detailed analysis of the conflict-management approach, see Kim, "China's Conflict-Management Approach," 5–38.

4. Ryosei Kokubun, "Changing Japanese Strategic Thinking toward China," in *Japanese Strategic Thought toward Asia*, ed. Gilbert Rozman, Kazuhiko Togo, and Joseph P. Ferguson (New York: Palgrave Macmillan, 2007), 155.

5. For Prime Minister Miyazawa's speech at the National Press Club, see Ministry of Foreign Affairs of Japan, *Gaiko Seisho 1992* [1992 Diplomatic Bluebook] (Tokyo: Ministry of Foreign Affairs of Japan, 1992).

6. Statement by Japanese Foreign Minister Taro Nakayama in July 1991.

7. Rumi Aoyama, "Chugoku no tai-Nichi gaiko to Nicchu kankei" [China's foreign policy toward Japan and Japan-China relations], in *Go bunya kara yomitoku gendai Chugoku* [Understanding contemporary China by examining five fields], ed. Ryoko Iechika, Tang Lang, and Yasuhiro Matsuda (Tokyo: Koyo, 2005), 253–65.

8. Ming Wan, *Sino-Japan Relations: Interaction, Logic, and Transformation* (Washington DC: Woodrow Wilson Center; Stanford: Stanford University, 2006), 177.

9. The term "friendship framework" was coined by Ryosei Kokubun in 2001. See Ryosei Kokubun, "Reisen shuketsugo no Nicchu kankei: 72-nen taisei no tenkan" [Japan-China relations after the Cold War: switching from the '1972 Framework'], *Kokusai Mondai* [International Affairs], no. 490 (January 2001): 42–46.

10. Tadao Ishikawa, "Minzoku-shugi no yukue ga shoten" [The focus is on what will happen to nationalism], *Asahi Shimbun*, November 11, 1995.

11. "Chugoku no kyoi meguri funkyu, yoto boei chosa kaigi" [Ruling party defense study group meeting in disagreement over 'China threat'], *Asahi Shimbun*, November 25, 1995.

12. "Nihon no sanseiu, Chugoku no osen ga eikyo" [China's pollution the cause of Japanese acid rain], *Asahi Shimbun*, January 16, 1991.

13. Ministry of Foreign Affairs of Japan, *Gaiko Seisho 1992*.

14. "Kawaru kankyo, Nihon no sentaku wa? Nichibei anpo zadankai" [Symposium on the US-Japan alliance: what are Japan's options in a changing environment?], *Asahi Shimbun*, November 21, 1995.

15. Saori N. Katada, "Why Did Japan Suspend Foreign Aid to China? Japan's Foreign Aid Decision-making and Sources of Aid Sanction," *Social Science Japan Journal* 4, no.1 (2001): 39–58.

16. Yoshihide Soeya, "Taiwan in Japan's Security Considerations," *China Quarterly* 165 (March 2001): 141.

17. Speech made by Japanese Foreign Minister Aso in November 2006. See Ministry of Foreign Affairs of Japan, "Speech by Mr. Taro Aso, Minister for Foreign Affairs on the Occasion of the Japan Institute of International Affairs Seminar 'Arc of Freedom and Prosperity: Japan's Expanding Diplomatic Horizons,' November 30, 2006," http://www.mofa.go.jp/announce/fm/aso/speech0611.html.

18. "Higashi Shinakai shinshutsu wa tomaranai" [Advance in the East China Sea is not stopping], *Voice* (June 2006): 62–71.

19. Mineo Nakajima, "Higashi Ajia kyodotai wa genso da" [East Asia community is an illusion], *Voice* (February 2006): 129–35.

20. Li Shogen, Akio Takahara, and Yasuhiro Matsuda, "Chugoku wa 'kyoi' ka—anzen hosho no jirenma o koeru taiwa o" [Is China a 'threat'? Dialogue tries to overcome the national security dilemma], *Sekai* 756 (September 2006).

21. "China Is Not a Threat: Koizumi: Neighbor's Growing Economic Power Called an 'Opportunity,'" *Japan Times*, April 13, 2002, http://search.japantimes.co.jp/cgi-bin/nn20020413a1.html.

22. Hideo Ohashi, "The Sino-Japanese Economic Relations under the Koizumi Administration," *Senshu Keizaigaku Ronshu* [Economic bulletin of Senshu University] 42, no. 3 (March 2008).

23. "Kyoi-ron yori risuku-ron"[More a theory of risk than a theory of threat], *Asahi Shimbun*, March 28, 2002.

24. Nippon Research Center, "Findings of Joint Public Opinion Poll on Relations between Japan and China" (November 26, 2007), http://www.nrc.co.jp/english/pdf/071126.pdf.

25. Based on a public opinion survey on public safety conducted by the Japanese Cabinet Office in 2006.

26. "Kokkyo o koeru kankyo hozen" [Environmental protection that transcends borders], *Asahi Shimbun*, October 5, 1990.

27. "Kosa no nagare, Nicchu chosa" [The flow of yellow sand—a Japan-China survey], *Asahi Shimbun*, April 19, 2001; "Rainendo kara kosa gensho no jittai kaimei e" [Clarifying the state of the yellow sand phenomenon from next fiscal year], *Asahi Shimbun*, August 22, 2001.

28. Takao Ikeuchi, "Rising Smog Levels Threaten Health, Crops; China Link Seen," *Japan Times*, November 28, 2007.

29. "Laboratory Tracks Acid Rain's Seasonal Roots," *Japan Times*, June 24, 2000; "Sanseiu vs. kosa" [Acid rain vs. sandstorms], *Asahi Shimbun*, April 1, 2008.

30. Prime Minister Koizumi's statement in November 2005 that "the better [US-Japan] bilateral relations are, the easier it will be for us to establish better relations with China and neighboring countries" illustrated the tendency in Japan's foreign policy of weighing bilateral relations between Japan and the United States above its Asia policy. See "Simplistic View in a Complex World," *Japan Times*, November 26, 2005, http://www.japantimes.co.jp/weekly/ed/ed20051126a1.htm.

31. Ma Licheng, "Dui Ri guanxi xinsiwei" [New thinking toward Japan], *Zhanlue yu Guanli* [Strategy and management] no. 6 (2002): 42–47; Shi Yinhong, "Zhongri jiejin yu waijiao gemin" [Sino-Japanese rapprochement and diplomatic revolution], *Zhanlue yu Guanli* no. 2 (2003): 71–75.

32. Rumi Aoyama, *Gendai Chugoku no gaiko* [Contemporary foreign policy in China] (Tokyo: Keio University Press, 2007), 453–5.

33. "Tai-Chugoku do suru!" [How to deal with "anti-China-ism"!], *Asahi Shimbun*, January 31, 2001.

34. In May 2002, five North Korean refugees attempted to enter the Japanese Consulate in Shenyeng to seek asylum. Chinese police offers entered the consulate compound to drag the North Koreans out and arrest them.

35. Eric Johnson, "Yellow Dust Storms Getting Worse," *Japan Times*, April 22, 2008.

36. Most of these activities are conducted by foundations like the Obuchi Foundation (starting in 1997) or the Japan International Cooperation Agency.

37. According to a 2008 joint opinion poll conducted by the China Daily, Genron NPO of Japan, and Peking University, 38.8 percent of Chinese surveyed said they are concerned about the safety of Chinese food.

38. According to a 2008 joint opinion poll conducted by the China Daily, Genron NPO of Japan, and Peking University, 53.9 percent of Japanese respondents raised the history issue as an obstacle for future China-Japan relations.

39. Based on a 2007 public opinion survey conducted by the Daily Yomiuri.

12 | Chinese Public Perceptions of Japan and the United States in the Post–Cold War Era

FAN SHIMING

THE WORD FOR "perception" in Chinese literally means "observation and interpretation" or "interpretation through observation." Perception is thus considered to be the result of the subjective or psychological cognition of the observer rather than the objective reflection of the object that is being observed.

In his famous book, *Perception and Misperception in International Politics*, Robert Jervis introduces the cognitive variable to explain state behavior by saying, "It is often impossible to explain crucial decisions and policies without reference to the decision makers' beliefs about the world and their images of others. That is to say, these cognitions are part of the proximate cause of the relevant behavior."[1] While Jervis focuses mainly on the perceptions held by foreign-policy makers, the public's perceptions of foreign countries also matter in understanding policy choices and international relations. Mainstream public opinion might not necessarily be shared or accepted by decision makers, but it sets up the atmosphere for policymaking, delivers messages to foreign countries, and can be used by both domestic and foreign politicians to justify their choices. Moreover, in many instances, the people's understanding of international relations is based more on the perceived world rather than the real one.

There is no single, commonly shared perception of either Japan or the United States among the Chinese public. Perceptions vary depending on individuals' socioeconomic or peer group, the topic, and the particular point in time, and thus are always diverse and dynamic. One can, however,

identify some broadly shared opinions as being representative perceptions of a certain country within a given period of time. This chapter tries
to present and characterize Chinese public perceptions of Japan and the
United States in the post–Cold War era and analyzes the reasons behind
these views.

Conceptualizing Chinese Perceptions of Japan and the United States

Chinese Views of America: Ambivalence, Suspicion, and Diversity

Prior to China's reform and opening policy, the United States was regarded
by the Chinese people as a declining, warlike "paper tiger" whose working
people lived in a state of misery, or what is called in Chinese "deep water and
hot fire."[2] Since the early 1980s, however, the image of America has changed
greatly in China, and it has come to be viewed as a source of both fear and
fortune. As a popular Chinese TV drama says, "If you love a person, send
him to New York City, for it's heaven; if you hate him, send him to New York
City, for it's hell."[3] The United States has long been regarded in China as a
paradoxical mixture: it is the most developed, free, and powerful country,
but at the same time is a peremptory, belligerent, impervious hegemon.
The post–Cold War Chinese perception of America has reinforced that
"beautiful imperialist" image.[4] At least since the mid-1990s, surveys have repeatedly shown that the Chinese public views the United States as the most
impressive foreign country for its "richness," "advancement," and "power,"
as well as for its abuse of military force against others.[5] It is perceived by
many Chinese people as the most popular destination for overseas study
(see table 1), a very attractive land for emigration (see table 2), and the most
important partner for the Chinese economy (see fig. 1).[6] At the same time,
however, it is also perceived as the country that most interferes in Chinese
domestic affairs (see table 3), is most threatening to China's security (see
tables 4 and 5), and is the most arbitrary bully in world politics.[7]

This "love-hate" complex has turned into a strong suspicion of American
intentions toward China, especially since the mid-1990s, when China rose to
the status of a real power and the United States became the only superpower.
Recognizing that the US economic and military advantage continues to
grow, many Chinese people are increasingly concerned about the possibility that the purpose and practice of American power, both regionally and
globally, might be detrimental to China. Based on the Taiwan Strait crisis

Table 1. Most desirable destinations for overseas study, 2004

Expected destination for study abroad	Percentage of respondents
US	22.1
Australia	19.6
UK	12.5
France	10.5
Japan	7.0
Germany	4.7
ASEAN	2.2

SOURCE: Horizon Research Consultancy Group, "Survey on the World in the Eyes of Urban Chinese People," 2004.

Table 2. Expectations of emigration to United States (percent), 2007

Country	Life for emigrants to the US is seen as . . .			
	Better	Worse	Neither	Don't know*
Morocco	52	7	17	24
China	45	14	9	32
Argentina	43	12	24	20
Jordan	37	22	29	12

SOURCE: Pew Research Center, "Global Unease with Major World Powers," June 27, 2007, 28.

* Includes those who say they do not know anyone who has moved to the United States.

Table 3. Reasons cited by Chinese who said they dislike the United States, 1998

Reason for disliking the US	Percentage
Criticism of China's human rights	26.9
US international behaviors	26.1
US interference on Taiwan	25.2
US response to China's re-entry into WTO	10.9
Criticism on China's birth control	3.4
Other	6.7
Not sure	0.8

SOURCE: Horizon Research Consultancy Group, 1998.

Table 4. Chinese perceptions of the threat from the United States and Japan (percent), 2001

Country	Strongly disagree	Disagree	Agree	Strongly agree
Statement 1:	Each of the countries listed below, in your view, has hostile intentions against our country's vital interests and security.			
US	4.7	20.9	54.0	20.3
Japan	5.9	26.7	52.9	13.9
Statement 2:	Each of the countries listed below, in your view, has the military and/ or economic power that poses a real and immediate danger to our country.			
US	1.8	9.2	69.4	15.2
Japan	1.8	20.7	62.7	7.3

SOURCE: Adapted from Chen Jie, "Urban Chinese Perceptions of Threats from the United States and Japan," *Public Opinion Quarterly* 64, no. 2 (Summer 2001).

Table 5. Countries perceived by Chinese people as unfriendly toward China (percent), 1999 and 2004

1999		2004	
US	70.3	US	74.4
Japan	52.6	Japan	66.3
Indonesia	16.3	India	9.2
India	15.4	Vietnam	6.0
Vietnam	6.1	Indonesia	4.9
UK	5.9	UK	4.8
Russia	2.0	DPRK	2.8
DPRK	2.0	Singapore	2.3
ROK	1.4	Russia	2.3
Australia	1.4	ROK	1.6

SOURCE: Horizon Research Consultancy Group, "Survey on the World in the Eyes of Urban Chinese People," 1999 and 2004.

of 1996, the reinforcement of the US-Japan alliance in 1997, the Belgrade embassy bombing in 1999, the EP-3 spy plane incident in 2001, and many other incidents, the United States is seen as intending to make trouble on the Taiwan issue, to restrain the greater role that China deserves in world affairs, to engage China on terms that favor US dominance, and even to contain China.[8] The tone that was set in China in the late 1980s—that China should learn from and cooperate with the United States—encountered

Figure 1. Countries perceived by Chinese as China's most important
economic partners, 1999 and 2004 (percent)

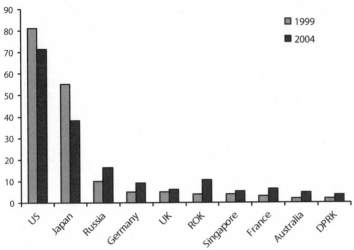

SOURCE: Horizon Research Consultancy Group, "Survey on the World in the Eyes of Urban Chinese People," 1999 and 2004.

criticism and challenges from emerging nationalist sentiment. Since 9/11, as Washington has clearly focused on an antiterrorism campaign, Chinese suspicions have not been relieved much. As one top Chinese international relations scholar observes, popular suspicions have gone beyond bilateral, conventional problems to more global, nontraditional issues like "financial security, energy procurement, environmental protection, climate change, the trade balance, intellectual property rights, product quality and safety, and so on" that are more relevant to China's domestic agenda.[9] Some are wondering if the United States—or at least certain hostile American groups such as the so-called "Blue Team" in the US Congress—is trying to use new means to circumscribe China's emergence. A best-selling book titled *Currency Wars* (Huobi zhanzheng) shows the typical anxiety in recent years that Wall Street is conspiring to trap and ruin the Chinese economy.

A group of intellectuals who are labeled the "New Leftists" echo the popular worries about the United States from another perspective. They identify capitalism and globalization as the major sources of problems in post–Cold War China and hegemonic America as the source of international instability. They appeal for more state intervention, more social and economic equality, and even a reconfirmation of some pre-reform policies in China, while questioning China's continuous marketization and integration into the world system. They look for remedies from Western critical thinking like the Frankfurt School, dependency theory, Orientalism, or postmodernism. Some New Leftists covertly showed their sympathies with the 9/11 attackers while openly opposing the American War in Iraq in 2003.[10] Interestingly, prominent members of the New Leftist School were educated in US universities, and some even call themselves New Deal liberals.[11] It is difficult to say how much New Leftist advocacy has influenced policy, especially foreign policy, but the popularity of this school cannot be neglected when China faces complex social and economic problems, and so the pressure it is placing on policymaking is apparent.

Despite the suspicions and challenges that exist, mainstream Chinese political elites have been insisting since the mid-1990s that China is facing "the best international environment" since the founding of the People's Republic of China (PRC), which can be interpreted as implying that there is no imminent menace coming from the major powers, especially not from the United States. They avoid using words like "strategic competitor," "adversary," or "enemy" to define the United States and instead try to promote such concepts as "strategic partner" or "stakeholder" in public statements to stress the necessity and possibility of bilateral cooperation. While realists support China-US cooperation based on their assessment of the power balance between the two, according to which the United States is still unchallengeable (see table 6), constructivists also support bilateral cooperation since mutual trust is only produced through communication. For those who believe that the sources of problems in China are still the lack of a mature market and the lack of rule of law—both of which originated with the old Chinese system—the New Leftists' charges regarding marketization and American dominance simply distract from an investigation into the domestic roots of the issues. They believe that

Table 6. Perceptions of the global balance of power, by country (percent), 2006

	China will replace US as dominant power in...				
	10 years	20 years	50 years	Will not replace	Don't know
India	32	24	9	24	12
US	11	22	10	47	9
Russia	10	17	13	45	15
Japan	7	19	13	59	3
China	4	13	20	34	29

SOURCE: Pew Research Center, "Publics of Asian Powers Hold Negative Views of One Another," September 21, 2006.

the integration of China into the Western-dominated (or US-dominated) system has generally favored China's development. The overall Chinese attitude toward America thus remains diverse and ambivalent.

Chinese Views of Japan: Retrospection, Coldness, and Emotion

In contrast to their post–Cold War ambivalence toward the United States, the Chinese public's perception of Japan can only be described as having turned increasingly negative (see fig. 2). The image of Japan as a "modern, friendly neighbor" that was formed in the 1980s quickly gave way to that of a remorseless, vexatious, and stubborn "small man" that is still defined in the early 21st century by its wartime history of aggression against China.[12] An array of surveys have shown that unfavorable ratings of Japan did not stop rising in China until 2006. When people are asked what they think of first when they think of Japan, responses like the Nanjing Massacre, the Yasukuni Shrine, and the old Japanese army rank high (see fig. 3). The Chinese public widely believes that Japanese society is still overwhelmed by militarism and nationalism, and they fail to recognize its democracy, peace-oriented reforms, and international contributions (see fig. 4). Even while acknowledging that the Japanese people are polite, diligent, and community oriented, the Chinese public generally perceives them as warlike, cruel, selfish, and untrustworthy.

Figure 2. Internet user attitudes toward foreign countries, 2003 (percent)

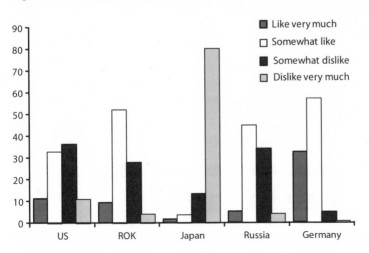

SOURCE: Horizon Research Consultancy Group, 2003.

Figure 3. Images associated with Japan among Chinese students, 2005–2007 (percent)

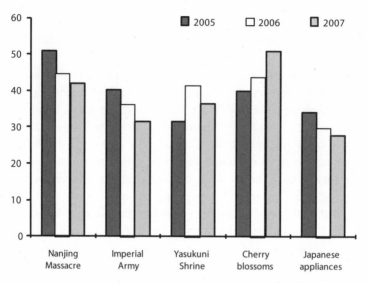

SOURCE: Peking University, China Daily, and Genron NPO, 2005, 2006, and 2007.

Figure 4. Chinese perceptions of prevailing political ideology in Japan, 2007

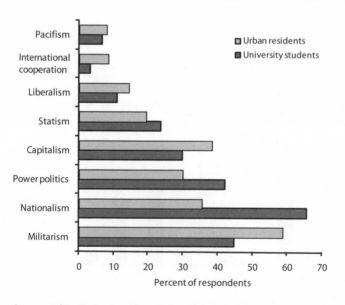

SOURCE: Peking University, China Daily, and Genron NPO, 2007

Nor do the Japanese receive much positive attention when the Chinese public thinks of Japan's power and its international position. For most Chinese people, Japan is seen as struggling not only with economic stagnation, political reform, and domestic aging but also with its "failed Asian diplomacy."[13] The strengthening and reorientation of the Japan-US alliance is first and foremost aimed at China. Japan's efforts to play a larger role in peacekeeping operations are just a reflection of its intention to militarize, and its bid for a permanent seat on the UN Security Council without having correctly accepted its past wrongdoing is perceived as objectionable. In the eyes of the Chinese public, Japan is moving toward the right and causing alarm. While Prime Minister Koizumi's visits to Yasukuni Shrine hurt Chinese feelings, Japan's energy diplomacy in Russia just as intentionally hurt Chinese interests. Accordingly, Japan has followed the United States in polls as the number two threat to China's security (see fig. 5).[14]

These sentiments gave rise to several anti-Japan incidents in 2004 and 2005. Still, there is at least a minimum amount of pragmatism that prevents the Chinese public from identifying Japan as "the enemy." The importance of China-Japan ties in Chinese foreign relations is recognized by a majority of people as being second only to those between China and the United States; most people support cooperation with Japan on regional affairs, especially on nontraditional issues; more often than not, bilateral economic relations are regarded as a win-win game instead of a zero-sum one; and extremist

Figure 5. Threats to China's security as perceived by the Chinese, 2007 (percent)

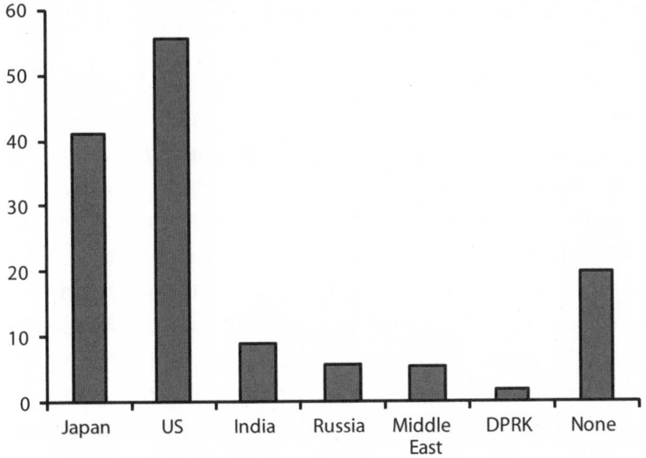

Source: Peking University, *China Daily*, and Genron NPO, 2007.

suggestions like boycotting Japanese goods have been rejected by young people.[15] The "diplomatic revolution" argument raised by a few Chinese scholars did not win public or political support but helped to deepen the understanding of China-Japan relations. Thanks to the way that Beijing and Tokyo have addressed the difficult challenge of rebuilding ties since the end of the Koizumi administration, the Chinese public's perception of Japan has ceased its downward slide, but it remains in a fragile position.

Comprehending Chinese Perceptions of Japan and the United States

Chinese perceptions of the United States and Japan naturally do not spring from thin air. Instead, a "5-E" formula can be employed to interpret the sources of Chinese public attitudes toward these two countries:

$$\text{Perception} = \text{Egocentrism} + \text{Events} + \text{Emotion} + \text{Education} + \text{Experience}$$

Egocentrism Egocentrism here means that the public's perceptions of foreign countries are mainly a reflection of the values, memories, confidence, and orientation of its own country, instead of the objective reflections of the outside world. Existing studies have found that individuals' attitudes toward specific foreign countries and foreign policies are significantly influenced by subjective "predispositions that affect the interpretation of evidence."[16] Egocentrism can also be supported by Professor Jervis's argument on cognitive consistency, in which people tend to interpret information using their existing frame of reference and refuse those facts that are seen as inconsistent.

In the case of Chinese perceptions of the United States and Japan, egocentrism is almost self-evident. The Chinese perception of US hegemony (*badao*) apparently comes from its own humiliating history, its traditional affection for benevolent rule (*wangdao*), and its adherence to the Five Principles of Peaceful Coexistence.[17] Most Chinese refuse to accept Japan as a democratic and peaceful country mostly because of their memories and stereotypes rather than reality. Egocentrism can also explain why the US image improved in China when American popularity was declining in most other parts of the world (see table 7), since China-US relations were seen in China as being satisfactory.[18] Also, the reason why most Chinese are optimistic about China-US relations and their future (see fig. 6) may be closely connected with the country's own rising confidence (see table 8). To understand elite support for a modest, cooperative Chinese diplomacy,

Table 7. Public image of the United States, by country, 2002–2006

	Percentage whose view of the United States is "very/somewhat favorable"				
	2002	2003	2004	2005	2006
China	—	—	—	43	49
Great Britain	83	80	73	70	69
France	71	58	53	64	65
Germany	70	67	68	65	66
Russia	67	65	64	61	57
Indonesia	65	56	—	46	36
Turkey	31	32	32	23	17

Source: Pew Research Center, "America's Image Slips, but Allies Share US Concerns over Iran, Hamas," June 13, 2006.

Figure 6. Chinese expectations for China-US relations, 2004 (percent)

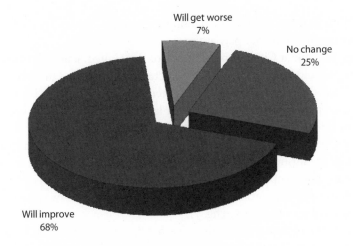

Source: Horizon Research Consultancy Group, "Survey on the World in the Eyes of Urban Chinese People," 2004.

egocentrism matters too, since in the past 30 years there has been a basic consensus in China that its international strategy should be firmly oriented toward domestic development.

Events "Events" refers to those historical and contemporary incidents or prominent events that provide analogies or a basis for reasoning in public perceptions. Of course, revolution and war usually shape collective

Table 8. Shift in domestic confidence levels, by nation (percent), 2003–2006

	Respondents who are satisfied with the state of their own nation			
	2003	2004	2005	2006
China	48*	—	72	81
Jordan	42	59	69	53
Great Britain	46	38	44	35
Russia	28	26	23	32
India	9*	—	41	31
United States	50	39	39	29
Japan	12*	—	—	27
France	44	32	28	20

Source: Pew Research Center, "America's Image Slips, but Allies Share US Concerns over Iran, Hamas," June 13, 2006.

*Summer 2002

perceptions in terms of how one nation sees another, but unexpected incidents can also come into play at times.

When we look at Chinese perceptions of the United States and Japan in the post–Cold War era, we find that fluctuations are linked to events in China-US and China-Japan relations. Whenever negative events happen, public perceptions of the United States or Japan turn sharply unfavorable. The 2001 EP-3 spy plane incident aroused strong Chinese criticism of US hegemony, while Prime Minister Koizumi's visit to Yasukuni Shrine apparently made the shrine into a symbol of Japan in China. General impressions of Japan in China improved remarkably in 2007 after Prime Minister Abe suspended prime ministerial visits to Yasukuni Shrine and the two premiers visited each other's capital (see fig. 7).

Event-driven perceptions may fluctuate, but they are not transient. Events can activate underlying memories and emotions that make up the framework in which perceptions are formed. For example, when we look back on China-US relations in the 1990s, events can be linked together in the public's mind to empirically prove existing arguments for US conspiracies, hostility, or hard-line policies targeted at China. Events may also arouse emotions, which can further complicate matters.

Emotion Cognition is balanced by emotion. Emotions are sentiments that may distort perceptions of values and events. Under most circumstances, when we say somebody is "emotional," we consider it to be a temporary release of a strong feeling that keeps that person at a distance from "normal"

Figure 7. Chinese impressions of Japan, 2005–2007 (percent)

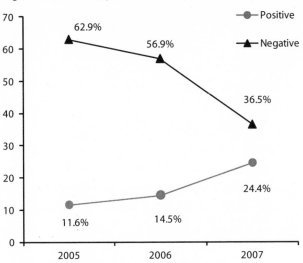

SOURCE: Peking University, China Daily, and Genron NPO, 2005, 2006, and 2007.

feelings and reality. Emotions sometimes affect Chinese perceptions of Japan and America. In the case of Japan, for example, although Japan became China's largest trading partner in 2002 and Chinese-Japanese economic relations have been crucial to China's development, a 2003 poll found that respondents regarded Japan as just the fifth most important actor for China, following the United States, ASEAN, Russia, and Germany. Researchers believe that emotion played a role in those results.[19] Another survey showed that the more people like Japan, the more significant they deem the bilateral relationship to be (see table 9) and the more probable it is that they will buy Japanese products.[20] The emotion factor shows a stronger influence over Chinese buying behavior toward Japanese products as compared with American and Korean products.

Emotion sometimes adds volatility to situations, but it cannot dominate people's perceptions and behavior, especially when it goes against basic reason and pragmatism. Studies have also shown that many people still purchase American and Japanese products even if they hold unfavorable opinions of those countries. As one Chinese news report noted in 2004, the newly rich people in China "hate Japan but still love Japanese products."[21]

Education The education that respondents receive is also relevant to their perception of foreign countries. Education does not necessarily mean

Table 9. Emotion and perception of Sino-Japanese relations (percent), 2003

| Issue | Perception | Netizens*, by opinion of Japan | | | |
		Like Japan	Do not like Japan	No opinion	Overall
Importance of China-Japan relations	Important	91.3	50.7	81.2	53.4
	Not important	6.7	43.3	9.6	40.8
	Don't know	1.5	6.0	9.2	5.8
Evaluation of present bilateral relations	Good	16.5	15.3	27.5	15.4
	Bad	48.0	72.2	54.1	70.6
	Don't know	35.6	12.7	18.3	14.0
Expectations of future relations	Optimistic	14.5	16.0	28.8	16.1
	Pessimistic	37.4	76.0	45.4	73.4
	Don't know	48.1	8.1	25.8	10.5

SOURCE: Horizon Research Consultancy Group. 2003
* "Netizen" refers to an individual who is actively involved in online communities.

school learning. Education from family, school, and other sources not only shapes individual value systems but also provides the background knowledge against which people gauge issues. Preliminary research by this author shows that, although Chinese middle school textbooks emphasize patriotism, national identity, and sovereignty in history and ethics teaching, information directly related to Japan and the United States is still limited. Popular publications, TV dramas, and films may have a greater level of psychological permeation, but that is difficult to measure. Most Chinese appear to rely heavily on the Chinese media for information about Japan rather than on textbooks (see table 10), and young people rely on the Internet in particular. Discussions via "new media" played a central role in the understanding of, and actions against, Japan in the spring of 2005.[22]

Alastair Iain Johnston has noted that different educational levels affect Chinese public perceptions of the United States and concluded that better education generally produces warmer feelings toward the United States among the Chinese public and lessens the sense of threat.[23] A Peking University–China Daily–Genron NPO joint survey conducted in 2005 also found that students in different disciplines or majors held discrepant opinions on certain sets of issues. For instance, students studying the Japanese language were less negative in their general perceptions of Japan than those who had never learned Japanese; people with science backgrounds in Chinese universities seemed more critical of Japan and more radical about China's approach to bilateral relations than those studying

Chinese Public Perceptions of Japan and the United States

Table 10. Sources of information about Japan in China (percent), 2007

Source	College students	Urban residents
Chinese news media	90.2	87.8
Chinese films and TV dramas	36.6	37.2
Japanese films and TV dramas	24.6	9.6
Other people's comments	20.3	11.2
Family, friends	10.6	11.9
Chinese governmental information	10.5	10.9
Personal experience	6.7	5.8
Chinese books (including textbooks)	5.6	40.6
Japanese books	3.9	3.9
Japanese news media	3.8	8.8
Other	1.5	0.1

SOURCE: Peking University, China Daily, and Genron NPO, 2007.
NOTE: Respondents could select more than one response.

the humanities; and students of international studies were more inclined toward cooperative and pragmatic ways of dealing with Japan (see tables 11, 12, and 13).

Experience Experience provides an important supplement to—or can even be a decisive factor in—people's perceptions of other countries or cultures. Experience can sometimes adjust misperceptions caused by egocentrism, emotion, events, or education. Experience provides direct and real raw data upon which perceptions can be based. In the case of China-Japan relations, studies reveal that people who have been to Japan have a more positive perception of Japan than those who have not.[24] Most Chinese people, however, have not been to Japan—less than 4 percent of students and 2 percent of urban dwellers in China have visited Japan, and 62.3 percent of students and 92.4 percent of city dwellers do not have any Japanese acquaintances. More than 90 percent of Chinese people base their understanding of Japan mainly on Chinese newspapers and television.[25]

Interviews also confirm that students change their impressions of Japan after visiting that country.[26] Similarly, in a study on public perceptions of China-US relations, a number of differences were found between those who had overseas experience and those who did not (see table 14).[27]

Table 11. General impressions of Japan among Chinese university students (percent), 2007

	Students studying Japanese	Students not studying Japanese	All students
Very good	0	0.5	0.5
Relatively good	16.7	4.5	4.8
Not good or bad	53.3	34.9	35.4
Relatively bad	23.3	37	36.6
Very bad	3.3	21.8	21.3
Don't know	3.3	1.3	1.3

SOURCE: Peking University, China Daily, and Genron NPO, 2007.

Table 12. University student attitudes toward Japan's bid for a permanent seat on the UN Security Council (percent by major), 2005

	Respondent's field of study				
	Humanities	Social sciences*	Science	International studies	All students
Support	1.2	1.1	0.9	0	0.8
Against	66.8	71.7	83.4	52.4	71.1
Conditionally support	27.5	26.7	13.5	46.0	25.8
None of our business	0.8	0	0.4	0.4	0.4
Don't know	3.6	0.5	1.8	1.2	1.9

SOURCE: Peking University, China Daily, and Genron NPO, 2005.
* Does not include international studies

Table 13. University student attitudes toward the Diaoyu [Senkaku] Islands dispute (percent by major), 2005

	Respondent's field of study				
	Humanities	Social sciences*	Science	International studies	All students
Should land on the island	21.5	22.6	31.4	16.9	24.6
Should shelve the dispute	31.2	34.4	27.6	56	35.8
Should apply international law	43.7	38.7	35.7	25	35.6
Should tolerate proactive measures by Japan	1.6	3.2	3.6	1.2	2.6
Don't know	2.0	1.1	1.8	0.8	1.5

SOURCE: Peking University, China Daily, and Genron NPO, 2005.
* Does not include international studies

COMPARING CHINESE PERCEPTIONS OF JAPAN AND THE UNITED STATES

When comparing what the Chinese people like or dislike about the United States and Japan and why, some interesting observations emerge.[28] First, most Chinese dislike the United States mainly because of its foreign policies and international behavior—especially toward China—and not because of its domestic values, culture, institutions, or political leadership.[29] This has been repeatedly discussed in Chinese writings and proven through empirical studies.[30] In a poll taken in 2001, when most people were very critical of American foreign policy, 66 percent of the respondents gave favorable ratings to the general US domestic situation.[31] In short, what the Chinese dislike about the United States is its arbitrary, condescending, interfering, and hegemonic international behavior rather than its internal democracy, freedom, or economic and scientific achievement. However, when it comes to Japan, the Chinese show little admiration for its values,

Table 14. Impact of experience on perceptions among Chinese people, 2001

Do you agree that . . .	People with international experience		People without international experience	
	response	%	response	%
. . . US hegemony threatens world peace?	yes	35.1	yes	51.2
	(92.8 percent responded yes among those who had visited the US)			
. . . your general impression of the US is good?	yes	82.5	yes	62.6
. . . American people are friendly to the Chinese people, but the US government is unfriendly?	no	56.7	yes	57.7
. . . US media coverage of China is . . . . . . fair but not accurate?	yes	47.4	yes	31.2
. . . not fair and not accurate?	yes	36.1	yes	46.6
. . . the embassy bombing was caused by wrong intelligence?	yes	9.3	yes	4.4
	absolutely not	59.8	absolutely not	80.2
	(21.4 percent responded yes among those who had visited the US)			

Source: Yu Xunda, Chen Xudong, and Zhu Jiping, "Zhongmei guangi: gaizi minzhong de kanfa" [China-US relations—perceptions from the public], in *Shijie Jingji yu Zhengzhi* [World economics and politics], no. 6 (2001).

culture, or institutions. What the Chinese appreciate about Japan is mostly practical things, such as home appliances, and the spirit behind them, such as seriousness, diligence, and teamwork. What the Chinese dislike most about Japan is of course its attitude toward history, which is deeply rooted in Japanese values and culture. The history dispute strongly overshadows the Chinese people's understanding of contemporary Japan.

Second, there is also a difference in the intensity and breadth of people's like or dislike of the United States and Japan. Anti-American sentiments, though sometimes strong and violent, are more event driven and can fluctuate with specific occurrences. Once an incident has passed, emotions fade, and China-US relations seem to improve overnight. Anti-Japanese sentiments, however, seem more persistent and ingrained, although they are often aggravated by incidents as well. Events trigger emotions, and those emotions reinforce stereotypes and transcend the events themselves. So China-Japan relations often seem to deteriorate overnight. Moreover, anti-Americanism in China is more directed at the US government and not at the American people, whereas anti-Japanese sentiments are very easily extended from individual leaders or the government to the people or the nation as a whole. As Chen Shengluo notes, people in China usually call those who are fond of the United States "pro-America," but they call those who are fond of Japan "national traitors," a word much more negative and intolerable in Chinese political culture.[32]

Third, the nature of anti-Americanism and anti-Japanese feelings differs. China-US confrontation is perceived in China more as a power struggle in which realism is employed. Compromise is accepted by the public mostly because of the power balance between the two countries. Ideological competition exists more between the two governments and less among the people of the two countries. China-Japan disputes, however, are perceived more through a moral lens. It is not just about power but about "who is right and who is wrong, who is good and who is evil."[33] The moral conflict exists not only between the two governments but also between the two peoples. Thus it is less likely that the Chinese public will tolerate any Japanese behavior that is seen as incorrect, such as textbook revisions or the Yasukuni Shrine visits, which reflect Japanese values about history and beyond.

In Chinese perceptions of both the United States and Japan, we see possible common psychological deviations, as mentioned by Robert Jervis: (1) perception of planning—incidents like the embassy bombing and the EP-3 spy plane incident, viewed together with policies on human rights, currency, and other issues, tend to be seen as evidence of scheming or conspiracies against China's rise rather than as accidents or confusion; (2) perception of unity—there is a tendency to interpret the attitudes of individual Japanese toward history as the dominant or even unanimous position in Japan, without recognizing the existence of any plurality or diversity in that nation; (3) wishful thinking—there is a tendency to base perceptions on one's own expectations and fears, which are the result of historical memories, instead of on reason and reality, which creates, for instance, the image of present-day Japan as a militarist state; and (4) cognitive distortion or dissonance—contradictory images of America exist among the Chinese people, and even within individual Chinese people, and there is a lack of balance between the image of the warlike, cruel, selfish, untrustworthy Japanese and that of a polite, serious, community-minded people.[34]

CONCLUSIONS AND RECOMMENDATIONS

The Chinese public's knowledge of the United States and Japan is still indirect, superficial, and fragmented, and is naturally based on Chinese values, experiences, social context, and a tendency to be inward looking. This way of thinking is understandable, but it needs to be improved.

More than a few wise people have appealed for Chinese public perceptions of Japan and the United States to be more comprehensive, deep, and rational. A greater focus on the internal political, social, and cultural factors of the two countries is recommended. For instance, some Chinese scholars suggest that religion in the United States should not be neglected when people attempt to understand America, including its international behavior.[35] Repeated calls have also been made for a more balanced and less emotional perception of Japan. One Chinese writer, for example, argues that the image of declining Japanese power is not accurate if one considers the broader framework with a cool head.[36]

This chapter has applied a 5-E formula to interpret Chinese perceptions of the United States and Japan. The first E, egocentrism, reminds us how people's perceptions tend to reflect their own situations; the second E, events, helps explain the fluctuations in public perceptions of the two countries; the third E, emotion, plays an important role in creating misperceptions and distortions; the fourth E, education, is especially meaningful in understanding differences; and the final E, experience, may result in adjustments that produce a more balanced and constructive perception.

Public perceptions of the United States and Japan should be seriously considered against the backdrop of expanding public participation in policy discussions in China. Never in the history of the PRC has the Chinese government paid as much attention to public voices or feelings in its decision making as it does today. But this trend in China should only continue if the public demonstrates informed, balanced, and rational thinking. There is both a dark side and a bright side when public opinion plays a function in decision making. The dark side, as discussed by Taylor Fravel in this volume in relation to the Diaoyu [Senkaku] Islands case, is the potential for the public to play a trouble-making role or to create obstacles to governmental reconciliation. The bright side, on the other hand, is the potential to provide the government with a basis for different policy choices or for bargaining. We should expect a more strategic vision from decision makers and academia; they must provide better leadership and education to shape Chinese perceptions of the United States and Japan in order to prevent relations from being derailed by public outcries. It is critical that we incorporate discussions of ways to manage public perceptions or public emotions into governmental dialogues, as is already being done between China and Japan.

Based on the 5-E formula analysis, a number of measures can be prescribed to improve Chinese perceptions of the United States and Japan:

- Direct, effective, people-to-people interchange must be enhanced so that ordinary people have more opportunity to *experience* the perceived countries. There is a Chinese saying, "seeing is believing," even if you just discover part of the truth. There are plenty of travelers between China and Japan already, but the actual communication occurring does not seem to be very effective. People-to-people interchange must involve not only seeing another country but talking with the people there as well. Communication produces experience, and experience produces better perceptions. In this regard, the Chinese, Japanese, and US governments should maintain or expand grassroots exchange programs, enhance student exchanges, loosen visa restrictions, and support more Track 2 dialogues.

- Media coverage of the perceived countries should be improved so that ordinary people better grasp *events*. Studies confirm that the media is the general public's primary source of information on what is happening, and that the "new media" is more trusted in China than in Japan and America.[37] The media does not just inform but also interprets, sets the agenda, and influences opinions. Media coverage and the public perception of a foreign country are therefore closely connected, and sensational coverage of trilateral relations by the media for commercial reasons should be firmly rejected.

- Greater support and encouragement should be given for the participation of thoughtful opinion leaders in public discussions so that the general public is better *educated*. An open, accommodating public discussion results in an informed public. To be sure, there are always problems with who is thoughtful and whether personal risks are involved, but opinion leaders should take responsibility. The existence of egocentrism makes clear the significance of empathy in perceiving others, and that can only be learned through more experience and education.

It might not be realistic to expect public perceptions of foreign countries to ever be free of egocentrism and emotion. However, greater experience and education and a stronger grasp of events can balance egocentrism and emotion to some extent and adjust misperceptions in the Chinese public's view of the United States and Japan.

NOTES

1. Robert Jervis, *Perception and Misperception in International Politics* (Princeton: Princeton University, 1970), 28.
2. Yang Yusheng, *Zhongguoren de Meiguo guan* [Chinese views of the United States] (Shanghai: Fudan University, 1996), 234–51.
3. This saying was from a 1990s TV show, *Beijingers in New York*.
4. This term was used by David Shambaugh in his book, *Beautiful Imperialist, China Perceives America, 1972–1990* (Princeton: Princeton University, 1993).
5. An opinion poll in 2001, for example, found that 94.6 percent of respondents fully agreed or basically agreed that "the United States is the most advanced country in terms of science and technology"; 90.5 percent chose the US economy as "most competitive"; 81.5 percent regarded the United States as "militarily far ahead of other countries"; while 82.9 percent believed that "American hegemonic policies endanger world peace." Yu Xunda, Chen Xudong, and Zhu Jiping, "Zhongmei guangi: gaizi minzhong de kanfa" [China-US relations—perceptions from the public], in *Shijie Jingji yu Zhengzhi* [World economics and politics], no. 6 (2001).
   In another analysis of the American image in Chinese public discourse, "hegemonic country" (which has a negative connotation in Chinese, equal to "arbitrary power politics") is the word most used to identify the United States. See Qian Hao and Qian Xiaoming, "Dazhong huayu zhong de Meiguo yu Zhongmei guanxi" [American image and Sino-US relations in public discourse], in *Guoji Jingji Pinglun* [International economic review], no. 3–4 (2003).
   Opinion surveys conducted by the China Youth Daily in May 1995 and the Horizon Research Consultancy Group in 1995, 2002, and 2003 also show that "rich," "developed," "powerful," and "war events" are the terms identified most frequently by the Chinese public when they think of America. See Zhang Chun, "Lengzhan hou Zhongguoren de Meiguo guan" [Chinese perception of America after the Cold War], in *Kaifang Shidai* [Open times], no. 3 (2004).

6. In a survey by the Horizon Research Consultancy Group and Sina.Com in 2003, the United States was regarded as one of the most important countries for future Chinese economic development by 86.8 percent of the respondents, far ahead of ASEAN (38.5 percent), Russia (37.1 percent), Germany (32.4 percent), and Japan (31.6 percent). See *Xinlang-lingdian diaocha baogao: Zhongri minjian guanxi* [Sina-Horizon poll report: people-to-people relations between China and Japan], http://www.sina.com.cn.

Another survey, conducted by *Huanqiu Shibao* in 2006, also confirmed that China-US ties were chosen as the most influential or important bilateral relationship for China by 78 percent of the respondents, far surpassing China-Japan ties (48.7 percent), China-Russia ties (19.8 percent), China-Europe ties (13.2 percent), and China-Africa (6.2 percent). See *Huanqiu Shibao*, December 31, 2006, as cited by Gao Jing, "Beijing Daxue xuesheng de Zhongguo guojia anquan guan fenxi" [An analysis of national security perceptions of Peking University students], master's thesis, Peking University, 2007.

7. A total of 64.3 percent of respondents regarded the United States as the major threat to China's development and power in the long run. Yu, Chen, and Zhu, "Zhongmei guanxi."

8. See Niu Jun, "Hou lengzhan shiqi Zhongguoren dui Meiguo de kanfa yu sikao" [Chinese perceptions of America in the post–Cold War era], in *Guoji Jingji Pinglun* [International economic review], no. 7–8 (2001).

9. Wang Jisi, "America in Asia: How Much Does China Care?" *Global Asia* 2, no. 2 (2007): 24–28.

10. Xiao Shu, "Zhongguo bufen xinzuopai renshi xuanze yu kongbu zhuyi zhanzai yiqi" [Some Chinese New Leftists chose to stand by terrorism], in *Sichao* [Thoughts], ed. Gong Yang, 364 (Hong Kong: CASS, 2003); and http://www.dw-world.de/dw/article/0,,781844,00.html.

11. Gan Yang, "Zhongguo ziyou zuopai de youlai" [The origin of Chinese liberal leftists], in *Sichao* (Thoughts), ed. Gong Yang, 110.

12. The "Chinese-Japanese War" is the most widely known event of modern Japanese history in China, while the "history problem" consistently ranks number one (with more than 70 percent of respondents) as the top bilateral issue. The data come from polls done by Peking University, China Daily, and Genron NPO in 2005, 2006, and 2007.

In a 2006 poll by the Pew Research Center, 81 percent of Chinese respondents said that "Japan has not apologized sufficiently for its military actions in World War II." "Publics of Asian Powers Hold Negative Views of One Another," September 21, 2006.

13. In surveys conducted by Peking University, China Daily, and Genron NPO, "Losing trust of neighbors and diplomatic crisis" has repeatedly been listed as the number one or two problem facing Japan.

14. In a 1997 poll by China Renmin University and a 2007 joint poll by Peking University, China Daily, and Genron NPO, Japan was named as the greatest threat to China's security by 21.1 percent and 41.2 percent of respondents respectively, following the United States' 39.9 percent and 55.6 percent.

15. See the joint surveys in 2005, 2006, and 2007 by Peking University, China Daily, and Genron NPO.

16. Chen Jie, "Urban Chinese Perceptions of Threats from the United States and Japan," *Public Opinion Quarterly* 5, no. 2 (2001).

17. The Five Principles for Peaceful Coexistence, which were agreed to by China and India in 1954, include mutual respect for sovereignty and territorial integrity, mutual nonaggression, noninterference in each other's internal affairs, equality and mutual benefit, and peaceful coexistence.

18. According to *Huanqiu Shibao* surveys in 2005, 2006, and 2007, the total percentage of respondents who chose "very satisfied," "satisfied," or "possible to be satisfied" with

China-US relations were 70.9 percent, 79.8 percent, and 74.7 percent respectively. See Gao Jing, *Beijing Daxue xuesheng de Zhongguo guojia anquan guan fenxi* (An analysis of national security perceptions of Peking University students).

19. See "Xinlang-lingdian diaocha baogao: Zhongri minjian guanxi" [Sina-Horizon poll report: people-to-people relations between China and Japan].

20. Ibid.

21. "Zhongguo xin fu jieceng: taoyan Riben, ai Ri huo, mengxiang Meiguo" [The newly rich Chinese: repulsed by Japan, love Japanese products, dream of America], *Guoji Xianqu Daobao*, November 19, 2004.

22. Fan Shiming, "The Internet and Political Expression in China," in *Nation-State and Media*, ed. Kenji Suzuki (Tokyo: Asahi Shoten, 2007).

23. Alastair Iain Johnston, "The Correlates of Beijing Public Opinion Toward the United States, 1998–2004," in *New Directions in the Study of China's Foreign Policy*, ed. by Alastair Iain Johnston and Robert Ross, 340–78 (Stanford: Stanford University Press, 2006).

24. Peking University–China Daily–Genron NPO joint surveys, 2005 and 2006.

25. Peking University–China Daily–Genron NPO joint surveys, 2007.

26. Personal interviews with a group of Peking University PhD students who have joined a program and visited Japan.

27. Data taken from Yu, Chen, and Zhu, "Zhongmei guanxi."

28. Professor Chen Shengluo of China Youth University for Political Science offers an excellent analysis in his paper, "Zhongguo daxuesheng de Meiguo guan he Riben guan bijiao" [A comparison of Chinese university students' perceptions of the United States and Japan], in *Zhongguo Qingnian Zhengzhi Xueyuan Xuebao* (China Youth University Review), no. 6 (2006).

29. China was not among the countries that most dislike American ideas about democracy in a global survey by the Pew Research Center in 2007. "Global Unease with Major World Powers," June 27, 2007.

30. Zi Zhongyun, *Leng yan xiang yang* [See the world with a cool head] (Beijing: San Lian, 2001). See also, Wang Jisi, "Meinyu yu yeshou" (Beauty and the beast), in *Meiguo Daguan* [American panorama], no. 8 (2001); and Fan Shiming, "Ai hen jiaorong zhong de fanmei zhuyi" [Anti-Americanism in the love and hate complex], in *Guoji Zhengzhi Yanjiu* [Studies of International Politics], no. 2 (2005).

31. Yu, Chen, and Zhu, "Zhongmei guanxi."

32. See Chen Shengluo, "Zhongguo daxuesheng de Meiguo guan he Riben guan bijiao," 29.

33. Ibid, 28.

34. See Robert Jervis, *Perception and Misperception*, 319–27, 356, and 382.

35. Wang Jisi, "Renshi Meiguo he renshi ziji" [Understanding America and understanding ourselves], *Nanfeng Chuang* [For the Public Good], January 23, 2006; and Yu Zhiyan, "Shuaxin Zhongguoren de Meiguo guan" [Update Chinese perceptions of America], *Nanfang Renwu Zhoukan* [Southern people weekly], April 11, 2007.

36. See Zhao Xiao, "Riben jingzhengli: Shuju zhong jian zhenxiang" [The competitiveness of Japan: data tell the truth], *Nanfeng Chuang*, October 1, 2004.

37. Polls by Peking University, China Daily, and Genron NPO suggest that around 90 percent of the Chinese and Japanese people know about each other through the news media in their respective countries. Other research on perceptions of China-US relations also indicates that the news media ranks first as an information source in China. See Yu, Chen, and Zhu, "Zhongmei guanxi," 34.

About the Contributors

Rumi AOYAMA is a professor at Waseda University.

Gerald CURTIS is the Burgess Professor of Political Science at Columbia University.

FAN Shiming is an associate professor and associate dean at Peking University's School of International Studies.

M. Taylor FRAVEL is the Cecil and Ida Green Career Development Associate Professor of Political Science at the Massachusetts Institute of Technology.

GUI Yongtao is an associate professor at Peking University's School of International Studies.

Ryosei KOKUBUN is the dean of Keio University's Faculty of Law and Politics.

Yasuhiro MATSUDA is an associate professor at the Institute for Advanced Studies on Asia at the University of Tokyo.

Andrew OROS is an associate professor of political science and international studies at Washington College.

Saadia PEKKANEN is the Job & Gertrud Tamaki Professor at the University of Washington's Henry M. Jackson School of International Studies and adjunct professor at its School of Law.

Katsuhiro SASUGA is an associate professor in the Department of International Studies at Tokai University.

WANG Jisi is the dean of Peking University's School of International Studies.

ZHANG Haibin is an associate professor at Peking University's School of International Studies.

Index

Japan Center for International Exchange

Founded in 1970, the Japan Center for International Exchange (JCIE) is one of the few major independent, nonprofit, and nonpartisan organizations active in the field of international affairs in Japan. JCIE believes that Japan faces a major challenge in strengthening its contributions to the international community in cooperation with other countries and actors around the world. Operating in a country where policymaking has traditionally been dominated by the government bureaucracy, JCIE plays an important role in broadening debate on Japan's international responsibilities by conducting international and cross-sectoral programs of exchange, research, and dialogue.

JCIE operates in cooperation with its New York–based counterpart, JCIE/USA, and it sponsors a wide range of projects with the collaboration and cosponsorship of institutions around the world. These include policy research and dialogue on cutting-edge issues in international relations, leadership exchanges, and efforts to strengthen the contributions of civil society to domestic and international governance. Through these, JCIE aims to create opportunities for informed policy discussions; it does not take policy positions.

JCIE receives no government subsidies; rather, funding comes from private foundation grants, corporate and individual contributions, and contracts.